twentieth-century residential architecture

twentieth-century residential architecture

RICHARD WESTON

Abbeville Press Publishers
New York • London

First published in the United States
of America in 2002
by Abbeville Press
22 Cortlandt Street
New York, NY 10007

First published in Great Britain in 2002
by Laurence King Publishing Ltd
71 Great Russell Street
London WC1B 3BP

ISBN 0-7892-0740-0

Designed by Keith Lovegrove
Picture research by Mary-Jane Gibson
Printed in Hong Kong

contents

introduction

Throughout the twentieth century the house has commended itself as the most appropriate and responsive vehicle for testing ideas and expressing an architectural position in built form. A history of the twentieth-century house is also, therefore, to some extent a history of the leading ideas of the century's architecture: the scope is enormous, and this book is intended to be inclusive but not comprehensive. Despite the global approach it was decided at the outset not to include Japan because it would be impossible to do justice to the diversity and depth of the designs produced there. But to every rule there must be an exception and ours is Tadao Ando. His work is of such international importance that to omit it would be to impoverish any account of the house during the last quarter of the century. I trust that most readers will discover many if not all of their favourite houses here, as well as some unexpected delights, and those less familiar with the subject matter will, I hope, find sufficient contextual information to situate the houses in the wider currents of architectural development.

The book is organized thematically rather than strictly chronologically. The first chapter begins where many histories of modern architecture begin, in the middle of the nineteenth century, and then moves on to the *fin de siècle*, where ideas belonging to the dying century culminate and mingle with premonitions of things to come. The second chapter deals with the larger incarnations of the classic Modern (with a capital 'M') house, and the third with the smaller 'machines for living in' advanced as solutions to the housing problem. The latter includes Le Corbusier's Unité d'Habitation at Marseilles, because of its pivotal role in his development and the trajectory of post-war architecture, and also a tiny block of apartments in Israel which vividly illustrates many of the ideas and deserves to be better known. Otherwise, I have stuck to the principle that this is a book about houses, not apartments or housing (although one or two seminal housing developments have been allowed in).

The fourth chapter follows the dissemination and adaptation of modern architecture in diverse places, climates and cultures. To capture the variety of approaches it ranges across five continents and decades, but excludes the USA and Scandinavia to which the next two chapters are devoted. The seventh chapter examines the episode of stylistic Post-Modernism in the 1960s and 1970s and the broader post-modern critique, with particular reference to the issues of 'place' and 'dwelling'; in a book of this scope it seemed wise not to tread too deeply into the murky waters of post-modern theory. The final chapter reviews houses built primarily during the last quarter of the century: the selection attempts to illustrate the bewildering diversity of approaches and forms that characterize our own *fin de siècle*, but makes no claims to being definitive.

The house remains the basic building-block of the man-made environment and in the West, at least, is still closely identified with the nuclear family, even when that unit in its traditional form accounts for less than half of the households in many countries. Other histories of the twentieth-century house could and will focus on issues of psychology, family structure and the changing roles of women and developments in biulding technology – such as frame construction and central heating, which made the open plan possible. This book makes no attempt to address these issues, or to examine the domain of mass house-builders, whose products remained largely untouched by modern architectural thought.

Opposite Koshino House, Ashiya, Japan, 1982, Tadao Ando. Built as a 'bastion of resistance' against the consumerism that was sweeping Japan, the Koshino House is closed to its suburban neighbours but open to nature.

the house as a work of art

1859 may seem an unlikely point to begin a history of the twentieth-century house. And at first sight Red House, completed that year in Bexleyheath, Kent, by the young English architect Philip Webb, does not appear especially innovative, its brick walls, steep-pitched tiled roofs and gothic arches looking more medieval than modern. But to Hermann Muthesius, who came to London in 1896 as cultural attaché at the German embassy and eight years later published an influential account of English domestic architecture entitled *Das englische Haus*, it exhibited 'independence and originality' in every aspect of its design. These sentiments were echoed forty years later by Nikolaus Pevsner in his seminal 1936 book, *Pioneers of the Modern Movement* (better known by its later title, *Pioneers of Modern Design*): 'a building of surprisingly independent character,' he declared, 'solid and spacious looking and yet not in the least pretentious.'

Red House Bexleyheath, England, 1859, Philip Webb

To its many admirers, Red House represented a key moment in the development of architecture. Nineteenth-century architects, bemused by the possibilities of new, industrially produced materials such as cast iron and large sheets of glass, and confronted by unprecedented building types like factories and railway stations, which engineers seemed better equipped to tackle, were obsessed by the issue of style. The authority of Classical architecture, largely unquestioned since the Renaissance, was challenged and a host of styles revived – Egyptian, Greek, Romanesque, Gothic. Many designers flourished amid the spirit of eclecticism, but to others the new freedom seemed more like licence. What they sought was not a confusing multiplicity of styles, but a new style to capture the 'spirit of the age' – an elusive concept for which German has a special word, *Zeitgeist*.

Red House stood for the rejection of easy stylistic eclecticism and gratuitous ornament. It embraced simplicity and sought to ground architectural expression in the nature of building materials and construction. Unlike most middle-class villas of its day, it did not imitate grander – typically Italian – architecture, but was content to draw on the English vernacular. It was not without stylistic features, nor stylistically consistent – the roofs and arches are gothic, sash-windows Queen Anne, and the picturesque arrangement looks back to monastic architecture – but the ensemble was novel and, internally, bolder and more original.

But what made Red House so important had as much to do with its owner as the undoubted virtues of its design. Like many of the houses we will explore, it was a manifesto in bricks and mortar, space and light; not just a house, but the embodiment of a vision for a new way of living. Webb's client was William Morris, a young designer and propagandist who became one of the most influential figures of his day, and his house was intended to exemplify the values of the Arts and Crafts movement he led. Disgusted at the vulgar eclecticism of Victorian architecture and design, Morris became an implacable enemy of industrialization and the sham products that poured relentlessly from its factories which, to compound the folly, made slaves of their workers. He valued the intrinsic qualities of materials and workmanship, and believed all true art was rooted in craftsmanship and 'joy in making'. These ideas helped to redefine the way we look at buildings and objects, and Morris's example established the house as a vehicle for personal artistic expression.

We have become so accustomed to the idea that an original designer of talent such as Philip Webb has the right – even duty – to break with tradition, to reject outmoded styles and to design freely in response to his client's requirements, that it is difficult to realize just how revolutionary a proposition it was at the time. And it is in this sense, above all, that Red House embodies the spirit imbuing the houses discussed in this book: for the first time in the history of architecture, the private house – as opposed to the mansion or palace – became the focus of the most advanced ideas of the day.

The idea of the house as a work of art, promoted by magazines like *The Studio*, caught on like wildfire towards the end of the nineteenth century and domestic commissions from enlightened patrons frequently offered architects the greatest opportunities for innovation. The most original English Arts and Crafts architect, C. F. A. Voysey, was born just two years before Red House was built. Perrycroft, completed in the Malvern Hills in 1894, is typical of his early work. Its white pebble-dashed walls, broad slate roofs peppered with tall chimneys, small-paned windows grouped into horizontal bands, and battered piers owed more to vernacular buildings than recognized architectural styles. Markedly simple by the standards of the day, these features led historians and critics of teleological inclination such as Pevsner to see it as 'anticipating' the whitewashed surfaces of the 1920s, an idea Voysey himself never understood. Internally, Perrycroft remained a fairly traditional composition of individual rooms, albeit functional and progressive in its arrangements – the servants' rooms, he said, should be 'cheerful, not shabby and dark'. Later, in the double-height halls and studied asymmetry and informality of the principal rooms of houses such as Broadleys of 1898, built on a magnificent site overlooking Lake Windermere, Voysey began to open up the internal spaces in a way that was taken further in the work of his younger contemporary, M. H. Baillie Scott.

The medieval-looking, half-timbered hall and pargeted plaster frieze in the drawing room of a house such as Blackwell – sited, like Broadleys, overlooking Windermere and completed by Baillie Scott in 1900 – are misleading. They do not strike the modern viewer as especially progressive, but the consistent attention to detail and the determination to give each space a distinctive character have a hitherto unmatched consistency. This yields an organic quality which led Muthesius to hail Baillie Scott as 'the first to have realized the new idea of the interior as a work of art'. This integrating vision was quickly extended to the outdoors, and turn-of-the-century English houses are notable for their use of pergolas, sunken areas and artful steps to achieve a fusion of house and garden, an interplay raised to exceptional heights in the partnership of Edwin Lutyens and the doyenne of Edwardian gardeners, Gertrude Jekyll.

In Britain, by far the most original realization of the ideal of the house as a work of art came in Scotland in the work of Charles Rennie Mackintosh. His masterpiece, the Glasgow School of Art, was won in competition in 1896 in the name of his employers Honeyman and Keppie. It took several years to complete and he burst onto the international scene in 1900 by winning a special prize – no first was given, and Baillie Scott won second – in the competition to design a 'House for an Art Lover' organized by the magazine *Zeitschrift für Innendekoration*. The contrast between the two designs could hardly have been greater: Baillie Scott's, a fantasy of turrets, gables, chimneys and proliferating

Overleaf Red House, Bexleyheath, England, 1859, Philip Webb. Built for the young William Morris, who later wrote, 'If I were asked to say what is at once the most important production of Art and the thing most to be longed for, I should answer A BEAUTIFUL HOUSE.' Red House stood for the rejection of stylistic eclecticism and belief in truth to materials which were central to the Arts and Crafts movement.

rooms, assembled with artfully contrived inconsistencies; Mackintosh's, a bold massing of clear volumes which doubtless owed something to Voysey but whose impact was wholly original and, unlike most Arts and Crafts houses, thoroughly urban. Internally, it showed the openness and complexity beloved of Baillie Scott, but under altogether tighter control.

The House for an Art Lover was not built – or at least not for ninety years, when a posthumous version was completed in Glasgow as a commercial venture – but two years later the publisher Walter Blackie commissioned a house at Helensburgh, west of Glasgow on a site overlooking the Firth of Clyde, which gave Mackintosh the opportunity to put theory into practice.

The Hill House Helensburgh, Scotland, 1902, Charles Rennie Mackintosh

Externally, The Hill House is overtly Scottish – the debt to the Scottish Baronial style is more conspicuous than that to Voysey – and characterized by Mackintosh's remarkable talent for giving order and tension to a seemingly disparate collection of windows, which on analysis turn out to be both functionally placed and organized into a complex series of dynamic or partial symmetries.

Internally, the same organizational talent is set to work on the individual rooms. In the drawing room, for example, Mackintosh projects a light-filled bay beyond the main volume of the house. It has an enticing built-in seat and two doors leading out into the garden, and to complement this openness the 'winter end' of the room is intimate, gathered around the fireplace and lit by a single, small window. A large recess, designed to house a piano or act as an informal stage for the children's theatrical performances, shares the same ceiling height as the window bay. Both are defined by the continuous shallow cornice that runs around the interior: below it, the colours are white or pale; above it, darkness reigns.

The main bedroom exhibits the same attention to use, and even greater formal control. The pervading atmosphere is unmistakably feminine. This is an intimate realm that the husband entered only after changing in a separate dressing room, from where a door led directly into the square alcove housing the bed, above which is a shallow barrel-vaulted ceiling. At its end the bed is elaborated with an abstract flower motif and adjacent to it a small cupboard of drawers sits below a tiny, shuttered window in a curved bay, slightly shallower than a semi-circle, echoing the ceiling. The washstand is built-in, and backed by decoration that could almost be an adaptation of Mondrian's mature style of the 1920s. In fact, it is underpinned by a complex modular arrangement that echoes the plan of the house and is integrated with a rose motif.

Mackintosh's motifs were generally rooted in nature, flowers in particular, and transformed into artistic form by the use of geometry. In the inner hall and staircase we see him at the height of his powers. The double-layered structure of beams and joists is fully exposed and stained black, and a series of full-height timber slats enclose the stair and are echoed on the walls as a kind of wainscoting, framing a three-dimensional volume as lines and planes in a way that seems unmistakably modern. Each slat tapers slightly, like a plant stem, and at their tops they divide into two branches around an inset of pink glass; on the wall a decorative frieze, half-geometric, half-organic, suggests flowering plants.

The abstraction and geometric control that pervade Mackintosh's work were seen as alien and exotic by many in Britain, but found numerous admirers on the

Above Blackwell, Windermere, England, 1900, M. H. Baillie Scott. The medieval-looking hall is the focus of a house which exemplified the new ideal of the interior as a work of art in which each room has a distinctive character suited to its purpose.

Opposite Perrycroft, Colwall, England, 1894, C. F. A. Voysey. Spectacularly sited in the Malvern Hills, Perrycroft's exterior is typical of Voysey's combination of broadly treated surfaces and idiosyncratic details, whilst inside a new openness in planning was becoming apparent.

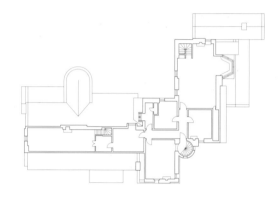

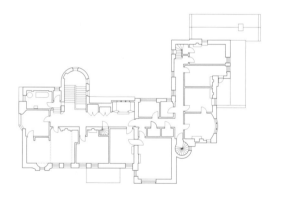

Above and opposite The Hill House, Helensburgh, Scotland, 1902, Charles Rennie Mackintosh. Picturesquely planned around a masterfully orchestrated circulation route, externally the house evokes memories of Scottish Baronial architecture. Internally, however, geometry and abstraction from nature rule, as seen in the light-filled bay projected from the living room.

10m

30ft

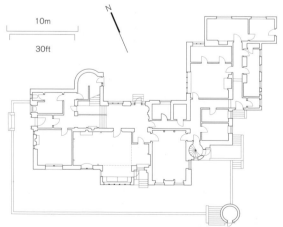

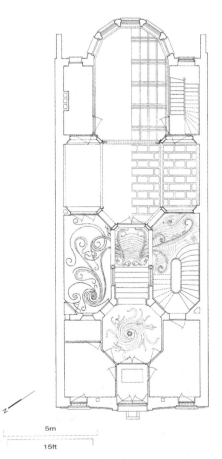

Continent, above all in Vienna. In The Hill House he was given control over every detail and the cumulative effect of this synthesis of space, light, decoration and furniture is overwhelming. The decorative elaboration can easily blind us to the imagination and discipline with which Mackintosh's ideas were grounded in responses to patterns of use, and proved an embarrassment to later critics. Eager to claim him as a pioneer of the more austerely functional virtues of the International style of the 1930s, they attributed the decorative qualities, wholly without foundation, to the influence of his wife, the talented artist Margaret Macdonald.

In continental Europe the search for new forms culminated in the Art Nouveau style that flourished for little more than a decade either side of 1900. In architecture, the first breakthrough came in Brussels with Victor Horta's Hôtel Tassel of 1892–3. The Kingdom of Belgium had been established as recently as 1830, in the wake of Napoleon's defeat. By the 1890s, when the country was thriving economically, Brussels had a reputation as an emancipated city that played host to a lively cultural avant-garde and was a home to many innovators before they were accepted in their countries of origin. Like London, but unlike other major continental cities, its expansion was based on terraced houses – the larger being known as *hôtels* – rather than apartment buildings.

Hôtel Tassel Brussels, Belgium, 1892–3, Victor Horta

The façade of Horta's *hôtel* gives little away. The bowed front and restrained use of stone are notably elegant but only the exposure of a single iron beam below the cornice declares the originality of what lies within. Once inside you enter a dark lobby, where the only daylight enters surprisingly and somewhat mysteriously from *within* the house. A day-lit cloakroom leads to an octagonal vestibule, positioned a metre (3 feet) lower than the floor, a stage from which to view the interior that opens on several different levels. Seven steps rise into a light-well bay, which functions almost as a tiny *cour d'honneur*. Its internal façade is framed by steel piers – at the time a daring breach with domestic decorum; to one side is the roof-lit winter garden, an exotic world of curvilinear metalwork, bamboo chairs and tropical plants, and to the other, mirroring it in plan, the main stair – a design of great geometric complexity which must have delighted Horta's client, who was a Professor of Descriptive Geometry. On the floor, serpentine decorative motifs writhe out into the adjacent spaces, while overhead arching steel beams are supported by a cast-iron column whose capital blossoms into thin iron tendrils, which seem designed to hold down rather than support the stair floating above.

Spatially, the Hôtel Tassel was unusually intricately worked, and Horta took the openness further in later designs such as the Hôtel Solvay, where the three principal rooms were divided by folding doors which could open to form a continuous, differentiated space. The 'honest' exposure of metal structure, derived from French Rationalists such as Viollet-le-Duc, and the determination to look to nature rather than to previous styles for inspiration in the design of the tendril-like ornaments were equally remarkable. In this Horta's work appears remarkably modern, but in other respects it was very much a product of its time, and nowhere can this be better grasped than in the small salon of the Hôtel Tassel. Isolated from the street and garden by the entrance spaces and dining room, and

5m

15ft

Opposite Hôtel Tassel, Brussels, Belgium, 1893, Victor Horta. The serpentine motifs which swarm across the plan and walls of the Hôtel Tassel are quintessentially Art Nouveau, but architecturally the house's greatest innovation lies in the use of structural iron. This permitted a spatial openness which Horta took further in the Hôtel Solvay, **above**, completed nearby in 1900.

Below Castel Orgeval, Villemoisson, France, 1905, Hector Guimard. Medieval fantasies combine with typical Art Nouveau curvilinear forms to create an organic whole which seems to grow from the site.

looking into the light-well through obscured glass, it presented a private, inner world in which every element, functional and decorative, was integrated into a symphonic whole. For all the use of nature as a source of inspiration, the artificiality of the result is striking. Like the Symbolist poets and painters by whose ideas he was influenced, Horta was trying to create a synthetic paradise through which art could challenge the assumptions of a society increasingly committed to the blind pursuit of technological progress.

Shortly after the completion of the Hôtel Tassel Horta's fellow countryman, Henry van de Velde, built a house for himself at Uccle outside Brussels, replete with organically inspired furniture. It brought him an invitation to design four rooms for the Salon de l'Art Nouveau opened by Samuel Bing in Paris in 1895, the shop that gave the new style its name and was intended, according to Bing, to be a 'meeting ground for all young spirits anxious to manifest the modernness of their tendencies'. Art Nouveau found most of its patrons among the *nouveaux riches*, anxious to display their wealth through an art as distinctive and individual as their lifestyles.

Notable among the 'young spirits' whom Bing influenced was Hector Guimard, best known as the designer of the celebrated Paris Métro entrances but also architect of several outstanding houses. Among these the demolished Castel Henriette (1899–1900) in Sèvres and Castel Orgeval at Villemoisson near Paris were outstanding. Both combined suave Art Nouveau details with wilfully rustic vernacular stonework, suggesting an almost medieval character. Castel Orgeval seems to grow spontaneously from its site, while Castel Henriette was notable for an extraordinary plan in which two orthogonal systems crash obliquely together. This leads a functionally expressive sequence of volumes to explode into a hybrid of load-bearing masonry and structural frames surmounted by picturesque roofs, terraces, balconies, chimneys and, to crown the composition, a campanile-like look-out tower. Superficially, Hôtel Guimard, the house and studio Guimard completed for himself in Paris in 1912, has little in common with these precocious works. But the plan, which melds oval volumes with diagonal axes, reveals a similar, if less violent, fascination with colliding geometries, and the exterior, with its swelling, bulbous forms so redolent of organic growth, looks back, ultimately, to medieval precedents.

In the German-speaking world the new style was christened Jugendstil, and its greatest flowering came in Austria, among the group of artists and architects known as the Secessionists. In architecture their mentor was Otto Wagner, a fervent advocate of building as the basis of design, who believed that a modern style was being forged by engineers who were the masters of the new materials. The young Secessionists, led by the painter Gustav Klimt, seceded in 1897 from the same Academy at which Wagner taught, in protest at its conservatism, and much to his colleagues' astonishment and outrage he joined them two years later. In his lectures Wagner argued for bright, well-ventilated houses with simple furnishings. His influence was enormous: he was an exemplar for Josef Olbrich and his students included Josef Hoffmann and Rudolf Schindler, who later left Vienna to work for Frank Lloyd Wright.

The rectilinear style of Art Nouveau that characterizes the work of the Viennese was developed by Olbrich and Hoffmann in the late 1890s, and taken

Above Hôtel Guimard, Paris, France, 1909–12, Hector Guimard. Stone and brick seem to flow and congeal into drapery-like curves of suave sophistication.

Opposite Olbrich House, Darmstadt, Germany, 1900, Josef Maria Olbrich. Part of the artists' colony which flourished under the patronage of the Grand Duke of Hesse, Olbrich's house combined vernacular German forms with typical Secessionist refinement and decorative motifs of Vienna.

to Germany in 1899 when Olbrich accepted an invitation to join the artists' colony established by the Grand Duke of Hesse on the Mathildenhöhe in Darmstadt. It was the most extravagant piece of artistic patronage in Europe and until his premature death in his early forties Olbrich flourished in the new surroundings, completing not only the central education and exhibition buildings, with their celebrated 'Wedding Tower', but also a string of large private villas around the park. One of the first, built in 1900, was his own house and studio. The exterior, with its distinctive gambrel roof, recalls rural German vernacular houses – a popular allusion at the time among practitioners of National Romanticism – while internally the planning, organized like most of his houses in Darmstadt around an open, multi-purpose living hall, was clearly indebted to Baillie Scott.

The synthesis was Olbrich's alone, however, and on closer examination nothing is as simple as it might appear. The roof, for example, is asymmetrical, with a hanging 'flower gallery' balancing the lower eaves opposite. The fenestration is similarly artfully balanced, with windows positioned in response to the spaces within and bound together by a horizontal frieze of blue and white tiles arranged chequerboard fashion – a trademark of the Secession style that may well have reflected the influence of Charles Rennie Mackintosh, whose work the Viennese greatly admired.

In 1903 Hoffmann and the artist Koloman Moser formed the studios and workshops known as the Wiener Werkstätte. In the spirit of William Morris their programme stated, 'We consider it our most noble duty to regain for the workers a joy in work and an existence worthy of a human being.' This faith in art to bring about, as Olbrich put it at the dedication ceremony of the Darmstadt colony, an 'increase in prosperity' and an 'equalization in social conditions' may seem naïve, but was widely held at the time. In practice, however, Hoffmann was more interested in artistic than social or political questions. He did not believe that it was 'possible to convert the masses' to an appreciation of art and was happy to satisfy 'the few' who could appreciate his refined, abstract style of geometrically pure forms. Two years after the foundation of the Werkstätte he was given the opportunity to create a *Gesamtkunstwerk* – total work of art – in Brussels. The clients were Adolphe Stoclet, a Belgian financier who had lived in Vienna, and his wife Suzanne, a beautiful Parisienne whom he had married against his family's wishes. Their brief was to create a house in which to exhibit their ever-growing collection of art and to entertain the artistic élite of Europe – the guest book (designed by Hoffmann, naturally) contains the names of Diaghilev, Paderewski, Stravinsky, Cocteau and Anatole France.

The site was ideal, situated almost on the edge of the built-up area on the Avenue de Tervueren, a continuation of the prestigious Rue de la Loi. It enjoyed fine views south over woods and parkland and to take maximum advantage of these Hoffmann arranged the extensive accommodation as an axially composed sequence of en-suite rooms forming a linear block facing the road. The major reception spaces, such as the hall and dining and music rooms were expressed as boldly projecting bays, establishing a subtle interplay of crossing axes that extended out into the garden. The planning was highly accomplished but not especially innovative, still rooted in classical principles – unlike Mackintosh's

Palais Stoclet Brussels, Belgium, 1905–11, Josef Hoffmann

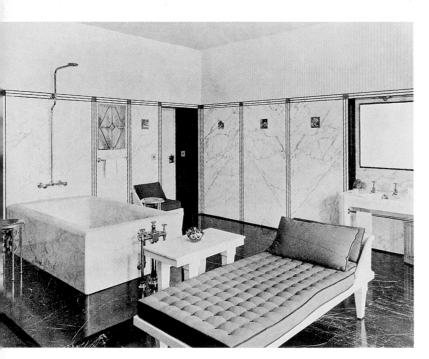

Above Palais Stoclet, Brussels, Belgium, 1905–11, Josef Hoffmann. Like every space in this ultimate *Gesamtkunstwerk*, the bathroom was designed down to the last detail to create an ambience of luxurious cleanliness.

House for an Art Lover, which may have influenced the massing. What makes Palais Stoclet one of the most remarkable achievements of the pre-war years is Hoffmann's handling of surfaces and the unrivalled sophistication and completeness of the interior decoration.

Palais Stoclet was built of brick and clad in large, thin slabs of stone, a perfect example of the 'slablike treatment of the surface' that Hoffmann's teacher Otto Wagner had proposed as a leitmotif of a genuinely modern architecture. The size of the slabs alone showed that they must be a thin veneer, not an ashlar wall, but like Wagner, who had famously used exposed fixings like 'nails' on his Vienna Postal Savings Bank, Hoffmann was at pains to emphasize that this was cladding, not solid masonry. He did so by marking corners and framing openings with thin metal profiles, like tautly stretched ropes which seem to spill down from the tower that forms the culmination of the massing. The result is striking, even disconcerting, completely undermining the expressed interaction of load and support that underpinned most previous architecture. In Palais Stoclet the windows are no longer holes in a wall but rectangular surfaces on – and in some cases, actually in front of – the wall. The volumes read as compositions of planes, emphasizing the geometric purity of the design, and the effect is so light as to feel almost unreal – after all, stone, even thin stone, is a heavy material. Hoffmann exploits the planar quality to dramatic effect in details such as the covered seating area carved out of the garden elevation, where the languorously sagging soffit and façade seem, thanks to the doubling of the mouldings, almost ready to slide down like a giant gate.

The interiors were designed collaboratively with his Secession colleagues, the individual artists and craftsmen being given exceptional freedom to develop themes and ideas of their own choosing within Hoffmann's framework. Every means at their disposal was deployed – changes of shape, proportion and volume; varied combinations of natural and artificial light; luxurious surface treatments and colour. In lesser hands the opulence could have been oppressive, but the refinement and control were masterly. Consider the dining room for example. The walls are recessed in three stages: dark Portovenere marble and macassar wood cabinets project furthest, recessed above them is a band of light Paonozzo marble, and above and slightly behind that, appear mosaic decorations by Klimt, also articulated by projecting and receding materials – the subtlety of which quite escapes the camera. Less opulent but no less remarkable was the ample main bathroom, with its walls of pale marble inlaid with strips of black marble and malachite, and furnishings and silver toilet articles purpose-made by the Wiener Werkstätte; it even opened onto a generous exercise balcony, reflecting the fitness cults that anticipated the obsession with health and exercise in the 1920s.

More completely than any other house, perhaps, Palais Stoclet exemplified the European ideal of the aestheticization of life, over which the architect and artist assumed a god-like control, transforming the dwelling from a setting for normal, everyday life into a higher realm consecrated by art. Early visitors reported that the Stoclets lived out this vision, achieving perfect harmony with their surroundings. Nothing was left to chance: in his obituary, their friend E. De Bruyn recalled that the flowers were always of one colour, and even M. Stoclet's cravat

Above, left and below Palais Stoclet, Brussels, Belgium, 1905–11, Josef Hoffmann. The axially controlled planning was stylistically conservative, but the stone revetment of the exterior transformed the building mass into a radically new interplay of volumes and planes. The supremely refined interiors, such as the dining room seen here, combine exquisite materials with decorations by Gustav Klimt and Wiener Werkstätte fittings and furniture.

10m

30ft

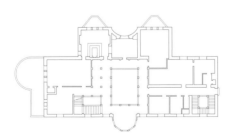

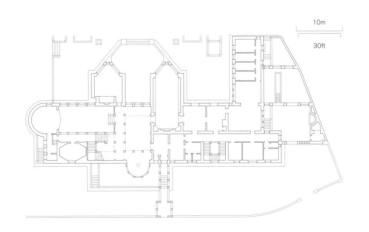

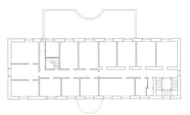

Above Kalela, Lake Ruovesi, Finland, 1895, Akseli Gallen-Kallela. The 'studio in the wilds' became a favoured model throughout Scandinavia at the turn of the century, nowhere better seen than in the painter Gallen-Kallela's home, which he modelled on a Finnish farmhouse and built himself.

Below Hvitträsk, Lake Vitträsk, Finland, 1901, Gesellius, Lindgren, Saarinen. The log-walls, exposed beams, giant fireplace (glimpsed on the right) and *ryijy* rug transform the living room into a fantasy of an ideal Finnish past.

Hvitträsk Lake Vitträsk, Finland, 1901, Gesellius, Lindgren, Saarinen

was chosen to harmonize with his wife's *toilette*. Eduard Sekler, author of the definitive account of Hoffmann's work, has suggested that Palais Stoclet embodies the 'ambiguity and uncertainty' that his contemporary Hugo von Hoffmannsthal believed characterized their epoch. The preciousness and exclusivity of the way of life it celebrated were destined to be swept away by the impending world war, but as we shall see in the next chapter its aesthetic premises were challenged well before then by one of the most incisive critical minds of the day, that of the architect Adolf Loos.

Nowhere, arguably, beyond its places of origin, did the ideal of the house as a work of art fall on more fertile ground than in Scandinavia, where the search for national identity – common throughout central Europe, Germany and the Nordic countries following the era of state formation in the nineteenth century – was especially keenly felt. Throughout Scandinavia the new ideal was the 'studio in the wilds' and artists led the way in showing how to live an authentic life away from the temptations of urban society. Artistically, the most compelling results came in Finland where progressive artists were struggling to assert cultural independence from Russian rule. The pioneer was the painter Axel Gallén, who changed his Swedish name to the Finnish Akseli Gallen-Kallela in 1906. In 1895 he completed a log-built studio home modelled on farmhouses from the remote region of Karelia, which he thought was free of Russian taint (erroneously, as later scholarship revealed).

Gallen-Kallela's example was followed by several leading Finnish artists, including the composer Sibelius and the architects Hermann Gesellius, Armas Lindgren and Eliel Saarinen, who came to fame as designers of the much admired Finnish Pavilion at the 1900 Paris World Fair. The following year Saarinen, with help from his partners, built a house and studio for the practice on a site at Lake Vitträsk, some 30 kilometres (19 miles) west of Helsinki – at that time still 'in the wilds', but close enough to the capital to enable them to pursue their work. The accommodation was organized in three wings around a courtyard. The earliest was modelled on the log and plank buildings of Karelia, and almost immediately acquired a rustic stone entrance tower; that to the south, with its logs, stone base, and steep tiled roofs seems to grow out of the dramatic site and has often been compared to English Arts and Crafts houses, but in fact was based largely on Finnish examples; finally, to the north and originally occupied by Lindgren, was another timber wing with a beguiling fantasy of a tower based on Finnish wooden churches which was destroyed by fire in 1922.

All too predictably the ideal of harmonious living in Hvitträsk – as the house was named – proved less durable than the architecture. Following realignments of the marital arrangements, Gesellius and Lindgren departed and the house was occupied by Saarinen and his wife Louise ('Loja') Gesellius, who enriched it with furniture, rugs and textiles. In keeping with Jugendstil practice, each room acquired its own character and ambience. The one-and-a-half storey high living room, with its exposed logs and beams, *ryijy* rug draped over a built-in bench, and giant fireplace, was modelled on the multi-purpose room known as the *tupa* of regional Karelian farmhouses. In other rooms the national tone was transformed by derivations from architects whom the Saarinens admired. The children's bedroom, for example, was a *petit-*

Above, left and below 'Lilla Hyttnäs' (Larsson House), Sundborn, Sweden, 1893–1919, Carl and Karin Larsson. The Larssons' widely influential vision of a relaxed domestic life, centred around children and celebrated in bright colours, natural materials, folksy details and unconfining clothes, was disseminated through Carl's paintings and books.

hommage to Charles Rennie Mackintosh, while elsewhere Viennese influence can be discerned.

Sweden produced nothing to match Hvitträsk architecturally, but the house the artist Carl Larsson created with his artist-wife Karin Bergöö became the inspiration for idealized images of domestic life whose influence were to ripple through the twentieth century. It all began modestly enough in 1893, with a small log house inherited from Karin's aunt. They added a studio two years later, made it their year-round home in 1901, named it Lilla Hyttnäs, and continued to expand the property so that the old building was all but engulfed in new construction. 'A home is not dead but living,' said Carl Larsson, 'and like all living things must obey the laws of nature by constantly changing.' In 1897 Larsson exhibited his watercolours of the house and in 1899, with an additional four images, they were published as the book *Ett hem* (A Home), which was immediately translated into German and went through several editions. Other books followed, all depicting an unprecedentedly relaxed family life, with children at its centre, lived close to the land and filled with sunlight and smiling faces. German translations emphasized the importance of light – titles included 'The House in the Sun' and 'Let the Light in!' – and notable visitors such as Diaghilev, Strindberg and the royal painter Prince Eugen helped spread the Larssons' fame.

Karin designed several pieces of furniture for Lilla Hyttnäs, made woven textiles and, influenced by the movement to reform women's clothes, developed a new style of dress, flowing and unconfined, for herself and her daughters. Larsson's globetrotting lifestyle was hardly in keeping with the homely life among the 'people of my own kind' whom he portrayed in his paintings and autobiography, but the images were compelling. The Larssons' vision made an immediate impact on numerous contemporaries, not least on Friedrich Alfred Krupp, founder of the industrial giant that bears his name and enthusiastic builder of housing for workers modelled on the Garden City ideal of the English reformer Ebenezer Howard. And it anticipated a vision of modern living that ultimately spread far from its Scandinavian origins. It was not simply national sentiment that led IKEA to sponsor the exhibition 'Carl and Karin Larsson: Creator of the Swedish Style' held at London's Victoria & Albert Museum in 1998, but also recognition of the debt the world's most successful furniture company owed to the aesthetic and lifestyle they pioneered.

Across the Atlantic the vision of a new form of house for new ways of living crystallized in the 1880s on the East Coast of the United States in what the historian Vincent Scully later christened the Shingle style. It drew on earlier Colonial architecture and a way of building Scully termed the Stick style. These native traditions were combined with the picturesque manner of the prolific English architect Richard Norman Shaw and the open, framed spaces and pierced screens of Japanese architecture, which had made a huge impression when a complete house was exhibited at the Philadelphia Centennial Exposition in 1876. Many of the new houses were built as vacation homes, several of the best in the fashionable Rhode Island resort of Newport (for example the Isaac Bell house, illustrated overleaf). Their architects, among whom the young New York firm of McKim, Mead and White were pre-eminent, exploited the more relaxed social requirements to open the interior to an unprecedented degree.

Opposite Isaac Bell House, Newport, Rhode Island, 1882–3, McKim, Mead and White. The light, shingled mass, large windows and generous porches exemplify the airiness of the so-called Shingle Style made possible by timber construction.
Below Winslow House, River Forest, Illinois, USA, 1893, Frank Lloyd Wright. The cruciform plan, with a great hearth at its centre, anticipates the organization and spatial continuity of Wright's Prairie Houses.

Their typical plan-type placed an English-style living hall at its heart and expanded the spaces horizontally into generous bay windows and porches. Vincent Scully's description cannot be bettered: 'Inside the variety was like that of a nineteenth-century landscape painting, where gradations of light – partly in full flood, partly shielded by porches; sometimes golden, sometimes thunderous – defined flickering interior landscapes at various levels, broader and more extensive than any that America had known before and flowing on to the outside through wide doors and echoing porches.'

The Japanese influence on American architecture was reinforced with the publication in 1886 of Edward Sylvester Morse's classic book *Japanese Homes and Their Surroundings*. It received a further boost with the exhibition of the Ho-o-Den temple at the 1893 World's Columbian Exposition in Chicago, where it was seen by a twenty-five-year-old architect of genius at the moment he was poised to launch his solo career. His name, needless to say, was Frank Lloyd Wright, and in the same year as the Exposition he designed a house and stables that anticipated by almost ten years his revolutionary Prairie Style. The client was William Herman Winslow, president of a highly successful ornamental ironwork firm and keen amateur typographer.

Winslow House River Forest, Illinois, USA, 1893, Frank Lloyd Wright

The site is on a large suburban lot in River Forest near Chicago, and the street elevation is divided into three horizontal bands: a brick base, which sits on a clearly defined stone foundation and rises beyond the first floor, terminating in a white cornice; a narrower, dark band made of strongly textured terracotta panels, punctuated by three windows which fill its height; and a deeply overhanging hipped roof. By separating the elements in this way Wright effected a radical simplification, further enhanced by binding together the entrance door and adjacent windows in a rectangular stone panel. The composition, however, is still strictly symmetrical – a public face guarding the private world within – and sits uneasily against the asymmetrical spaces that unfold behind. At their centre is a strongly emphasized fireplace: a 'fire burning deep in the solid masonry of the house' was, for Wright, the abiding symbol of home and here it greets the visitor immediately on entry. Placed three steps up on its own podium and set behind an arcaded screen, which Noris Kelly Smith has interpreted as a rood screen, it has the formality of a chancel with the hearth as its altar, an interpretation wholly in keeping, as we shall see, with Wright's religious view of the home. The principal rooms unfold around the fireplace, and you move through them along their edges, not centres. Traces of the Beaux-Arts planning that still characterized a house like Palais Stoclet are present, but at no point are you allowed to enter a space axially.

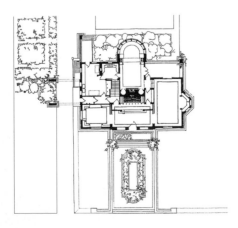

The Winslow House is impressive, but in the stables Wright built behind it we find something far more original. The upper level plan is cruciform, generated by two interpenetrating volumes, and the elevations are composed of continuous horizontal layers – anticipated in the house, but without any suggestion of the boxiness of traditional buildings. Each layer is free to assume whatever shape and dimensions the pressure of the spaces inside might dictate. For Wright 'letting the room within come through' was the key to what he called natural, 'organic' architecture and here, in the Winslow stables, the architectural means to realize that idea seem to have sprung to life fully formed. Spatially, it made

Gamble House Pasadena, California, USA, 1907–8, Greene and Greene

everything done in Europe before the Great War seem old fashioned, and it would take Wright himself several years to assimilate its possibilities.

Three years after completing the Winslow House Wright began a collaboration with his client on a book entitled *The House Beautiful*. The text was a popular sermon, distributed the previous year as a pamphlet, by the famous Unitarian minister William C. Gannett, a long-time friend of Wright's uncle. The book took three years of part-time work to produce, and ninety copies were finally printed on a press housed in Winslow's stables. Gannett's text, scattered with quotations from poetry and the Bible, was typical of the day, ornate in style and, to modern ears, cloyingly pious and sentimental. In keeping with the thought of his time, Gannett ascribed moral and religious value to the home, and throughout his long life Wright himself regarded it as both an almost sacred institution and the basis of American democracy. 'The ideal of beauty is simplicity and repose' was the book's central message, to be followed not only in the design and furnishing of the home but equally in the lifestyles of its occupants. The text was preceded by twelve exquisite photogravures of wildflowers taken by Wright, who was a keen photographer, and framed by elaborate but highly abstract graphic designs based on natural forms, in which the influence of the Viennese, Art Nouveau, the English and American Arts and Crafts movements and even Wright's love of Oriental rugs can all be discerned. But as with his architecture, Wright's ability to absorb and abstract yielded results that seem at the same time intensely personal and universal.

The influence of the Arts and Crafts movement and of Japan were just as keenly felt on the American West Coast where, above all in California, the challenge of developing completely new lifestyles for a culture still untainted by industrialization, in a climate that encouraged outdoor living, remained full of promise. This vision of California as a second Eden, ripe for innovation, would run right through the twentieth century and yield some of its outstanding houses. First among these were the so-called 'California bungalows', of which the recognized masters were the brothers Charles and Henry Greene. Born and schooled in the mid-West, where they received early encouragement to work with timber, they assimilated the lessons of the French Beaux-Arts system as students at the Massachusetts Institute of Technology in Cambridge. They moved to California in 1893, opened an office the following year, and in 1907 began work on their masterpiece, the Gamble House in their adopted town of Pasadena, now part of greater Los Angeles. The client was wealthy – a son of one of the founders of Procter and Gamble, the soap-makers – and his house large yet surprisingly intimate.

The Gamble House stands on a rustic rubble-stone plinth and was built entirely of timber: redwood framing externally, much teak internally. The plan, with its principal rooms organized axially around fireplaces, shows the influence of Wright, but is looser and more rambling, dissolving around the perimeter into generous balconies and sleeping porches from which vegetation spills out of large planting boxes. The open timber framing recalls earlier East Coast Stick style houses, but nowhere had the widely espoused ideal of natural living been so vividly achieved. The handling of the wooden structure shows a keen knowledge of Japanese practice, and as in

Above and opposite Gamble House, Pasadena, California, USA, 1907–8, Greene and Greene. With its integral terraces and sleeping-balconies the Gamble House exemplifies the relaxed way of life made possible by the equable Californian climate. The interior, a masterpiece of exposed timber structure and construction, is at its most compelling in the stair-hall.

Guy Hyde Chick House Berkeley, California, USA, 1914, Bernard Maybeck

Japan the construction was designed to move, to cope with tremors from the notorious San Andreas Fault. The pegged joints and metal straps – which bind the members together like thongs but enable them to slide when required – are marvellously refined and ornamental in effect, and all the structural elements are subtly tapered and rounded. The architects, who were also skilled carpenters, perfected many of the details on site and the craftsmanship and attention to detail are awesome.

The exterior quality is fully matched in the interior. A Live Oak rendered in stained glass fills the entrance doors and screen, and the living room, made entirely of teak, is a masterpiece of expressed structure and construction. Open trusses with sinuous corbelled brackets frame alcoves around the perimeter, and everything is exquisitely detailed down to the exposed fixings and art-glass lamps. Clouds drift across the bookcase glass and the tendrils of a vine climb up the fireplace tiles, displacing any possible doubts about the pervasive debt to Japan. Most inventive and memorable of all, however, is the main stair. A miracle of interlocking pieces of Burmese teak, it is almost animate in the way it seems to climb between floors. Dovetailed joints like interlocking fingers greet you beside the lowest steps, while above, the handrail zigzags its way up with muscular, animal grace. Each of the three sections of rail was carved from a single piece of wood, lending the whole a rare combination of constructive and sculptural power and marking it out as one of the supreme achievements of the Arts and Crafts movements on either side of the Atlantic.

The Gamble House was the most luxurious flower of a determination in California to develop bungalows and furniture appropriate to the new frontier. Its chief propagandist was Gustav Stickley, whose magazine *The Craftsman*, distributed from 1901 to 1916, was widely influential, and its most original talent was Bernard Maybeck, whose work fell into obscurity until its rediscovery in the 1970s. Although trained in the 1880s in that still mighty bastion of Classicism, the Ecole des Beaux-Arts in Paris, Maybeck developed a highly eclectic personal manner that drew on twelfth-century Gothic as freely as modern steel construction. Many of his early houses around San Francisco were inspired by the Swiss-chalet style, but he quickly stamped his own ideas on the type, tailoring each house to its site and owners, and endeavouring to make it embody an individual way of life. Interviewed in 1927 he said that, 'the thing to do is to make the home fit the family…. I never plan a home for a man until I have asked him a lot of questions. "What sort of woman is your wife? What kind of clothes do you both wear? What do you most like to read? Do you enjoy music?"'

Maybeck's chalet-style culminated in 1914 with the Guy Hyde Chick House in Berkeley's Chabot canyon. Framed in timber and clad in a mixture of vertical redwood boards, grey-green stained shingles and sand-finished plaster, it blends superbly with the native Live Oaks and the Japanese-inspired garden that threads among them. Large sliding doors connect the reception rooms to each other and, on every elevation, to outdoor paths and shallow terraces. Maybeck once defined architecture as 'landscape gardening around a few rooms'; the integration of house and garden here surpassed anything attempted by Greene and Greene and rivalled, in a more informal mode, the mature Prairie Style houses of Wright. The rooms were by no means as casually arranged as Maybeck's description might suggest, and on the upper floor three of the bedrooms have a strikingly novel feature: wardrobes that project beyond the volume of the house. They were not so much built-in as 'built-out', an idea Charles Moore later referred to as 'saddlebags' and were used to house kitchens, bathrooms and other service spaces. True to Maybeck's principles, the rooms reflected the life they were to accommodate. Most of the walls were plastered, but the living room was more refined, covered in dull gold velvet and trimmed in redwood, while in total contrast the boys' room upstairs, anticipating rougher treatment, was a timber world of board and batten walls and exposed beams and rafters.

Designed as war was breaking out in Europe, Maybeck's Chick House was but one of many built in the early 1900s in which we can see the culmination of ideas that had been maturing for half a century alongside hints of more radical innovations to come. The openness of its planning and effortless integration with the site anticipated ways of living that would not be widely adopted for several decades, but like all the houses we have explored in this chapter it looked back to the ideals of the Arts and Crafts movement with which the story of the twentieth-century house begins, more than forward to the possibilities of industrial production. Ideas and techniques that would ultimately transform the conception of the house from a handmade work of art into a 'machine for living in' had been developing throughout the nineteenth century, and it is to their consequences that we now turn.

Right and opposite Guy Hyde Chick House, Berkeley, California, USA, 1914, Bernard Maybeck. Combining native Californian timber-building traditions with Japanese influence, Maybeck fused house and garden, opening the principal rooms freely into each other and to the surrounding landscape.

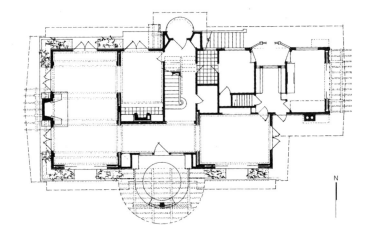

the modern house

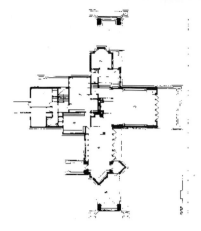

Above Ward Willits House, Highland Park, Chicago, Illinois, USA, 1901, Frank Lloyd Wright. With this cruciform plan Wright crystallized the idea of the Prairie House as an interpenetrating sequence of rooms, overlapping at their corners and pinwheeling around a central hearth.

Opposite Robie House, Chicago, Illinois, USA, 1909, Frank Lloyd Wright. Wright regarded it as the culmination of the Prairie House type, with a continuous living space inside and deeply overhanging cantilevered terraces and roofs expressing the 'strong earth line' Wright believed vital to any house.

The Modern house with a capital 'M' was born on the continent of Europe in the 1920s and quickly disseminated around the world. Externally, its walls were plain and unornamented, with large areas of glass, while internally separate rooms were replaced by a continuum of space made possible by a structural frame. The resulting 'open plan' reflected a new openness in living, the gradual breakdown of old social hierarchies, and a reduced dependence on servants. The first houses we could call modern with a small 'm', however, were built in the United States by Frank Lloyd Wright shortly after the earliest recorded use of the word 'modern' as a description of architecture. It occurred in the title – 'Moderne Architektur' – of Otto Wagner's inaugural lecture as professor at the Vienna Academy, given in 1895 and published the following year as a book. 'It may be regarded as proved,' Wagner said, 'that art and artists always represent their own epoch…. New forms originate from new construction, new materials, new human tasks and ideas.' Therefore 'all modern forms must correspond to new materials and the new requirements of our time, if they are to fit modern mankind.'

The search for a 'modern' style had been a preoccupation throughout the nineteenth century, underpinning the ideals of those who rejected the machine, like the exponents of the Arts and Crafts movement, as much as those who urged architects to embrace it, like Wagner. The engineer was widely seen as *l'homme moderne par excellence*, as a pupil of Emmanuel Viollet-le-Duc wrote in a paean of praise for the Eiffel Tower in 1889, and as early as the 1840s the American sculptor Horatio Greenough declared that 'form follows function' and compared steamships to the Parthenon. His assertion was popularized by Frank Lloyd Wright's mentor, Louis Sullivan, and Wright in turn quickly moved on from his Arts and Crafts roots to become a leading advocate of 'The Art and Craft of the Machine', as he entitled an important lecture given in Chicago in 1901. 'In the machine lies the only future of art and craft,' Wright declared, 'as I believe, a glorious future.' In the same year he designed the Ward Willits House in Highland Park, on the outskirts of Chicago: it is often called the 'first Prairie Style house' and in it Wright crystallized the ideas of form and space implicit in the Winslow House stables (see page 27).

The plan of the Willits House is cruciform, and on the ground floor the major rooms have open corners which interlock to form a continuous space that pinwheels around the central fireplace. The external form, horizontally layered and with low-pitched, deeply overhanging roofs which cantilever out to shelter porches and verandas, is a direct expression of this inner organization, and a response to the prairie landscape of the region. Only the vertical framing of the living room breaks the horizontal continuity, marking the double-height volume behind. Wright built the house using the standard American 'balloon frame' system, in which two-storey-high walls are framed in 10 x 5 centimetre (4 x 2 inch) timbers, sheathed and covered in stucco. Frames, trims and cover strips were all plain rectangular sections – he complained how difficult it was to get them without mouldings and so remain true to the simplicity he wanted to represent the 'art and craft of the machine'.

The clarity achieved in the Willits House was hard-won, the result of several years of experimentation, and Wright went on to exploit his innovations in a series of houses, many of them located in the Chicago suburb of Oak Park. Several of his clients were young engineers who shared his progressive ideals and had become managers of successful manufacturing companies. The thirty-year-old Frederick Robie was typical: an inventor who made bicycles and car parts in his father's firm.

Unusually, Robie found an urban corner site in south Chicago, near the University. It was tighter than Wright was used to working with and brought out what he considered to be the most extreme and conclusive expression of the Prairie House type. The Robie House has three floors, but at first sight it looks like a single, elevated level with a small addition emerging from the overhanging roofs; in fact there is also an almost invisible ground floor, like a basement above ground – Wright hated the ubiquitous American basement, believing it unhygienic. The house hugs the ground, yet the elevated brick walls and deeply undercut roofs appear almost to defy gravity: Wright's advocacy of building 'in the nature of materials' did not preclude the use, as here, of hidden steelwork to achieve the effects he was after. He was always sceptical of other architects' commitment to the 'honest' exposure of structure – 'I call it *indecent exposure*,' he said with characteristically caustic wit.

The horizontality is boldly reinforced by the stone foundation and lines of copings, and more subtly by the choice of a long Roman brick which is laid in thick, plain mortar beds but has narrower vertical joints pointed in coloured mortar to match the brick. Wright's attention to detail was total, and his specifications called for any exposed screw-heads to have their slots set horizontally: nothing was allowed to contradict the broad horizontals, the 'strong earth-line' which for Wright was always a vital expression of home and freedom in the open American landscape.

The Robie House plan has traces of the classic cruciform type, but to fit the site it was transformed into a long room with a vestigial cross-axis marked by the entrance, located out of sight around the back to ensure privacy, avoid breaking up the street frontage and heighten the sense of arrival. The fireplace, as we have come to expect, is at the heart of the house, sunk into the floor to suggest vertical continuity and opened above to allow an almost uninterrupted horizontal flow of space from living to dining room. Both ends of the main volume terminate in pointed prows framed by staggered piers, and the perimeter is enclosed by a ribbon of floor-to-ceiling doors and waist-high windows, all glazed with leaded lights of Wright's design. The composite effect is the dissolution of solid enclosure and the framing of space by folding planes – what Wright would later call the 'destruction of the box'. Artificial lighting, heating and ventilation are integrated seamlessly into the design: pierced wooden grilles above the windows conceal lamps which cast a gentle dappled light onto the floor, like sunlight through foliage, while the small globes suspended by the oak strips that weave their way back and forth across the ceiling reinforce the feeling of a folded plane floating above you.

Contemporary observers nicknamed the Robie House a 'ship of the prairie' and Neil Levine, the most thought-provoking recent interpreter of Wright's work, has likened his achievement here to the exactly contemporary Analytical Cubism of Picasso and Braque. Just as they fragmented figures into intersecting,

Robie House Oak Park, Illinois, USA, 1909, Frank Lloyd Wright

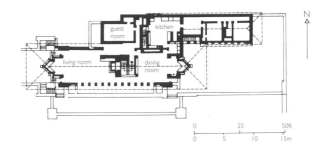

overlapping planes, Wright subjected the traditional image of the house – still secure in the Winslow design – to a series of transformations. He reinvented the dwelling as abstract planes that defined shifting geometric shapes in which traditional distinctions between wall and window, inside and out, cease to be valid. The real prairie may have been physically distant from Wright's Prairie houses, but he re-created its openness for their occupants through the abstraction of spatial continuity and horizontally stretched forms. This process reached its highpoint in the Robie House, which has a strong claim to be called the first fully modern house in which space itself is the prime medium of composition and the external forms are a direct expression of the habitable volumes within.

The same could almost be said of the extraordinary Torre de la Creu which stands just outside Barcelona. It was designed by Josep Maria Jujol, a talented former assistant of Antoni Gaudí now thought to be responsible for some of his finest ironwork and other details. The Torre contains a pair of houses and the plan is composed of six intersecting circles which rise as cylinders to various heights. Within the three larger, interpenetrating circles the rooms are subdivided orthogonally – a simple but clever move – and conventional horizontal circulation is replaced by the spiral stairs that occupy two of the smaller circles and bring light down into the interior. Everything flows from this singular plan which, as Le Corbusier would later declare, should be the 'generator' of the massing and surfaces. Torre de la Creu hardly conforms to our expectations of a 'modern' house – the formal elaboration seems vaguely Islamic, and it might well have been inspired by circular Romanesque churches in the region – but it is unique and utterly original, the forms ultimately Jujol's alone. In 1913, when he built it, only Frank Lloyd Wright had surpassed this level of spatial and formal innovation.

Torre de la Creu was destined to remain unknown, however: Jujol never rivalled its originality and had no impact on mainstream developments. Frank Lloyd Wright, on the other hand, had already produced a substantial body of work and would continue to build for another half century. His buildings may have been far away across the Atlantic and physically inaccessible to most, but increasingly architectural ideas would be promulgated in print. Two folios of Wright's work were published by Ernst Wasmuth of Berlin in 1910 and 1911 and they staggered the emerging European avant-garde. There, fully-formed, were compelling examples of that modern spatial art for which they were still searching. Wright's influence was clear as early as 1916 in the first concrete-framed house in Europe, a villa at Huis ter Heide designed by Robert van't Hoff, one of the few to see his work at first hand. Writing in 1918 another Dutchman J. J. P. Oud was in no doubt that Wright had 'advanced on the way towards the machine aesthetic' and 'laid the basis of a new plasticism in architecture'.

Closest among the Europeans to a comparable breakthrough, arguably, was the Viennese Adolf Loos; he was also the most acerbic critic of Art Nouveau. Loos launched his attacks as early as 1898 in Vienna's leading newspaper, writing about such ordinary things as underwear, men's hats and plumbing. Left to their own devices, he argued, the crafts unselfconsciously produced a 'modern' style, but they were being corrupted by style-mongers like the Secessionists. Loos thought these self-styled arbiters of 'taste' had no right to impose their

Torre de la Creu Barcelona, Spain, 1913, Josep Maria Jujol

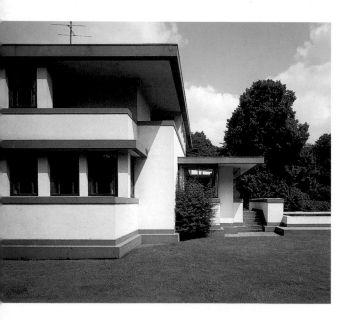

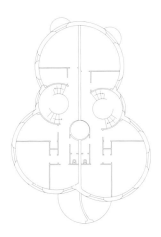

Above and right Torre de la Creu, Barcelona, Spain, 1913, Josep Maria Jujol. The spaces and external forms of this artfully asymmetrical pair of houses flow directly from the plan in a way which is thoroughly modern – despite the inventive but traditional-looking exterior.

Opposite Villa at Huis ter Heide, The Netherlands, 1916, Robert van't Hoff. The first concrete framed house in Europe, the villa was also first to have assimilated the lessons of Wright's Prairie Style.

values on others – in your flat, he said, 'it is you who are always right' – and he composed a story in which a 'poor rich man' commissioned an interior makeover (to borrow the term beloved of popular television home decorating programmes) by a thinly disguised Josef Hoffmann. He invited the master to see the completed interior, only for him to be horrified by the sight of the owner's embroidered slippers: '"But Mr Architect! have you already forgotten? You yourself designed them!" "Of course," thundered the architect, "but for the bedroom! They completely disrupt the mood here with these two impossible spots of colour. Can't you see that?"'

Loos famously inveighed against gratuitous ornament. His most celebrated essay was entitled *Ornament and Crime* (1908), often misquoted as 'ornament is crime', in which he argued that the 'evolution of culture marches with the elimination of ornament from useful objects'. In place of stylistic fripperies he advised his readers to study the everyday products of crafts and modern engineering: 'Behold the bicycle!' he urged, 'does not the spirit of Periclean Athens permeate its forms?' For Loos the Greeks still epitomized the ability to choose the 'one right form' and their modern counterparts were 'the English as a people, the engineers as a profession'.

Unlike many talented critics, Loos could match deed to word and the Steiner House he designed in Vienna in 1910 was the most austerely simple anywhere, its exterior relying solely on well proportioned, white rendered surfaces and large plate-glass windows. Two years later he completed the Scheu and Horner Houses. In 1934 the British journal *The Architectural Review* declared the former was the 'first in the world of which we can say without any sort of mental reservation that it is "modern" in our own specific sense of the word.' The *Review* was guilty of judging by appearances, however, as spatially the interiors were relatively traditional: arrangements of rooms, not compositions of space. In both there was also a radical disjunction between the austere exterior – a response to the anonymity of the modern city – and the intimate, private world of the interior with its panelled walls and exposed oak beams. This contrast was central to Loos's vision of the house as a shelter to the psyche as well as to the body and would persist in his work throughout the 1920s.

Around the period of 1912 to 1913 Loos began to have the germs of a spatial idea that blossomed after the war: 'This is the great revolution in architecture,' he declared, 'the planning of a building in volume.' He called his 'plan of volumes' a *Raumplan*, and viewed the building cube as a void to be filled freely with rooms of different volume, scaled in section as well as plan to fit the activities they contain. We first see the *Raumplan* fully at work in the Rufer House, built in Vienna in 1922. The exterior is almost completely cubic, broken only by a veranda and a roof terrace cut into the volume, and the windows are scattered, apparently at random, across the rendered surfaces. In fact, of course, they are positioned to suit the rooms within, and adjusted to achieve a dynamic balance externally. The plan revolves around a central column, which doubles as a central-heating flue, and the principal rooms – named music and dining – open around it on different levels. 'Floors', in their familiar guise, were beginning to disappear, something he took further in several subsequent designs, culminating with the Müller House of 1930 in Prague.

Above Horner House, Vienna, Austria, 1912, Adolf Loos. The idiosyncratic placement of the windows directly reflects the organization of the rooms and staircase within. The austere exterior was Loos's response to the anonymity of the modern city, in striking contrast to the inner life of rich materials to be discovered in the privacy of the dwelling.

Müller House Prague, Czech Republic, 1930, Adolf Loos

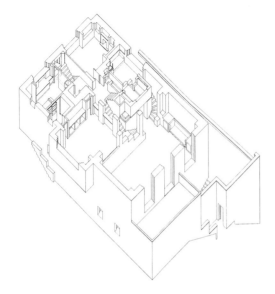

Schröder House Utrecht, the Netherlands, 1924, Gerrit Rietveld

On paper we can see that, in principle, the plan of the Müller House is organized on multiple levels around a central stair. But this stair is only reached after passing through an anteroom, turning left up seven risers onto a landing before the main hall, and then turning right and rising another half-level to reach the core. The interior verges on the labyrinthine: few rooms share the same 'floor' and the identity of each is reinforced by varied proportions and unique surface treatments. The latter were grounded in Loos's commitment to the theory of cladding articulated by Gottfried Semper in the mid-nineteenth century, and based on a radical division between structure and enclosure. Semper traced this idea back to animal skins or carpets hung from a timber framework. To emphasize that his finishes were (almost literally) only skin deep, Loos favoured veneers of highly figured stone and wood, deploying them both to assert the uniqueness of each room and, by allowing the material of one space to invade the next, to ensure a degree of ambiguity and continuity.

Although Loos's writings were widely admired – several essays were reproduced in the magazine *L'Esprit nouveau* founded in 1920 by Amedée Ozenfant and Charles-Edouard Jeanneret (who soon restyled himself Le Corbusier) – his work had little impact on mainstream developments. His way of composing was, in some respects, more fully three-dimensional than the 'open plan' which, by the mid 1920s, came to define the Modern house. But he still thought in terms of rooms, and the truly radical innovation of European Modernism, anticipated by Wright, was to reinvent the house as a continuous spatial field. The first time we see that idea fully realized is in the Schröder House in Utrecht, a collaboration between the client, Truus Schröder-Schräder, and Gerrit Rietveld, who studied architecture in the evenings after training as a furniture-maker. In this capacity, from 1917 to 1918, he created one of the first and most unforgettable icons of modern design, the 'Red and Blue' chair.

Truus Schröder-Schräder was married to a lawyer but preferred to socialize with the avant-garde and immerse herself in books on philosophy, art and architecture. She tried, often against her husband's wishes, to implement progressive educational ideas for her three children and when he died young in 1923 decided to make a new start in a new home. She found a small plot at the end of a terrace facing open country (now, sadly, occupied by an elevated motorway and, beyond it, more housing, including some designed by Rietveld). Rietveld had previously worked on the Schröder's flat, and other small conversions, but had never designed a new building. He brought a strong personal vision about form and space to the task, but few preconceptions about what a house should be, and so the design evolved in response to the liberated life Truus wanted to live. Architect and client became – possibly already were – lovers, but although Rietveld kept an office in the house, he only moved in after the death of his wife in 1958.

Mrs Schröder-Schräder decided to live at first floor level, to enjoy the views, and wanted to be in close contact with her children whom she thought should be educated by mixing with the artists and intellectuals she entertained. To circumvent building regulations, the ground floor was designed with relatively

Above Müller House, Prague, Czech Republic, 1930, Adolf Loos. The cubic form belies the complex sequence of rooms organised on many levels within, where the materials and colours are chosen to create an appropriate atmosphere – as seen in the contrast between the children's suite (**right**) and the formality and luxury of the principal reception room (**below**).

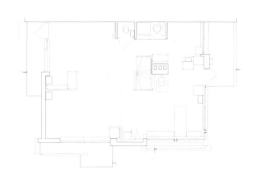

Above Schröder House, Utrecht,
The Netherlands, 1924, Gerrit Rietveld.
The ground floor plan (**below**) was
conventional, the upper floor (**top,
centre and right**), which Mrs
Schröder-Schräder occupied,
unprecedented in its openness.
The space can be transformed by
sliding and folding partitions and
furniture, and is articulated by coloured
planes: 'the destruction of the box'
announced by Wright was complete.

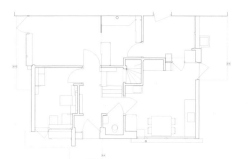

conventional rooms, including a built-in garage – novel at the time, especially as she didn't have a car – and the first floor was left open and called simply 'attic'. It proved to be the most important attic in the history of architecture. Near its centre Rietveld placed a tight, winding staircase, lit through the flat roof by a cubic skylight. In the rear corner, tucked against the party wall, was Truus's room, which could open into the living area via a folding door. The rest of the space could be completely open, or subdivided by thin sliding partitions into living space, a room for her two girls, and one for her boy.

With a craftsman's eye for detail Rietveld redesigned everything in the house in light of the aesthetic principles explored in his furniture. The windows, framed by differently coloured strips of wood, could be either closed or secured fully open at 90 degrees to the façade so as not to introduce a jarring diagonal (there were several sizes of opening to allow for different rates of ventilation). Broad sills were provided for ornaments and plants – very Dutch, like the bench beside the entrance – and all the furniture was either built-in or of Rietveld's design.

Every detail reflected the organizing principle of the house: the definition, but not containment, of space by sticks and planes. To emphasize their autonomy they were variously coloured, and either freestanding or slipped past one another to avoid conventional corners. To open the interior to the garden and countryside, columns retreated from the corners, which could be completely dissolved by opening the windows. The result was a complete *Gesamtkunstwerk*, like the Palais Stoclet, but free of inner tensions between the modernity of the surfaces and a classical plan. And whereas the houses we considered in the last chapter all too easily, as Adolf Loos realized, became aesthetic tyrannies, Rietveld's masterpiece was liberating and receptive to ordinary living: Truus Schröder-Schräder dwelt there happily until her death in 1985.

The Schröder House was the first building to match the widely shared post-war dream of a new world, rebuilt from the ground up on new aesthetic, social and political principles. In the Schröder House, as in all the greatest modern houses, the architectural means were developed and deployed in the service of a new vision for living. To Rietveld and his client, clarity and simplicity were articles of faith as much as artistic means. Truus Schröder-Schräder's ideas about the family, the role of women in society, and the shared responsibilities of individuals were central to the making of her house, and Rietveld's unsurpassed achievement was to create an environment in which simple acts like closing partitions or raising and lowering a table assumed ritual significance as part of a conscious celebration of daily life.

In the absence of evidence to the contrary, it might be tempting to suppose that the Schröder House was an inhabitable version of a Mondrian painting. Rietveld, like Mondrian, was embraced by Theo van Doesburg, leader of the Dutch De Stijl movement, but he arrived at his key ideas largely independently and never fully subscribed to theirs. He worked by instinct rather than theory and in this respect was an unusual figure among the pioneers of modern architecture, with whom ideas frequently ran ahead of the ability – or opportunities – to realize them. This was the case with Le Corbusier who began promoting his revolutionary vision in earnest in *L'Esprit Nouveau* in 1920, and then in 1923 assembled the articles to form the book *Vers une architecture*. It was translated into English in 1927 and published, slightly misleadingly, under the title *Towards a New Architecture*. It proved to be one of the most influential books on architecture ever written.

Like Loos in Vienna, Le Corbusier began by attacking his *bêtes noires* – the overblown, worn-out Classicism of the Ecole des Beaux-Arts and the, to him, absurd idea that architecture could be reduced to a superficial question of 'style'. After reminding his fellow architects of the timeless means of their art – the control of mass, surface and plan (which, as we noted above, he called the 'generator'), and the use of geometrically ordered 'regulating lines' to control proportions of the locations and sizes of openings – he went on to explain, for 'eyes which do not see', the aesthetic virtues of engineering structures and machines. He illustrated his arguments with American grain silos (pictures of which were in circulation in Europe before the war) and other engineering works, comparing in a famous pairing of images a 1907 Humber with the early Greek temple at Paestum, and a racy 'Grand-Sport' Delage of 1921 with the Parthenon. His message was that whereas it had taken over a century and a half to achieve the refinement of the Greek temples, it took only fourteen years to move from the 'primitive' to the 'classic' phase in car design. This progress, he argued, was driven by a process he called 'mechanical selection', a Darwinian view of industry which he believed resulted in functionally perfect *objets-types*. The comparisons were persuasive but like much propaganda, at times devious: the Delage was a handcrafted product, not mass-produced like the famous Model T Ford.

Vers une architecture culminated in a call for mass-produced houses to meet the housing shortage afflicting Europe in the wake of war, a call later summed up by a phrase that has entered the language: 'the house is a machine for living in' (although 'a machine for living' might have been more accurate). To confound any narrowly mechanistic interpretation, Le Corbusier defined beauty and a sense of proportion as key features of this 'machine'. The design of compact houses for low-paid working families preoccupied many leading architects in the 1920s, not least those at the Bauhaus, the most influential art and design school of the century, and will be considered in detail in the next chapter. Here we will concentrate on the spatial ideas that were more fully realized in larger, private commissions.

Le Corbusier's new vision of space was made possible by replacing load-bearing walls with structural frames. It was implicit in the Dom-Ino house he developed in 1914 in response to the early devastation of the war in Flanders, but it took him a decade, he later explained, to realize its architectural possibilities. These he duly published at the Weissenhof Exhibition of new housing in Stuttgart as the 'Five Points of a New Architecture':

1. Columns (he called them *pilotis*) to raise the house in the air, freeing the ground for the movement of people and vehicles.
2. A *roof garden* on the *flat roof*, to replace the ground lost by development.
3. Extending the *pilotis* through as a structural frame to free the external walls and partitions, enabling the latter to be freely arranged to suit the planning requirements – which he termed the *plan libre*, or free plan.
4. Disposing windows and terraces as required by the interior to create what he called a *free façade.*
5. Long horizontal windows – *fenêtres en longueur* or ribbon windows – to give an even, generous distribution of light.

Villa Stein Garches, France, 1926–8, Le Corbusier

As principles go these are an odd mixture of construction, functional organization and aesthetic preference. Ribbon windows certainly do not give the light distribution he claimed, but they do differ radically from the upright stance of conventional windows, which is what he needed to express the continuous, 'flowing' space within. They were all seen for the first time in the modestly sized Cook House built on the outskirts of Paris in 1926, on a site overlooking the Bois de Boulogne. To emphasize its machine-like modernity the entrance, with its curved front and narrow band of windows, recalls the cockpit of the 'Goliath' biplane illustrated in *Vers une architecture*, while the wing-like roof canopy is supported by columns as slender as those holding the plane's wings together. Internally, the compact form did not allow much room to demonstrate the virtues of the *plan libre* – even after, to his client's cost and annoyance, Le Corbusier 'stole' an extra half metre (1.5 feet) from the neighbouring property – but three-quarters of the main level is a continuous open space, with the living room itself occupying a double-height volume. On the bedroom floor the partitions demonstrate their freedom by artfully evading the columns and wrapping sinuously around a wash-basin and built-in table.

In the vastly larger villa at Garches, begun the same year and completed in 1928, Le Corbusier exploited the new possibilities to the full, carving terraces at various levels out of the broad rectangular block and interlinking and interpenetrating spaces vertically and horizontally to form a continuous whole of great complexity. The clients could hardly have been more exciting: the Stein family – the legendary Gertrude, Leo, Michael and his wife Sarah, one of Matisse's most important patrons – wished to share it with their friend Gabrielle Colaço-Osorio de Monzie and her daughter. Michael Stein was a classic example of the 'new man' whose virtues were extolled in *L'Esprit Nouveau* and described by Le Corbusier's colleague Charlotte Perriand as the 'type of individual who keeps pace with scientific thought, who understands his age and lives it: the Aeroplane, the Ocean Liner and the Motor are at his service; Sport gives him health; his house is his resting place'. And like Madame de Monzie, who owned several châteaux in the South of France, he was also passionate about art and rich enough to build on the grand scale.

The freedom of the *plan libre* came into its own in accommodating the clients' intricate living arrangements and they in turn fell in love with their new house and garden, nicknaming it Les Terrasses. They disappointed Le Corbusier by insisting on furnishing it with their heavy antiques, and he conspicuously omitted all furniture, save for some casually placed white Parisian chairs on the terrace, from the photographs in the first volume of his *Oeuvre complète*.

Like several of Le Corbusier's larger houses of the 1920s, that at Garches seems to engage in a dialogue with the master of the Classical villa, Andrea Palladio. The column grid alternates between wide and narrow bays, and the spaces are similarly layered in contrasting zones from front to back. Centrality, a hallmark of Classicism, is asserted and then denied: the ribbon windows force the eye to the edges, and incidents are scattered around the perimeter of the plan. The front elevation is a masterpiece of subverted symmetries, geometrically controlled by hidden regulating lines: ribbon window balances garage door;

Above and left Villa Stein, Garches, France, 1926–8, Le Corbusier. Artfully asymmetrical and layered in plan and elevation, the Villa Stein was a sophisticated re-working of the compositional norms of the Classical villa, designed to accommodate the clients' unusually complicated domestic requirements.

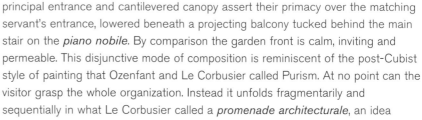

Villa Savoye Poissy, France, 1928-30, Le Corbusier

principal entrance and cantilevered canopy assert their primacy over the matching servant's entrance, lowered beneath a projecting balcony tucked behind the main stair on the *piano nobile*. By comparison the garden front is calm, inviting and permeable. This disjunctive mode of composition is reminiscent of the post-Cubist style of painting that Ozenfant and Le Corbusier called Purism. At no point can the visitor grasp the whole organization. Instead it unfolds fragmentarily and sequentially in what Le Corbusier called a *promenade architecturale*, an idea inspired by the ascent to the Acropolis in Athens, which he brought to a peak of perfection in the house with which this phase of his work culminated, the Villa Savoye in Poissy.

The site for the villa is now hemmed in by trees which screen a large school, but it was originally open and enjoyed fine views over the Seine valley. So, like Palladio in his Villa Rotunda, Le Corbusier opted for a square plan to address the four horizons. But in place of the central room with its dome, he placed a ramp around which the promenade through space unfolds. In fact things are not quite so simple: the square is defined by a classically incorrect four-by-four bay system ('incorrect' because there is a column, not a visually restful open bay, at the centre) and extended by cantilevers along the direction of approach to imply an understated major axis, along which the ramp, in turn, is displaced off-centre. The visitor is greeted by a true 'elevation', a flat plane which touches the ground, but all the other sides are undercut at ground level by a curving screen of glass and metal whose radius was defined by the turning circle of a Voisin car, to be driven in the gap between the columns into the three-bay garage – M. Savoye, another New Man, also liked his cars.

You enter the house on axis at the centre of the curved screen and are greeted immediately by the ramp and, to its left, a freestanding pedestal wash-basin, an industrially produced *objet-type* that almost inevitably brings to mind Marcel Duchamp's notorious urinal 'fountain'. As the ramp gently rises and turns to ascend to the first floor, views open invitingly to the right – where the sculptural stair, bathed in sunlight, corkscrews up and out of sight – and then to the left, enabling you to see through a triangle of glass, across the open terrace, through the corner of the living room and out to the landscape framed by the ribbon window. The living room, glimpsed during your ascent, opens to the terrace via almost 10 metres (32 feet) of full-height glazing, half of which can slide open courtesy of a hand-crank. The terrace retreats beneath the roof slab into an outdoor room from where, in one of the defining views of the new ideal of interpenetrating spaces, you can see directly out through the glassless ribbon window, back through the living room to the landscape, and up to the roof garden and sky.

The ramp obligingly appears outside on the terrace to continue the promenade that culminates on the roof. You arrive, on axis with an opening framing a view towards the Seine, in a 'solarium' defined by a freestanding wall – originally painted pink and blue – whose plan recalls a guitar in a Cubist painting. The roof is planted with low shrubs and paved, partly with slabs like the terrace, partly with gravel like the driveway framed below, but despite these landscape materials it feels more like the deck of a ship, an image Le Corbusier prompts with the funnel-like enclosure of the stair and white-painted, nautical steel-tube handrails. What he wants us to experience here, beneath the sun and surrounded by pure form, is

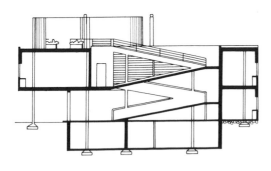

This page and opposite
Villa Savoye, Poissy, France, 1928–30, Le Corbusier. Floating like an ocean liner in a meadow outside Paris, this weekend house marks the culmination of Le Corbusier's 1920s villas. Organized as a winding 'architectural promenade' around the ramp (**opposite, centre and bottom**), which leads to the roof-top solarium and (originally) open views over the Seine valley. The full-height glazing to the living room (**left and above**) can slide away to unite interior and terrace; the small planters frame a roof-light in the garage below, which further opens the house vertically.

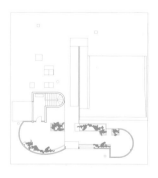

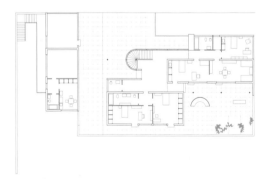

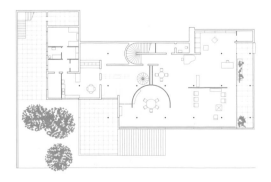

Above, below, opposite and overleaf Tugendhat House, Brno, Czech Republic, 1928–30, Mies van der Rohe. Like all Mies's buildings, this exceptionally large house is organized as spatially independent layers. The open-plan living floor sits below the bedrooms and is articulated by free-standing planes of luxurious materials; the entire south-facing glazed wall can disappear into the basement, transforming the interior into an open belvedere with splendid views of distant parkland.

what he called 'architecture's purest gift, mathematical lyricism'.

The Villa Savoye is a work of consummate artistry in which freedom and order coexist in subtle and ever-shifting tension. The architectural order, posited by the column grid and latent symmetries, recalls the disciplines of Classicism but is everywhere responsive to patterns of use and to the presence of the observer. One notices, for example, how the ramp is framed by two rows of columns, not divided by them as the grid would require, and that these are then doubled to mark a rectangular place of arrival. Elsewhere, individual columns step aside to free a room – there are none in the generous garage – or move slightly to engage with a partition: freestanding columns are always round, engaged ones square. Space is designed to be experienced, not as a formal end in itself, and the experience is inseparable from movement, upwards and outwards, towards the landscape and sky, towards nature.

Le Corbusier described the house as 'a place that gives birth to happiness' and architecture as 'a floor bathed in light', and in houses like the Villa Savoye the 'natural joys' of *soleil, espace et verdure* ('sun, space and greenery') are framed and represented in heightened form. The main bathroom, for example, is en suite with the master bedroom and internal, but opens to the sky through a roof light which unexpectedly fills it with sun. For all the rhetoric about machines and an engineer's aesthetic, these houses are profoundly humane, designed to reconnect us to nature and to elevate the dwelling to the status of a temple to the family. They bring to mind Baudelaire's desire for '*luxe, calme et volupté*' ('luxury, calm and voluptuous') a phrase used as the title of a celebrated painting by Matisse – and achieve this feeling using the purest of architectural means, 'volumes brought together in light', to use part of a famous definition in *Vers une architecture*. In this respect Le Corbusier differs significantly from the only European to rival him in talent, the German Mies van der Rohe. The son of a stonemason and heir to the German tradition of *Baukunst*, the 'art of building', Mies always retained a love of craftsmanship and fine materials. Echoing Hegel's belief in the *Zeitgeist* he defined architecture as 'the will of an epoch translated into space; living, changing, new'. He aimed to free architecture from 'problems of form' and return it to 'problems of building'.

Between 1919 and 1924 Mies exhibited a series of seminal projects, each based on a specific material. By reducing architecture to its structural essentials he anticipated its trajectory over the next few decades – variations on his Glass Tower and Concrete Office Building would be built worldwide in the 1950s and 1960s. The 1923 project for a Brick Country House was composed solely of straight and L-shaped brick walls and planes of glass. Mies was certainly familiar with the innovations of Frank Lloyd Wright and De Stijl – the pinwheeling pattern recalls some of Wright's plans, and more directly a 1917 painting, *Rhythms of a Russian Dance*, by Theo van Doesburg – and his idealized house combined the abstract quality of the Dutch exemplars with a determination to stay close to the 'nature of materials': the drawings show every brick, laid in Flemish bond. Mies built several fine brick houses during the 1920s, but none had the spatial freedom of this early project. The breakthrough came with the German Pavilion at the Barcelona Exhibition of 1929 and the Tugendhat House in Brno completed the following year, when Mies also took over as director of the Bauhaus.

Brno became an important industrial centre in the late nineteenth century, the population reaching 100,000 at the turn of the century. New suburbs blossomed, including Cerná Pole where, as part of his wife Greta Weiss's dowry, Fritz Tugendhat acquired a large sloping plot, facing south over parkland towards the city. They married in 1928 after putting in hand the construction of their house, which they entrusted to Mies on the basis of the initial design for the German Pavilion seen on a visit to Berlin the previous year. Tugendhat was a successful cloth manufacturer and the couple's combined resources were considerable: the

Tugendhat House Brno, Czech Republic, 1928-30, Mies van der Rohe

first thing to be said about the Tugendhat House is that, at 2,000 square metres (21,000 square feet), including a generous basement, it is very large indeed – something not always grasped in photographs and drawings.

The house occupies a sloping site and is entered at the upper level, between two pavilions containing the bedrooms. Thanks to the travertine floor, full-height translucent glass and dark, palisander-veneered doors and wall panelling, the atmosphere is calm, inward-looking, and quietly opulent. You descend via a broad dog-leg stair and emerge into the vast living space. Directly ahead, filling the short side, is a winter garden bursting with exotic plants. To your right, glimpsed between the straight plane of pale onyx that screens the library and a semi-circle of highly figured red- and brown-streaked macassar enclosing the dining alcove, is a wall of cast glass which not only runs the full 24-metre (79-foot) length of the space but can disappear, as if by magic, into the basement, transforming the entire living area into an open belvedere overlooking the garden. All the furniture was designed by Mies, some of it, like the 'Brno Chair', especially for the house, and the materials – emerald green leather, ruby velvet and white vellum – are luxurious and colourful. Each piece had its appointed place, where it was meant to remain, frozen in time – an aesthetic vision very different from that of Le Corbusier's *plan libre*.

Believing that a 'clear structure is the basis of the free plan', Mies maintained the regularity of the grid throughout most of the interior; a few columns are replaced by walls, but for the most part the grid reads clearly as a counterpoint to the freestanding partitions and furniture. The columns are cruciform, made of eight steel angles clad in polished, highly reflective chrome: slender and shiny, they hardly appear capable of bearing the load. The floor is finished in ivory-coloured linoleum – a modern material par excellence in the 1930s – which by day assumes an almost identical tone to the white ceiling. At 3 metres (10 feet) the ceiling height is sufficiently generous for the space not to appear cramped, and the space is contrived to ensure that your eye level is poised halfway between the floor and ceiling planes. As Robin Evans has pointed out, in the similarly dimensioned German Pavilion at Barcelona the classical symmetries banished from the plan reappear in section in a way that reinforces the feeling of a 'floating world' of reflective surfaces and luxurious materials transfigured by light. It was perhaps this which inspired a contemporary critic to remark that Mies here showed how to 'elevate oneself above purely rational and functional thinking . . . into the realm of the spiritual.'

The Tugendhats, who were Jewish, fled their house in 1938. It was eventually taken over by the Communist authorities and during the 1960s the living room

was used as a gymnasium to help rehabilitate disabled children – many of the interior details survived, but the floor was painted bright red. It was restored, minus the original furniture and many of the fittings, in the late 1980s.

Maison de Verre Paris, France, 1928–32, Pierre Chareau

The Maison de Verre in Paris by Pierre Chareau, assisted by the Dutchman Bernard Bijvoet, suffered a different sort of neglect: forgotten by all but a few cognoscenti until the 1960s. But by the 1980s it had achieved cult status and was acclaimed by some, rather extravagantly, as the 'greatest house of the century'. Realized between 1928 and 1932 and designed down to the last detail, here was a very different vision of the 'machine for living in', singular and grand.

The house was wedged in between and under surrounding apartments and both elevations were made almost entirely of glass bricks of the type normally found in public lavatories: laid in four-brick-wide panels, they established the 91-centimetre (36-inch) module that runs throughout the design. Industrial steel sections were riveted together to form the main structure – they look as if they might have escaped from a factory – and the interior bristles with endlessly inventive details: bookcase balustrades, a lift-out-of-the-way ship's stair and warm-air filled hollow steel floors. The bathrooms, which eventually found many imitators, are screened by curving panels of finely perforated aluminium, and duralumin was used to make sleekly efficient wardrobes and drawers. It seems an unlikely home and office for a gynaecologist, although Chareau's attention to the hygienic virtues of clear air, natural light and durable materials was exemplary, offering a different vision of architectural modernity to that of Le Corbusier, who was a regular visitor during construction. In place of the classical disciplines of form, proportion and space modelled by light, Chareau – an interior and furniture designer by training – toiled in his workshop producing what he described as 'a model executed by craftsmen with the aim of industrial standardization': virtues calculated to appeal to new generations of designers after 1945.

From its inception, the pioneers of the new architecture had seen it as international in spirit and scope. The first Bauhaus book, published in 1925, was dedicated to 'International Architecture', and lecturing in Buenos Aires four years later Le Corbusier looked forward to an improbable utopia when rooms everywhere could be conditioned to a standardized 18°C (64°F). This faith was grounded in the widely felt need to transcend the national differences that had led to war and to build a new world order based on rational, supposedly universal, values. Modern art and architecture could be as international as modern science and technology because it was believed that, 'all men react unanimously to broad daylight or full night, or red or black, or love or death', to quote *Foundations of Modern Art* by Le Corbusier's former colleague Ozenfant.

In light of such beliefs, the new architecture was designed to appear universal, independent of specific materials, sites or cultural traditions. Despite its proponents' belief that their ideas transcended traditional ideas of style, it was almost inevitable that sooner or later someone would christen it the 'International Style'. It happened in 1932, at New York's Museum of Modern Art (the first such in the world), courtesy of Henry-Russell Hitchcock and Philip Johnson who used it as the title of a book published to accompany an exhibition of almost a hundred buildings from sixteen countries. The exhibition travelled to eleven other cities in America but

Above and opposite Maison de Verre, Paris, France, 1928–32, Pierre Chareau. Enclosed by glass brick panels framed in steel, the house was conceived as a cage of light, wedged into a tight Parisian courtyard. Internally the planning is intricate and the detailing endlessly surprising and inventive – riveted factory-style columns, book-case balustrades and warm-air filled floors.

made little impact; the book, on the other hand, travelled the world and did.

Hitchcock and Johnson defined the new style by three features: the treatment of a building as a *volume* defined by surfaces, not as a mass; *formal regularity*, resulting from proportional control and orderly structure; and the *avoidance of applied decoration* – superficial, stylistic criteria that missed the spatial essence of the new 'style'. Frank Lloyd Wright figured in the exhibition – which had the less exclusive title 'Modern Architecture: International Exhibition' – but not the book; his former assistant Rudolf Schindler, whom we met in the last chapter as a student of Otto Wagner, was not in either. He probably ruined his chances by explaining with his submission, 'I am not a stylist, not a functionalist, nor any other sloganist.'

Schindler was, however, an exceedingly good architect and his Lovell Beach House, completed in 1926 in Los Angeles, flaunted a gymnastic structural frame containing cleverly worked spaces that owed something to Loos's *Raumplan*. It was one of the most inventive houses of the decade and, although far from orthodox, certainly met all of Hitchcock and Johnson's rather woolly criteria. The house ran slightly over budget and Schindler lost his client to his supposed friend and fellow Austrian emigré, Richard Neutra. Lovell, a fanatical advocate of natural remedies, vegetarianism, exercise and nude sunbathing, and author of a column entitled 'Care of the Body' for the *Los Angeles Times*, commissioned a house in the Hollywood Hills from Neutra; it eventually cost more than twice the estimate on its completion in 1929. The design was steel-framed, relaxed and rambling, in a way that Californian houses tend to be, and featured inventive details such as suspended aluminium light troughs and a Model T Ford headlamp to light the staircase. Lovell promoted his house vigorously, opening it regularly to an amazed public: 15,000 came, making the 'Health House', as it was soon known, an instant star and ensuring its inclusion in Hitchcock and Johnson's canon.

In the same year that the Health House opened in Los Angeles, in Copenhagen Arne Jacobsen exhibited a project for a circular 'House of the Future', complete with a helicopter on its roof terrace. He also moved into his own house of white-painted brick: like many, it looked thoroughly modern, thanks to large areas of glass and corner windows, but the plan was still relatively conventional. In 1930 the Stockholm Exhibition, co-ordinated by Gunnar Asplund, disseminated the new ideas widely in Scandinavia, while in Italy Figini and Pollini showed their Electric House at an exhibition of decorative art in Monza. In the same year, the Swede Sven Markelius demonstrated his mastery of modernity in his own house in Nockeby, and Amyas Connell built 'High and Over' in Amersham, England. This was the first British house to look authentically modern, although the Corbusian motifs could not disguise Connell's abiding love of Classicism, plain for all to see in the symmetrical Y-shaped plan extending into a formal garden.

Although it accounted for a tiny proportion of new buildings, the International style proved attractive to clients worldwide who were eager to assert their modernity. In Norway Arne Korsmo became an inventive exponent, as witnessed by houses like Villa Damman of 1934, and the same year in New York William Lescaze built his own house, adapting the new style to the constraints of a

Lovell Health House Los Angeles, California, USA, 1927–9, Richard Neutra

Above Lovell Beach House, Los Angeles, California, USA, 1926, Rudolf Schindler. Behind the boldly exposed frame the planning reflects the influence of Adolf Loos, whose work Schindler knew before leaving Vienna to work for Frank Lloyd Wright.

Above and overleaf Lovell Health House, Los Angeles, California, USA, 1927–9, Richard Neutra. The Health House was built in the Hollywood Hills for the same client as Schindler's Beach House. A well known journalist and advocate of healthy living, Lovell promoted his Health House assiduously, helping to make it the best known emblem of the new architecture in the USA.

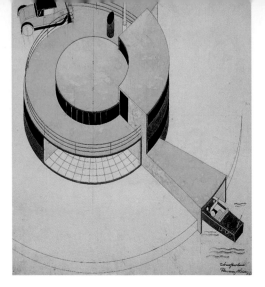

Above House of the Future (exhibition project), Copenhagen, Denmark, 1929, Arne Jacobsen. Replete with roof-top helicopter pad, the house offered a playful interpretation of the radical new spirit of modernity.

Below Stockholm Exhibition, Stockholm, Sweden, 1930, Gunnar Asplund *et al*. Arguably the best of many staged to promote the new ideas, the Stockholm Exhibition marked the official arrival of modern architecture in Scandinavia, where it flourished in the social-democratic political climate.

narrow mid-terrace plot. By 1932 Spain and Mexico could boast fine examples, such as Josep Lluis Sert's Galobart House and Juan O'Gorman's studio and apartment for Frances Toor in Mexico City. With its deep blue walls and Venetian red stair the latter clearly referred to the Mexican vernacular – but also to the 'machines for living in' that Le Corbusier had designed at Pessac. The mid-1930s saw the completion of several fine houses in Italy. Notable among them were Luigi Figini's own house in the Villagio dei Giornalisti in Milan in 1935, an essay in the Corbusian manner raised high on square *pilotis* and capturing a tree in its courtyard, and the richly layered Villa Bianca in Seveso, completed in 1937 by Giuseppe Terragni, one of the most formidable talents of his generation.

Modern architecture spread extensively through Eastern Europe, where private houses, such as Jozsef Fischer's Villa Hoffmann in Hungary, were outnumbered by dwellings and flats for workers, and it was taken to Palestine by Jews fleeing the Nazis. The most notable among them was Erich Mendelsohn, but again flats rather than private houses predominated, so much so that Tel Aviv can probably boast more 'Bauhaus' buildings than any other city. A group of talented young modernists led by Rex Martienssen flourished in South Africa and were honoured with a dedication by Le Corbusier in the 1936 edition of the first volume of his *Oeuvre complète*. Most of the houses built around the world were competent essays in the new manner rather than notably innovative, however, and during the 1930s the most far-reaching developments came from reinterpretations of the new ideas in light of local traditions, cultures and climates, which we will examine in Chapter 4.

The European examples we have so far considered are 'modern' in a particular sense of the word: they exemplify a set of ideas about spatial continuity and functional organization, and exhibit a marked preference, as Hitchcock and Johnson spotted, for simple volumes, regularity, and the avoidance of applied decoration. These aspects of the modern style were interrelated, but by no means always interdependent, and a significant competing set of ideas, sometimes described by the misleading term 'Expressionist', was largely banished from the official canon of the International style because of its love of what the mainstream saw as arbitrary irregularity. The leading theorist of this strand of thought was Hugo Häring, and its most gifted practitioner Hans Scharoun.

Häring rejected aesthetic dogma and set himself the task of challenging Le Corbusier, whom he saw as a representative of 'Latin Classicism', determined to impose geometric forms on life. Nature was Häring's model, and he believed that after centuries of oppression by arbitrary geometry, 'light constructions, with elastic and supple materials' offered the freedom to respond organically to building programmes. He illustrated his ideas in 1923 with a 'house shaped by use and movement'. Although conceived independently, it might have been intended as a direct, organically functional response to Mies's Brick Country House exhibited that same year. Where Mies's design was a differentiated field of space which left the viewer to speculate how it might be inhabited, Häring's showed every piece of furniture to illustrate how completely the walls wrapped themselves around the life to be lived – in places quite literally, around specific tables and chairs. By the 1940s Häring would go so far as to show coat hooks and a pair of gloves left on the hall table placed to receive them.

Above Villa Damman, Oslo, Norway, 1934, Arne Korsmo. The villa is organized around a double-height living room, which was running the full length of the house high, blank walls to display pictures.

Below Lescaze House, New York, USA, 1934, William Lescaze. Dispensing with a sub-basement, the house steps boldly forward of its terraced neighbours.

Above 'High and Over', Amersham, England, 1930, Amyas Connell. Modernist surfaces and volumetric composition are deployed around a classically symmetrical plan.

Left Figini House, Milan, Italy, 1935, Luigi Figini. Le Corbusier's 'Five Points' are reinterpreted in the light of Italian Rationalism. The long, narrow volume is entered from below via an external staircase.

Right Villa Bianca, Seveso, Italy, 1937, Giuseppe Terragni. The house is a richly layered composition of volumes and planes by the most gifted Italian architect of his generation.

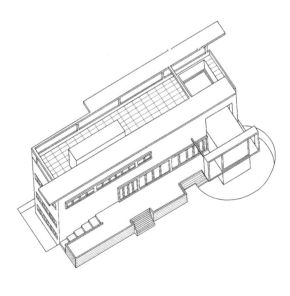

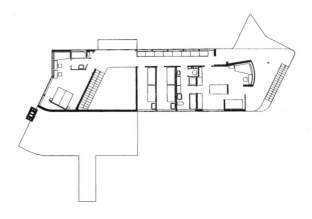

Schminke House Löbau, Germany, 1932–3, Hans Scharoun

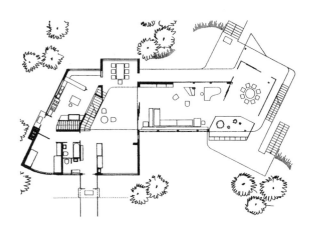

Melnikov House and Studio Moscow, Russia, 1927, Konstantin Melnikov

Hans Scharoun was deeply influenced by Häring's ideas, but by no means unresponsive to the visual power of Le Corbusier's work. Even in the absence of other evidence one might surmise as much from an early perspective sketch of his finest house, which shows the owner's car sweeping under a boldly projecting terrace, suggesting a likely debt to the Villa Savoye. The house was built from 1932 to 1933 for the wealthy industrialist Fritz Schminke, on a site in Löbau near the Czech border, and in most other respects is in total contrast to the Villa Savoye. Where Le Corbusier was generic and enjoyed exploiting the tension between a complex programme and a regular form, Scharoun was specific and allowed the exterior to expand and contract in response to spatial and functional pressures within.

The site for the Schminke House was challenging. Entered from the south, it enjoyed a spectacular distant view to the north-east – never an easy combination to resolve. In response these conditions Scharoun placed the main body of the house facing south, but turned the east and west ends to align with the site boundary. In the process the solarium at the eastern end was neatly aligned to the view – Scharoun labelled it *Blickachse* (view axis) on some of the plans. This in turn prompted him to align the main staircase on this same diagonal, creating a powerful dynamic element at the heart of the plan, greatly enriching the pattern of movement through the house, and establishing the shifted geometry as a second orthogonal system, in counterpoint to the dominant east-west alignment.

The planning is functionally zoned, and while the spaces flow together in the modern manner, they are also clearly identified as well defined territories designed for specific patterns of use. Bays push or swell out to accommodate activities. A free-standing fireplace is placed to give focus to the living room, around whose perimeter long, immovable ranges of seating define places to sit. Lighting specific to each area is provided – ceiling light for the dining table; place-lamps for the piano, hearth and sofa; spotlights for bookshelves and flowers. The composition culminates in the fully glazed solarium and winter garden, below which the ground falls away dramatically, leaving the house and terraces to soar over the landscape. The views here, seen across an interior bathed in light, are as beguiling a celebration of the virtues of sun, space, outdoor life and greenery as Le Corbusier's roof gardens.

Although he pursued ideas that differed radically from the mainstream, Scharoun is not difficult to accommodate in the narrative of the Modern house. But as we noted in the case of Jujol's Torre de la Creu, some houses refuse to conform to convenient classifications. One such is the extraordinary home and studio built for himself by Konstantin Melnikov, one of the most original architects of the post-Revolutionary period in Russia. Radical new ideas flourished for a decade after the 1917 Revolution but private houses, needless to say, did not: Melnikov's is the only one to become widely known. Even within the very different Soviet context, his design was singular and generated, like the Torre de la Creu, from intersecting circles – in this case two of equal size. The reasons continue to intrigue scholars. The cylinder was a favourite motif, and the work of Claude-Nicholas Ledoux, Russian Orthodox churches and the American grain silos beloved of European modernists have all

Above, top and opposite
Schminke House, Löbau, Germany,
1932–3, Hans Scharoun. The formal
language of the International Style is
here made responsive to the nuances
of site and programme – note how the
plan cranks to address a view and
variously swells to make places to eat
and sit, alone or in groups.
Right Melnikov House and Studio,
Moscow, Russia, 1927, Konstantin
Melnikov. Two intersecting cylinders
and a mysterious grid of hexagonal
windows contain and light a suite of
vertically interlocking rooms.

been suggested as possible inspirations: the result certainly has something of the monumentality of a silo.

The monumentality is reinforced by making the entrance part of a glazed slot running through the full four-storey height, while to the rear the rendered surface of the other cylinder is peppered with hexagonal windows, some with horizontal glazing bars, others with diagonals. This unique fenestration provides an extraordinary light in the double-height studio, and was achieved by replacing the brick walls with a network of diagonal columns, enabling Melnikov to make openings or carve out niches at will. The studio interlocks with the similarly double-height drawing room – the juxtaposition in section recalls Le Corbusier's project for a house in Carthage, made the following year. Finally, as if to confound any easy interpretation, Melnikov chose to furnish his revolutionary house with heavy, traditional pieces, providing an almost surreal contrast to the modernity of the architecture and making it all the more difficult to relate to contemporary developments elsewhere.

At first sight the design with which we conclude our exploration of the Modern House appears to belong comfortably in the mainstream, but for many years, if it was remembered at all, it was regarded as of only marginal interest. The site at Roquebrune, Cap-Martin, overlooking the Mediterranean, was remote and singular, but the house was well published and visited by leading Modernists – Le Corbusier took Rex Martienssen from South Africa there. It did not help that the owner and designer was a woman, Eileen Gray, still less that she was well known for her Art Deco furniture and interiors. The house was completed in 1929 and given the laconic name E.1027, not, Gray said, as a mark of machine-age anonymity but as a secret tribute to her confidant Jean Badovici, whose initials were the tenth and second letters of the alphabet – hence E. J.B.G.

Romanian-born and Paris-trained, Badovici was editor of *L'Architecture vivante*: launched in 1923, it was one of the main vehicles for disseminating modern architecture, but less polemical than a partisan journal like *L'Esprit nouveau*. Badovici provided technical advice, but the house was essentially Gray's own work. Le Corbusier, a close friend of Badovici, stayed there in 1938 and after his visit wrote a letter to Gray praising the 'rare spirit which has given the modern furniture and installations such a dignified, charming and witty shape.' And then, later that year, in an act whose motives have been the subject of much psychological speculation, he defaced it with a series of exclamatory and completely unsolicited murals.

The two-storey house was small – 160 square metres (1,722 square feet), twelve would fit comfortably inside the Tugendhat – and exquisitely adapted to the different levels of its rocky, coastal site, which Gray in turn adapted to create a seaside garden: the modernist living-machine and wild nature rarely achieved such a poetic and habitable fusion. The plan lacks Le Corbusier's rigour, but is intricately functional, and benefited from a furniture designer's eye applied to every detail. The house is filled with inventive, often witty furniture and while there are traces of Art Deco stylization (which Le Corbusier perhaps hinted at in his letter) everything springs from a rich imagination responding to the patterns of living. The plans feel almost like diagrams of frozen movement, with partitions

E.1027 Roquebrune, France, 1926–9, Eileen Gray

poised to slide, doors to swing, and furniture ready to transform itself by folding away or opening out to serve some unexpected purpose.

Gray's classic circular side tables adjust in height to sit by a sofa or over a bed, and around her own bed she made special places for books and even for a hot-water bottle – Häring would surely have approved! Blue night-lights recalled the romance of sleepless hours on trains speeding to distant climes; the canvas balustrade to the terrace could be removed to allow the low sun to warm her legs in winter; the kitchen could open completely to the courtyard via folding glass panels, enabling her maid to prepare food outside in the summer 'like peasant women'. Everywhere you look, every nuance of daily life seems to have been imagined and celebrated, and in this it recalls that other lyrical and intensely personal hymn to the art of living, the Schröder House.

Badovici devoted a whole issue of *L'Architecture vivante* to E.1027 and cast the preface in the form of an interview between a rationalist interrogator and Eileen Gray: 'We had to get rid of the old oppression,' she says, 'in order to be conscious again of freedom. But the intellectual coldness that ensued, and which corresponds all too well to the harsh laws of modern machinery, can only be a transition. It is necessary to rediscover once more the human being in the plastic form, the human will under the material appearance, and the pathos of modern life.' Her sentiments would find numerous echoes in the decades to come, as criticisms grew of what many came to perceive as the excessive rationalism of modern architecture, exemplified by some of the widely misunderstood 'machines for living in' of the next chapter.

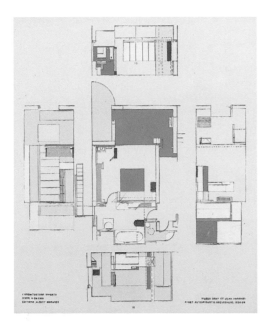

machines for living in

'We must create the mass-production spirit. The spirit of constructing mass-production houses. The spirit of living in mass-production houses. The spirit of conceiving mass-production houses.' With these typically stirring words Le Corbusier launched the penultimate chapter of *Vers une architecture*. While later critics and historians, like Hitchcock and Johnson with their 'International' style, tended to focus on the aesthetic implications of the new 'House-Machine', Le Corbusier left no doubt that what was at issue was a technical and social revolution, of which a new 'machine aesthetic' would be an expression, not an end in itself. A house for the 'common man' was, he concluded his polemic, 'the problem of the epoch. The balance of society comes down to a question of building…. Architecture or Revolution?'

In France, the context of this challenge was the Loucheur Act with its call for 500,000 new dwellings to be built well and cheaply to help restore the stock lost in the First World War. Le Corbusier was convinced industry was a sleeping giant waiting to be stirred into action and many of the building products required, he pointed out, were already being industrially produced - cements, steel girders, sanitary fittings, ironmongery, and so on. What was needed was the vision ('mass-production spirit') to change the way buildings were conceived, as well as industrialized building contractors and a system of national standardization to co-ordinate the disparate producers.

As predictions about the future of construction, these ideas proved prescient – dimensional co-ordination, rapid advances in building services, massive contracting firms and so forth have all become familiar realities – but the contention that 'a house will no longer be this solidly-built thing which sets out to defy time and decay… an expensive luxury by which wealth can be shown', but rather, 'a tool as the motor-car is becoming a tool' proved more problematic. The house, as Adolf Loos observed, is by nature conservative and despite being transformed by industrially produced components and ceasing to be a product of craft traditions, most prospective inhabitants, where they had a choice, proved stubbornly resistant to the aesthetic representations of modernity.

In *Vers une architecture* Le Corbusier illustrated various ideas for houses, including two basic types to which he returned throughout his life. The first, designed in 1919, he called the Monol. It was intended to exploit mass-produced asbestos panels. These were to be used to frame walls, which were then filled with rubble found locally, and covered in corrugated sheeting to form permanent shuttering for shallow concrete vaults. New materials like Eternit were widely exhibited in France in the 1920s as part of conventional-looking prefabricated houses designed to meet the same housing crisis, but most architects regarded them as unsuited to the Fine Art of architecture. The construction of Monol was inventive, and the forms it generated would be echoed in other materials by numerous modern architects; Le Corbusier himself reinterpreted them in the small weekend house and the Jaoul Houses we discuss in the next chapter. The second, designed in 1921–2, he called 'Citrohan' – a punning reference to the car manufacturer. This was a compact version of a Dom-Ino design like the Cook House. It had hollow concrete cross-walls in place of columns and a double-height living space with an open dining room and kitchen tucked under a mezzanine floor for bedrooms: he said the basic idea dawned on him in a Paris

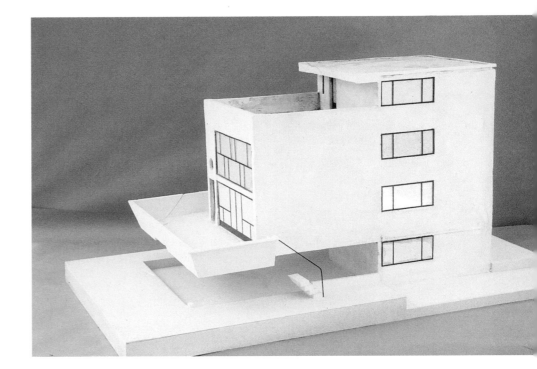

Right Citrohan House, project, 1921–2, Le Corbusier. This prototype was intended to be mass-produced, hence the punning reference to the French car-maker. Although it never went into production, the organization around a double-height living space established a spatial type to which Le Corbusier frequently returned.

Above Monol House, project, 1919, Le Corbusier. Designed for rapid construction using industrially produced materials – corrugated sheeting on the roof, asbestos panels for the walls – the Monol was a response to the massive housing shortages in France in the wake of the First World War

café with a similar arrangement. The ground floor was given over to the garage and 'servants well cared for' – this was no compact worker's house – and two further bedrooms were provided overlooking the roof-top solarium.

Le Corbusier was convinced he would find a major car manufacturer to build his mass-production houses, but the call finally came from the owner of a sugar refinery in Bordeaux, Henry Frugès. He wrote to Le Corbusier in November 1923 to commission a small group of workers' houses for his new sawmill in Lège. The basic unit was a smaller version of the Citrohan type. Despite numerous technical difficulties with the sprayed concrete construction and local ridicule for the 'Frugès cubes', the client decided to press on with a larger development in the fast-expanding rural suburb of Pessac. It became known as Les Quartiers Modernes Frugès.

Les Quartiers Modernes Frugès Pessac, France, 1924–6, Le Corbusier

The layout was based on garden-city principles, including an impressive gateway marked by a six-storey apartment block, but in other ways it was radically innovative. In one sector the open space formed a continuous realm in which traditional distinctions between front, back and side, public and private, were eliminated in favour of a continuous shared realm. In another the street was deliberately asymmetrical, with narrow, so-called 'skyscraper' *(gratte-ciel)* units framing open spaces at intervals along the street, across which was a more conventional two-storey terrace. Four standard house types were developed, all evolving from a spatial core 5 metres (16.5 feet) wide and planned around a single-flight transverse stair. The 'skyscraper' was the flagship, a free-standing back-to-back pair of houses extending vertically rather than horizontally and culminating in a roof garden accessible via an external stair, with a canopy and 'nautical' handrails to help evoke the image of a ship sailing through space.

Pessac was completed in 1926 and almost immediately favoured with a visit by M. de Monzie, the minister of public works. Three years later when M. Loucheur, the employment minister, came it was still empty, having fallen foul of local bureaucracy and outraged influential citizens. When it was finally inhabited the development soon fell into neglect, and pitched roofs, window shutters, stuck-on stone, scalloped window-boxes and a host of other details appeared to make the buildings look more like 'proper' houses. The biggest single source of outrage was the vivid polychromy. Henry Frugès later claimed that the colour schemes were implemented at his initiative but there is no doubt about Le Corbusier's enthusiasm for the idea. 'Architectural polychromy,' he exclaimed, 'takes possession of the entire wall and splashes it with pulsating blood, or clothes it in the fresh hues of a prairie, the bright luminosity of the sun, or the deep tones of the sky and sea. What power!' The colour was applied to ameliorate the drab grey of the concrete walls, but it also permitted the further manipulation of space and form, making one wall appear to recede, another to advance, shattering symmetry and destroying boxiness and the feeling of enclosure.

The reasons for the scheme's social failure are more complex than simple rejection of its unfamiliar aesthetic and layout. A tradition of workers' housing in Bordeaux was well established before the First World War. Its funding and management were geared to ensuring that the workers were financially tied to their properties through a savings scheme, and then encouraged to busy themselves in productive gardening and work around the house: with revolution

Above, below and opposite Les Quartiers Modernes Frugès, Pessac, France, 1924–6. This estate of workers' housing was the nearest Le Corbusier came to building 'mass-production houses'. The units were all planned using standard 5-metre-(6-foot-6-inch-) square units, the grandest being the tall 'skyscraper' double-houses (**opposite**).

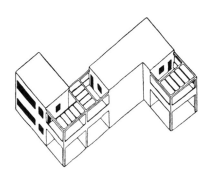

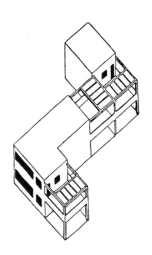

brewing in Russia and an active left wing in France, it was considered a social imperative to occupy workers' spare hours. Frugès and Le Corbusier, with boundless, ill-placed optimism, opted for a different funding system and believed that functionally planned, well ventilated and light-filled dwellings would not only create a healthy environment but also help free time for leisure pursuits and the arts. Their optimism proved ill founded, but when the houses were eventually restored in the 1980s they became sought-after as distinctive homes for middle-class families and urban professionals.

Weimar Germany, with its liberal democratic constitution and determination to break with the outmoded values that had led to war, provided a more favourable climate for experimentation than conservative France, where the dominant voices were calling for a return to the Classical tradition. There was already a strong housing reform movement, which was taken up after the war by the burgeoning women's movement. After five years of increasingly rampant inflation the economy began to stabilize in 1924 with the implementation of the Dawes Plan. US dollars were vital in the short term, but the acceptance of American ways of organizing workers and production methods was of more far-reaching significance. The enormous popularity of Henry Ford's autobiography, *My Life and Work*, which arrived in Germany in 1923, was seminal in spreading the message. It explained in euphoric prose the success of his production-line methods for making the Model T and was, incidentally, just as popular in Communist Russia, where Ford became an unlikely folk hero.

Against this background it comes as no surprise to hear the architect Bruno Taut argue that the 'problem of house-building today must be tackled along lines that are valid in industry for the production of machines, cars and similar objects. The success of Henry Ford in car production is in part based on the fact that he selects his raw materials in the best possible way…. Exactly the same can be applied to house-building.' What is slightly surprising is that these words came from the man who, in the immediate aftermath of the war, had dreamt of a chain of glass structures across the Alps as a symbol of the New World to be built out of the ashes of the Old. The road from visionary to advocate of industrialized building was not as long as it might appear, given the exalted language in which industry was frequently praised, and institutionally exactly the same path was trodden by the Bauhaus.

The industrialization of house building along Fordist lines meant the use of large-scale plant and machinery, efficient programming, centralization to form large efficient sites, and mobile building systems. And in order to have standardized dwellings like the Model T – *a Wohnford* (or 'living-Ford') as Sigfried Giedion, secretary of CIAM (Congrés Internationaux d'Architecture Moderne), called it in discussion with the Dutchman J. J. P. Oud – scientific methods had to be applied to both the building process and the design of the house or flat. Leaders of the women's movement persuaded the government to sponsor research in housing to help raise standards in the subsidized workers' accommodation being built across Germany. As a result of this and other pressures the RfG *(Reichsforschungsgesellschaft)* was established in 1926 to study all aspects of the design, construction and management of housing. It subsidized the use of prefabricated building systems on various projects, such as the Dessau-Törten estate designed under the direction of Walter Gropius, founder of the Bauhaus, and promoted experimentation in everything from housing layout to kitchen design.

The major focus for innovation in housing was Frankfurt where, in 1925, Ernst May, a native of the city, was appointed city planner and head of the department of buildings. May had trained as an architect in Darmstadt, where he was stimulated by contact with Olbrich, and then went to Munich to study city planning under the celebrated Theodor Fischer. He knew the pre-war innovations of Krupp in Essen and the small houses of Heinrich Tessenow, which later became sullied through identification with the goals of National Socialism. And he had met leaders of the avant-garde at an international conference on city planning held in Amsterdam in 1924, when he also saw the celebrated South Amsterdam expansion planned by Berlage and the work of Oud in Rotterdam. Out of these experiences he formed a clear vision for a New City and a New Home. It would become internationally known as *Das Neue Frankfurt* – the title of a magazine launched to publicize and celebrate the achievements – and the city would soon have to employ three guides for the people who flocked to see the acclaimed Römerstadt and other developments.

Tuberculosis and rickets were still familiar urban ills in Frankfurt, as in so many dense European cities (Le Corbusier's controversial planning ideas developed in part as a response to what he called 'tubercular Paris') and May waged reform under the slogan 'Light, Air, and Sun, a healthy life for all people'. He set about developing standards – the *Frankfurter Normen* – which included plywood doors with steel frames, unornamented hardware, a compact sit-up bathtub to save space and water and, most famously of all, the Frankfurt Kitchen.

Frankfurt Kitchen Frankfurt, Germany, 1926, Grete Lihotzky

Intended to be tailormade for 'modern women with little time for domestic cares', the new kitchen was seen as central to the new home. It was the work of Grete Lihotzky who came to work in Frankfurt from Vienna, where she had assisted Adolf Loos and amassed five years' experience designing kitchens for small apartments.

The original ideas for new kitchens came from America, where the social worker Catherine Beacher had analyzed, as models for small homes, the compact types made for Mississippi steamers and the ideas patented by Pullman in 1869 for use in his trains. In 1923, at an exhibition to promote the work of the Bauhaus, visitors to the Haus am Horn built specially for the show could see a kitchen by the brilliant Hungarian student Marcel Breuer, who soon went on to design several classic pieces of bent-metal furniture. His kitchen was the first in Germany to have a continuous run of work surfaces and wall cupboards.

Lihotzky said her models were the pharmacy and the laboratory, and her design method was derived from Christine Frederick's 1912 American classic, *The New Housekeeping. Efficiency Studies in Home Management*, which became the bible of household reform. Frederick analyzed domestic tasks using the work-study principles developed in America by Frederick W. Taylor to speed-up factory production, and Lihotzky in turn studied kitchen tasks to ensure that everything was within easy reach and efficiently placed: all aspects of a kitchen were examined functionally from first principles. The countless innovations, small and large, included storing crockery behind glass doors, keeping pans on sloping,

Right Frankfurt Kitchen, Frankfurt Germany, 1926, Grete Lihotzky. Designed after exhaustive analysis of the practical requirements, the kitchen was eventually installed in some 10,000 workers' apartments and houses. Many features that we now take for granted – continuous work-surfaces, wall cupboards, specialized storage units – were developed in the 1920s.

Above and opposite

Weissenhofsiedlung, Stuttgart, Germany, 1927, Mies van der Rohe (master-planner). Intended to introduce the new architecture to the wider German public, the Weissenhof presented designs by many of Europe's leading Modernists, and was occupied as permanent housing following the exhibition. The smaller of the two houses designed by Le Corbusier (**top**) was architecturally outstanding, whilst a terrace of five workers' houses by the Dutchman J. J. P. Oud (**above**) was particularly praised in the German press.

slatted shelves, a fold-away ironing board, and a bank of eighteen specially made aluminium containers. Known as *Schütte* when they went into production, these containers housed all kinds of dry goods and came complete with a tapering end for pouring.

The new kitchen was a small room (6.5 square metres, 70 square feet), separated for reasons of hygiene from the living area, from which it could be shut off, if required, by a sliding door. Ten thousand were eventually installed in workers' housing in Frankfurt, and the decision to replace the familiar kitchen-living room with the new arrangement had far-reaching implications, becoming the norm for several decades. Adolf Loos thought the trend misguided and in 1926, the year his former employee's design was completed, he defended the traditional living-kitchen for reasons that were social, not narrowly functional and hygienic. Cooking near the table was a sign of a high-quality restaurant – why should the working class not enjoy this pleasure, he asked? After all, the kitchen was the traditional gathering place for a family, and children love to be in it, near the fire, which heated the whole house and provided its natural centre; and moreover the arrangement did not cut off the housewife from her family while cooking. As we shall see, these sentiments would be echoed twenty years later, in almost exactly the same terms, by Le Corbusier in explaining the design of his Unité d'Habitation in Marseilles.

The early Frankfurt estates, based on industrially built two-storey houses of 60 to 70 square metres (645 to 753 square feet), still proved beyond the budget of factory workers to rent, let alone buy – even using the specially developed *Hauszinssteuer* mortgages, partly paid for by an unpopular tax on the city's better-off residents. The floor area had to be reduced still further, and houses changed for flats: they became known as *Existenzminimum* dwellings, and were made the subject of the 1929 CIAM congress (Congrés Internationaux d'Architecture Moderne) held in Frankfurt. One hundred and twenty delegates attended from eighteen countries – politicians, sociologists, psychologists, representatives of women's organizations and others, as well as architects – and just how minimal workers' housing could be, as well as the balance to be sought between individual and more collective forms, were fiercely debated.

In Frankfurt, housing with what May regarded as the 'absolute minimum' of 32 square metres (344 square feet) had been built the previous year, in a transit settlement for refugees. It quickly became permanent housing and was copied elsewhere, but after the stock market crash of 1929 and the ensuing economic chaos even this *Ration Wohnung* (Ration Flat) would prove impossible to provide for the many. By the time CIAM met there, Frankfurt's heyday as a centre of innovation was over. Responding to the darkening economic and political climate – the inexorable rise of National Socialism was by then all too obvious – May accepted an appointment as an advisor on industrial cities in the Soviet Union. When he left in 1930, 11 percent of the city's population had been housed in sanitary new accommodation but the *Hauszinssteuer* had dried up.

New approaches to living – *die neue Wohnkultur* – were a subject of wide interest in Germany and among the exhibitions held on the theme, one came to be seen as marking the moment at which the New Architecture reached maturity: the Weissenhofsiedlung in Stuttgart. It was organized by the Deutscher

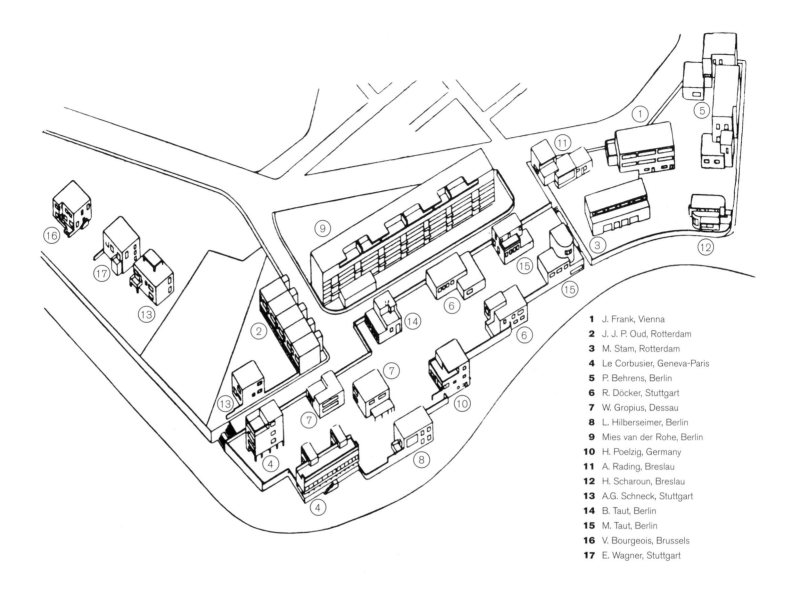

1   J. Frank, Vienna
2   J. J. P. Oud, Rotterdam
3   M. Stam, Rotterdam
4   Le Corbusier, Geneva-Paris
5   P. Behrens, Berlin
6   R. Döcker, Stuttgart
7   W. Gropius, Dessau
8   L. Hilberseimer, Berlin
9   Mies van der Rohe, Berlin
10 H. Poelzig, Germany
11 A. Rading, Breslau
12 H. Scharoun, Breslau
13 A.G. Schneck, Stuttgart
14 B. Taut, Berlin
15 M. Taut, Berlin
16 V. Bourgeois, Brussels
17 E. Wagner, Stuttgart

Werkbund, an association formed in 1907 to promote progressive ideas on art and design. It held several exhibitions before the war, and another in 1924 entitled 'Die Form', dedicated to promoting, as the invitation to participants stated, 'the extraordinary wealth of expression that can be embodied in pure form without the addition of any ornament'. A policy paper for the Stuttgart exhibition entitled 'Housing for a New Age' made it clear that they wanted projects geared to the city's pressing needs, not 'exhibition buildings or luxury homes' which, though 'technically irreproachable and architecturally strong and forward-looking', would be unsuited to everyday life.

Weissenhofsiedlung Exhibition Stuttgart, Germany, 1927

The overall planning of the exhibition, which was to become a habitable development, was entrusted to Mies van der Rohe, but his first proposal was not what the organizers anticipated: formalistic, uneconomic, overly complicated, unrelated to the city expansion plan – these were just some of the criticisms. Where his critics asked for 'evolution, not innovation', Mies explained that 'a New Home will extend beyond four walls. This is not a matter of producing to a layout as a pattern, in the old way; here, as also in the buildings, I want to break new ground.' He revised his design, but still managed to produce an innovative layout that shared an interest in the interplay of volumes similar to that of Le Corbusier at Pessac.

The choice of architects for the various buildings proved as problematic as their arrangement. It had more to do with political compromise between the different interest-groups involved than with producing the seamless demonstration of the New Architecture that Mies, if not the organizers, hoped for. Henry van de Velde was rejected because of his forthright attacks on Germany during the war, and Adolf Loos, who dearly wanted to be included, was eliminated because of his characteristically vigorous pre-war attacks on the Werkbund, which began life in the penumbra of Jugendstil as much as at the dawn of modernity. Mies thought that only left-wing architects should be appointed, Hugo Häring, who shared an office with Mies, argued that their intellectual rather than political views were more important. In the event twenty-one structures were commissioned from seventeen architects, with interiors by a further fifty-five designers. To accompany the model housing, a large exhibition entitled *Die Wohnung* (The Dwelling) was held in the city centre, and in his opening speech the mayor, Dr Lautenschlage, caught the ambition of both perfectly:

This exhibition departs markedly from outworn tradition. The idea behind it has sprung from the urgent needs of the present day: it is intended to serve immediate practical ends, and to show through drawings, models, furnishings, everyday utensils, and completed, permanent buildings, how by using simple means and taking up a minimum of space a comfortable, practical home can be achieved, satisfying every need and how, in particular, the harassed housewife can maintain her home with ease in the absence of unnecessary ornament, trinkets, and cumbersome furnishings.

I have quoted these remarks at length, because you almost have to pinch yourself to realize that they are the words of a politician, and spoken in 1927. In his introductory speech, Mies took the opportunity to set out the problem of the

New Home as being 'rooted in the altered material, social, and mental structure of our time' which was, he said, 'a problem of the new mind' and part of the 'great struggle for new forms of living'. His contribution to the exhibition took the form of a linear block of flats with flexible internal plans designed to emphasize the benefits of new construction techniques. Although externally, with its plain white surfaces and long strips of glazing, it looked radically new, the flexibility did not differ significantly from the contemporary plan studies of Alexander Klein, who preferred traditional exteriors. Walter Gropius contributed two houses designed to demonstrate the virtues of factory production. The first used conventional materials assembled as prefabricated panels, while the second was more radical, using an I-section steel frame infilled with cork insulation panels and clad with asbestos sheeting externally and Celotex-Lignat panels internally. The new construction, which did little more than translate timber-frame methods into steel, proved expensive. Visually, too, the results were far from appealing and they were widely criticized for looking 'like temporary barracks'.

Le Corbusier was asked to design for the 'educated middle class' and contributed two projects. The first was a gem based on the Citrohan house type, elevated on *pilotis*, which Mies called the 'most beautiful and best thing at the Weissenhof'. The second was a double villa, with planning, he said, like a sleeping car – by day it could be completely open, and then at night the small 'sleeping compartments' could be closed for privacy. Probably anticipating general puzzlement, Le Corbusier explained that it represented 'a way of living perhaps not common in Germany but which presents great advantages for the Parisian'. The professional and women's press were critical of both designs, but saved their most stinging remarks for the double villa. It might suit Parisians, they said, but it was irrelevant to the German search for a new culture of living and to the theme of the exhibition, which was widely assumed to be specifically housing for workers (which was not, of course, Le Corbusier's brief).

The designs that received the greatest approval were by Bruno Taut – whose vivid red, blue and yellow walls were the first realization of his 1919 'Call for Colourful Building' – and, widely singled out for praise, a small terrace by J. J. P. Oud, the city architect of Rotterdam from 1918 to 1933. To Erna Meyer, whose book *Der rationelle Haushalt* (The Rational Household) was a bestseller, Oud's row of five compact houses was wholly appropriate to German needs and skilfully designed to assist the housewife in her work. Oud's description stressed the practical features of his house-type: the serving-hatch – a key innovation of Functionalism – which made for easy contact between the living room and kitchen, which itself was large enough to eat in using a fold-down table; a separate utility room for washing and ironing; warm-air heating; and small holes in the doors to see where any lights had been left on and prevent wastage of artificial light.

Whatever the merits or failings of the individual designs, there is no doubt that the Weissenhof succeeded in bringing the new architecture to a much wider public, even if it was not the unified and unqualified triumph acclaimed by later, partisan accounts of the Modern Movement. Many, inevitably, were bemused. The hard Left dubbed the architects Salon Marxists, more interested in New Form for its own sake than in New Life; whereas to the burgeoning National Socialists they were Bolshevik Builders – the Nazis circulated a postcard in which the white buildings were transformed into an Arab settlement. But for the racist motivation it would have been rather amusing.

The new ideas on workers' housing diffused throughout the Continent and found fertile ground in the Netherlands where, following the Housing Act of 1901 and an increase in the Dutch population before the war, council-built workers' housing was in great demand. Oud's pioneering scheme in Rotterdam's Tussendijken district of 1920 was widely admired and at the time of the Weissenhof in 1927 he was at work on what proved to be his masterpiece, the

Kiefhoek Housing Development Rotterdam, the Netherlands, 1927, J. J. P. Oud

Kiefhoek development, also in Rotterdam. It was planned to minimum specifications for large families – two parents and six children – and each house had to be built for £213: 'All this,' said Oud, 'led me to look for a type, which one could think of as a Ford dwelling' – a concept that he had once discussed with Sigfried Giedion, secretary of CIAM. Despite the budgetary constraints he managed to achieve a dignified layout in which, as the English architects Alison and Peter Smithson later wrote, 'each change of road width, every set-back is made to speak of use'.

The majority of blocks in the Kiefhoek were aligned north-east/south-west, regarded as optimal at the time, but the layout was not dominated by rational lighting requirements, as happened so often in Germany, but based on a network of well-defined open spaces. Low brick walls accentuate the individuality of the dwellings, while the red doors and grey window frames reflected Oud's time as a member of De Stijl. Although he was skilled in meeting the demands of *Existenzminimum* accommodation, Oud never subscribed to the view that housing could be satisfactorily reduced to a narrowly defined 'functional' problem. In 1925 in his contribution to a collection of writings on architecture and the machine he wrote: 'I'm longing for a dwelling which satisfies all the demands of my love of comfort, but a house is more to me than a machine-for-living-in.'

During the 1930s, as we noted in the last chapter, the International Style found particularly fertile ground in Eastern Europe and Palestine, following the arrival of several German architects, including some trained at the Bauhaus. It was there, in the Upper Hadar district of Haifa – recently christened 'The Bauhaus on the Carmel' – that one of the most extraordinary expressions of the dwelling as a machine for living in of which I am aware was completed in 1940 by Theodor Menkes, who immigrated to Palestine from Vienna in 1934. Named the 'Glass House' after the all-glass enclosure of its stairs (subsequently removed, perhaps because of over-heating), it is a small, U-shaped block of one-room flats, originally built for bachelor British army officers and now occupied as social housing. The *Existenzminimum* dwellings occupy two sides of the U and the main stair the third; access to each of the four storeys is via open decks – the longer originally enjoying a clear view to the Mediterranean – along whose edges, at handrail level, are continuous plant boxes which were watered by pipes built into the soffit of the floor above.

The units are all identical and entered between a tiny bathroom and kitchen, which shows Frankfurt-like attention to detail. The square living room has a bed alcove placed behind the bathroom, and beyond it a door leads out to the recessed half of a two-metre- (6.5-foot-) square balcony, half of which also

Below 'Glass House', Haifa, Israel, 1940, Theodor Menkes. Designed as minimal bachelor housing for British army officers, this small block epitomized the Modernist vision of healthy, efficient living – there was originally a caged-in tennis court on the roof and a swimming pool in the courtyard.

Above and left Kiefhoek Housing Development, Rotterdam, The Netherlands, 1927, J. J. P. Oud. As City Architect of Rotterdam, Oud produced several outstanding workers' housing estates. Although his plans reflect the concern with 'rational' daylighting and serial production, Oud's projects never succumbed to the numbing repetition this frequently produced.

projects beyond the façade – an arrangement similar to that of the student hostel at the Bauhaus designed by Walter Gropius. The external walls of the bathrooms were originally made entirely of glass bricks, and the entrance doors are framed by the cast-iron drainage pipes. The kitchen and bathroom ceilings are both lower than the living room, enabling a bulkhead to be formed to allow cross ventilation. The communal facilities included a kitchen with dumb-waiter to bring meals to each level; a swimming pool in the courtyard, now sadly filled in but originally providing both recreation and evaporative cooling; and finally, and most striking, a steel-mesh cage housing a tennis court on the roof, reached via a steep stair of distinctly nautical provenance. Rarely can such modest resources have yielded such inspiring results. The building is currently in parlous condition, but if restored would make superb student housing. Almost unknown, it deserves recognition as an outstanding realization of the dream of the New Life.

Unité d'Habitation Marseilles,, France, 1947–52, Le Corbusier

It is a considerable leap to Le Corbusier's Unité d'Habitation in Marseilles, and I hesitated before including it in what is, after all, an account of the house rather than housing. But the Unité looms so large, in every sense, that to omit it seemed almost unthinkable. Its apartments were intended to have many of the qualities we associate with 'house' as opposed to apartment, and it marks, within the work of the century's most influential architect, the culmination of the strand of thinking we have been discussing. The Unité was realized from 1947–52 and remains Le Corbusier's grandest vision of a 'machine for living in', while at the same time marking his emphatic rejection of the machine aesthetic in which that vision was first cast.

Like the Dom-Ino, Citrohan, Monol and other would-be mass-production houses the Unité was promoted as a response to the demands of reconstruction after the devastation of war. Le Corbusier called it a 'vertical garden city' and said that, as in nature, its design began with the living cell. And that in turn revolved around 'the fire, the hearth', where the family should eat together – in his mind, modern 'fire' came down pipes or through wires. In the absence of servants, he argued, '*the living-room must be a kitchen, the kitchen a living-room*' – italicized for emphasis in the book about the project he published in 1953. We are back with Loos's criticism of the separate, Frankfurt-style kitchen: Le Corbusier also thought it essential that this age-old tradition of civilization 'be rehabilitated lest the modern family fall to pieces'. The key to preventing the family's dissolution, he thought, lay in efficiently planned and serviced homes. Privacy must be ensured by isolating the family from potentially noisy neighbours, and a range of support facilities should be close at hand.

The Unité was designed as an independent structural framework into which the individual apartments could be slotted – like wine-bottles in a rack, Le Corbusier said. In theory, they could have been mass-produced off-site, and a perfectly workable, prototype steel-framed unit was developed by Jean Prouvé, who specialized in industrialized construction methods. In practice, traditional on-site methods were eventually adopted – Prouvé said he never understood why – including the double-skin construction to ensure acoustic privacy (it actually proved too quiet for some, who felt isolated). The apartments were designed on two floors, like a house, and locked together in an ingenious cross-over section which gave each family a frontage and private balcony on both sides of the

Below and opposite and overleaf Unité d'Habitation, Marseilles, France, 1947–52, Le Corbusier. This vast block, riding the landscape like an ocean liner, contains 337 apartments, a small hotel and a range of communal facilities, and is crowned by the grandest of Le Corbusier's roof-gardens, dedicated to play, fitness, and the contemplation of sky and distant mountains.

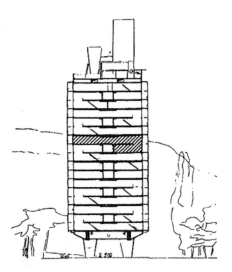

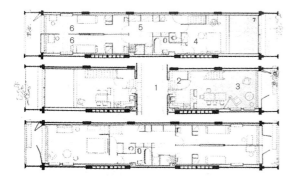

Above Unité d'Habitation, Marseilles, France, 1947–52, Le Corbusier. Typical floor-plans of two, two-storey apartments, organized around the shared 'internal street'.

building and enabled one broad corridor – he called them 'interior streets' – to serve three stories of accommodation. The living room was double-height, with the kitchen either under or on the mezzanine floor, as in the original Citrohan type. The parents had an en-suite bathroom, the children their own shower, and light reached the heart of the rooms thanks to full-height glazing protected by a concrete sunscreen or *brise-soleil*.

Twenty-three variants of the basic flat were designed, and the eighteen-storey block contained 337 apartments in all. On the roof – one of Le Corbusier's truly heroic spaces, addressing the coastal mountains – were a swimming pool, covered and open gymnasia, and, echoing the famous roof top test track of the Fiat factory near Turin, a running track. On the two floors below were a crèche and nursery, and half the seventh and eighth floors were occupied by other communal facilities – a co-operative store, smaller shops, restaurant, and an eighteen-room hotel.

The closest analogy to the Unité both in scale - it is 135 metres long (443 feet) – and contents is one of Le Corbusier's favourite 'machines', the ocean liner. But whereas the occupants of a liner are temporary and when at sea have no alternative to the on-board facilities, the Unité was permanently moored outside Marseilles and the residents preferred to go out for most of their shopping and recreation. The internal commercial and residential 'streets' were destined to remain no more than broad corridors, devoid of anything resembling the bustle of urban life. It was a magnificent yet flawed vision, a fragment of a larger proposal for the radical restructuring of the modern city to ensure the 'essential joys' of *soleil, espace et verdure*. These, however, mattered less to the residents than the traditional pleasures of urban life they sought outside. Well managed from the outset, unlike several late Unités, the Marseilles block was always popular and like Pessac is now inhabited predominantly by middle-class families.

Aesthetically, the Unité marked a radical break with Le Corbusier's work of the 1920s, where the geometric forms and sleek surfaces he believed would result from industrial production had either been simulated using blockwork and plaster, as in the Villa Savoye, or had to be painted over, as at Pessac, when sprayed concrete failed to live up to expectations. The abstract language of planes, smooth surfaces and slender columns was abandoned in favour of a delight in muscular, sculptural forms, and the roughness of raw concrete struck from grainy, timber-boarded shutters, which he christened *béton brut*. Stylistically, it would prove hugely influential for more than a decade to come.

The dream of machine-made houses manifested itself in other guises outside the architectural mainstream. To a visionary like the American Richard Buckminster Fuller the Europeans had not begun to come to terms with the real potential of new materials and mass-production. To do so he argued, the world's resources and means of production had to be looked at holistically, outmoded economic systems based on memories of scarcity and isolation replaced, and problems like housing stripped of their cultural baggage and seen, like a military operation, as a problem of logistics. His solution was to mass-produce houses as autonomous units and airlift them to anywhere in the world. The house would be designed to exhibit maximum strength at minimum weight, and like an aeroplane it would separate out compression and tension members and maximize the use of the latter. He called his first house 4D and published the designs in 1928; the following year it was given the name by which it became generally known – the Dymaxion House – by the Marshall Field store in Chicago, who used a mock-up as a futuristic stage-set for new furniture.

Dymaxion House Prototype 1928, Richard Buckminster Fuller

The Dymaxion House was a literal rather than metaphoric 'machine for living in'. The living areas were housed in a hexagonal, glazed enclosure hung, like a wire-wheel, from a central mast containing all the services. It was to be fully air-conditioned and cleaned using central compressed air and vacuum systems; laundry would be automatically washed, dried, pressed and placed in storage containers; clothes and food storage was based on revolving shelves. It was designed to be relatively independent of mains water: the atomizer bath would need only two pints of water, which would be filtered, sterilized and re-circulated after use, and the toilets would operate without water at all. And so it went on…. Much of the technology Fuller envisaged was not immediately to hand, but most of it now is – some, not surprisingly, developed to enable astronauts to survive in space.

Fuller was fond of rhetorical questions like 'Madam, how much does your house weigh?' to get people to think about the resources they used. The smart answer was, 'It doesn't matter, because it doesn't have to fly', but regardless of whether or not they were to be air-lifted, Fuller considered heavy compression materials like brick and stone hopelessly outmoded and priced his designs by the pound. He estimated the Dymaxion House could be mass-produced for 25 US cents per pound, only slightly more than Fords and Chevrolets in 1928.

Fuller provocatively offered the patents on his design to the American Institute of Architects, whose vice-president at the time was his father-in-law. They declined the offer, and passed a motion stating their opposition to all 'peas-in-a-pod-like repeatable designs'. He pressed on, designing the Dymaxion Bathroom from 1938 to 1940, which anticipated the industrially produced all-in-one units now available, and then, in 1944, the circular, metal-clad Dymaxion Dwelling Machine designed to exploit aeronautical techniques – unlike the earlier Dymaxion it got as far as a habitable prototype. Fuller's ideas took the Modernist dream of a universal industrial culture to a logical – in his own technocratic terms

conclusion, but to most his logic was fatally flawed by the absolute refusal to address housing as a cultural as well as a technical challenge. His example, however, exerted a continuing appeal to dreamers of technological utopias, such as the British Archigram group of the 1960s, and to High Tech architects fascinated by the idea of 'technology transfer' from more advanced fields such as aeronautics and sailing. The house-building system developed in 1985 by the British architect Richard Horden, for instance, used aluminium yacht-components.

The European rhetoric about 'machines for living in' and the *Existenzminimum* generally fell on deaf ears in the USA, where the impact of the First World War was less directly felt and the traditional balloon-frame was, in effect, an early form of system-building. Not surprisingly, it fell to a European to produce the most machine-like house included in Hitchcock and Johnson's exhibition *The International Style*. The Aluminaire House was designed by the Swiss-born Albert Frey in partnership with A. Lawrence Kocher, managing editor of the magazine *Architectural Record*. Frey had previously worked on the Villa Savoye

Below Dymaxion House, prototype, 1928, Richard Buckminster Fuller. Intended to be airlifted to anywhere in the world, this visionary prototype for an autonomous house used aircraft construction materials and techniques for lightness and envisaged a range of new technologies, some of which became a reality with the development of space travel.

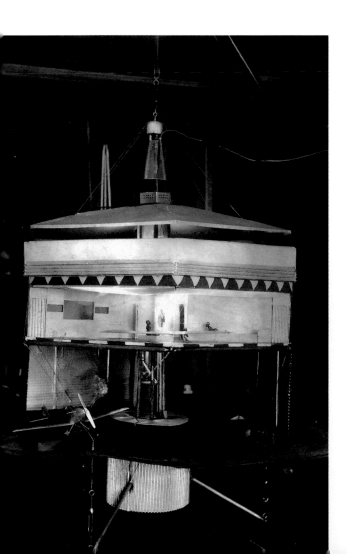

Opposite Dymaxion Dwelling Machine, prototype, Wichita, Kansas, USA, 1944, Richard Buckminster Fuller. More practical than the first Dymaxion, Fuller's later prototype was designed to use the spare capacity of the aeronautical industry following the end of the Second World War.

Above Aluminaire House, Syosset, New York, USA, 1931: Albert Frey and A. Lawrence Kocher. Made of aluminium and steel and prefabricated and erected in ten days, the design was based on the smaller of Le Corbusier's houses at the Weissenhof exhibition.

Left and below Yacht House, New Forest, England, 1985, Richard Horden. Incorporating aluminium yacht-building components, this housing system epitomized the idea of 'technology transfer', which continues to fascinate High Tech architects.

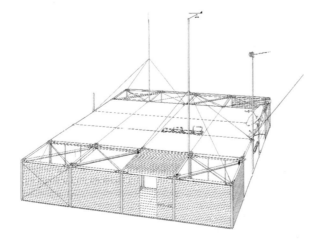

with Le Corbusier and greatly admired the freestanding house at the Weissenhof, which he took as a model for his, built in an exhibition hall in New York in 1931. The name was meant to conjure up aluminium, light and lightness, and the three-storey house was elevated on aluminium pipe-columns, fitted with steel-framed windows and doors, and clad in ribbed aluminium sheets. It was prefabricated and erected in ten days. Later it was dismantled in six hours and re-sited on Long Island, where it was altered and extended almost beyond recognition.

The architect who came closest to building a bridge between the technocratic utopia of Fuller and mainstream architecture was Jean Prouvé. During the 1930s he was preoccupied with exploring the architectural implications of new methods of construction. He developed factory-based techniques for manufacturing new components and for the off-site assembly of complete or sectional buildings which found fulfilment in the design of emergency dwellings during the Second World War, when 1200 six-metre-square (64.5-foot-square) units were ordered. They continued to be occupied during peacetime, proving their versatility by changing locations as well as occupants. Eight-metre-square (86-foot-square) versions were considered by the French government for large-scale use during reconstruction after the war, but only twenty-five trial houses were eventually manufactured, in 1949. After bureaucratic bungling these ended up scattered through France – some even turned up in Algeria – with the largest group at Meudon from which they took their name.

'Meudon' Prefabricated Housing Meudon, France, 1949, Jean Prouvé

Staying true to his conviction that 'the individual dwelling must be light and dynamic' and 'an expression of large-scale production and therefore characteristic of industry', Prouvé continued to design prototypes. Among these are two which merit special mention: the all-metal aluminium and steel Tropical House of 1949 which, with its outrigged external blinds and exemplary response to the climate, proved an inspiration to High Tech architects such as Norman Foster; and the prefabricated, two-bedroom, 50-square-metre (538-square-foot) house designed for the Abbé Pierre who helped provoke a national outcry about the housing crisis. 'A house built in less than seven hours', declared a headline in the Nancy newspaper *Républicain*, beside a picture of a tiny kitchen being craned into place, complete with five saucepans hanging ready for action. Prouvé also completed several private houses, including his own, built in Nancy in 1954. This was a relaxed assemblage of factory-made components which he used as a test-bed for new materials, including aluminium panels punched with small 'porthole' windows and laminated board panels for the roof. 'Everything Prouvé touches and designs', said Le Corbusier, 'immediately takes on an elegant plastic form, while at the same time he provides brilliant solutions to the problems concerning the strength of the materials and fabrication.'

Prouvé's buildings looked unashamedly factory made. In Britain similar attempts to marshal the defence industry's vastly enlarged manufacturing capacity to help meet the urgent need for housing were generally made to look as conventionally house-like as possible. The ARCON house, which the anonymously styled Architectural Consultants group developed in 1944, was an exception. It used a steel framework that gave flexibility in internal arrangement, and the rounded ridge and pressed steel cladding panels were expressive of

Above Tropical House, prototype, 1949, Jean Prouvé. This all-metal house demonstrated a concern with 'passive' climate control techniques which was well ahead of its time.

Opposite 'Meudon' prefabricated housing, Meudon, France, 1949, Jean Prouvé. Intended as a solution to the post-war housing shortages, only twenty-five of these eight-metre- (26.5-foot-) square houses were actually built, the largest group being in Meudon.

Right and below Prouvé House, Nancy, France, 1954, Jean Prouvé. The interior of his own house reflects Prouvé's relaxed yet thoroughly professional command of building technology. The plan opens to the south against an insulating, north-facing storage wall, and he used the fabric as a test-bed for new materials and components.

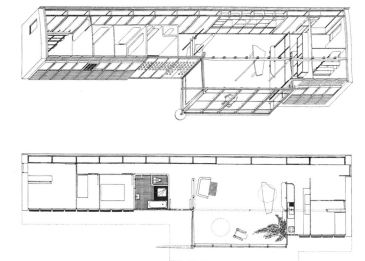

steel construction. Numerous factory-made, single-storey 'prefabs' – as they became known – were sited all over Britain in cities that had suffered serious bomb damage. They were meant to be temporary, but most long exceeded their projected life span, and some are still happily lived in over half a century later.

The humble British prefabs may not have looked much like the heroic 'machines for living in' espoused in the 1920s but the technology deployed in fabricating them was in fact highly sophisticated. Although they were genuine mass-production houses, in Britain, as in most parts of the world, the desire to live in houses that *looked* mass-produced did not exist, and the house-building industry quickly reverted to more traditional techniques. Behind the reassuringly familiar façades, however, the replacement of craft processes by industrial products gathered pace: the failure, if such it was, of the Modernist vision of the house as a 'machine for living in' was cultural more than technical.

Above ARCON permanent 'prefab' house, 1944, Architectural Consultants. Architecturally one of the most sophisticated of the prefabricated designs produced in Britain, this example is unusual for being a two-storey house.

Right British 'prefab' house, late 1940s. Although visually worlds apart from the visionary mass-production houses with which this chapter began, the British prefabs were genuinely mass-produced in large numbers using 'technology-transfer' from war-time industry – despite the reassuringly 'normal' exterior's attempt to suggest otherwise.

place, climate and culture

Above Villa de Mandrot, near Toulon, France, 1931, Le Corbusier. The raised courtyard framed by walls of local stone signals a departure from the abstraction and flowing spaces of his 1920s villas.
Below Weekend House, Paris, France, 1935, Le Corbusier. The vaulted Monol house type was here rendered in concrete, stone and turf – externally only the glass brick infill panels signal the house's modernity.

After moving to the USA in 1930 and establishing his credentials as an exponent of the new architecture with the Aluminaire house exhibited in New York the following year, the Swiss architect Albert Frey embarked on several trips across the country. He discovered a new wonderland of light, colours and materials and by 1940, when he decided to build his own, truly tiny house (32 square metres/344 square feet) in the desert near Palm Springs in California, his architectural aspirations had shifted decisively. The house was composed from planes of metal, plaster and glass, in the manner pioneered by Rietveld and Mies van der Rohe – it was from Mies, he said, that he learnt to extend a house into its site – but the colours and materials no longer represented the elusive spirit of the Machine Age, nor the universal truths of De Stijl, but were subtly attuned to the setting.

Aluminium, a shiny emblem of technology in the Aluminaire House, was now used to heighten by contrast and reflection our awareness of the colours and textures of the red-brown rocks of the Mojave Desert. Rose-red and sage-green walls echoed the flowers and foliage, midnight-blue curtains in the bedroom substituted for the night, while ceilings were a paler blue, like the daytime sky. Photographed in black and white, the colours of the International Style, Frey's house appeared orthodox. Comprehended in full colour, however, it represented an attitude that had begun to transform modern architecture in the 1930s and would become increasingly dominant as the century progressed. The spatial, formal and constructional innovations of the new architecture were to be inflected in response to specific places, climates and cultures, not deployed as a universal affirmation of modernity. In this chapter we will see this process at work over five decades in Europe and Central and South America, in India, South Africa and Australia. The United States, where so many significant private houses were produced, will be considered in the following chapter, followed by a briefer exploration of the most distinctive and influential tradition of house building to emerge in Europe following the Second World War, that of Scandinavia.

The first stirrings of the new attitude are to be found in a house Le Corbusier completed in 1931, immediately after the Villa Savoye. Designed for a rural site outside Toulon, the Villa de Mandrot has a U-shaped plan framing an elevated, south-facing courtyard, and is built with walls of local stone. The planning and use of reinforced concrete, Le Corbusier stressed in his description, demonstrated the 'ideas habitually exploited in our houses', but the change in attitude was clear, and confirmed four years later when he built the small Weekend House on the outskirts of Paris, not in the depths of rural France, using shallow barrel vaults and random rubble walls. Spatially, the design was a reinterpretation of the mass-production Monol type, but here the vault is closer to the peasant Catalan form rather than an attempt to exploit new materials. An understanding of the 'intrinsic qualities of materials' was, Le Corbusier still maintained, vital to advancing the cause of modern architecture, but those materials now included stone and turf – which covered the roof – as well as concrete and glass bricks.

In part the new attitude can be explained pragmatically, as a response to the technical problems afflicting his houses – the Villa Savoye, in particular, was plagued by leaks. Although some designers, most notably Mies van der Rohe,

Above Frey House I, Palm Springs, California, USA, 1940, Albert Frey. In black and white this tiny house looks like an orthodox exercise in planar modern architecture, but seen in colour it is revealed as a vivid response to the plants and rocks of the desert.

Right This adaptation to place is taken much further in the second house Frey built on the site between 1964 and 1971.

Villa Mairea Noormarkku, Finland, 1937–40, Alvar Aalto

Above Aalto House and Studio, Helsinki, Finland, 1935, Alvar Aalto. The L-shaped plan and use of timber boarding anticipate Aalto's Villa Mairea, whilst the volumetric composition suggests a debt to Walter Gropius's houses for the Bauhaus Masters in Dessau.

remained true to the vision of a universal modern style, the move towards an architecture more responsive to locality quickly gathered strength. One of the earliest and most influential critiques of 'an international, rootless modern architecture' began in Finland in the mid 1930s: the words are those of the country's finest architect, Alvar Aalto.

Aalto came to worldwide prominence as the designer of one of the major buildings of the International Style, the Tuberculosis Sanatorium at Paimio (1928–33), but he quickly became dissatisfied with what he saw as the one-sided rationalism of orthodox modern architecture. In a 1935 lecture entitled 'Rationalism and Man' he put forward nature as a model – 'formally rich and luxuriant' – and argued that supposedly rational, functional architecture had become just another style, 'a pleasant compôte of chromed tubes, glass tops, cubistic forms, and astounding colour combinations'. And even when 'rational', he argued, its rationality did not go far enough, applying only to aspects of the object, with results that lacked 'human qualities'. In the same year he gave this lecture Aalto demonstrated what he meant in his own house and studio in the outskirts of Helsinki at Munkkiniemi. The L-shaped form, wrapped around a roof garden and projecting over a ground-floor terrace, recalls the Masters' Houses designed by Walter Gropius for the Bauhaus staff in Dessau. But in place of crisp plaster surfaces we are confronted by lime-washed brickwork, weather-boarding, and bamboo-like poles for climbing plants.

The sources of his inspiration are not hard to guess: the International Style was being reinterpreted in the light of Mediterranean vernacular houses and Finnish timber buildings, lightened by contact with Japan. Any doubts on this score are quickly dispelled by the Villa Mairea, one of the century's great houses, completed in 1940. Aalto began work on the project in late 1937 and the clients, as so often with major modern houses, were wealthy industrialists, Harry and Maire Gullichsen. Maire had studied painting in Paris in the 1920s and owned an important collection of modern art; she was also heir to the vast Ahlström timber and paper company of which Harry, following their marriage, became managing director.

In the wake of liberation from Russia in 1917 the Finns were acutely conscious of their native traditions and in the 1930s the 'birch bark' culture, as it was deprecatingly known by the modernizers, was still in the ascendant. Industrialists like the Gullichsens, on the other hand, eager to establish Finland's place in the wider world and build export markets, were sympathetic to the progressive ideas emanating from the Continent. Their brief to Aalto was to design them a large summer house both modern and Finnish, on their estate at Noormarkku outside Pori on the west coast. Aalto's friend Gustav Strengell used to refer to the Munkkiniemi house and studio as the 'modern Niemelä', the name of a re-created farmstead in the nearby folk museum on Seurasaari island. It needed insight to see Niemelä there, but with the Villa Mairea the inspiration came out into the open: it was conceived less as a single structure than as a collection of buildings, earth mounds and planting framing a courtyard, a perennial form of settlement in much of Finland.

Historically, the first building a peasant farmer would erect was the sauna, and in the villa it can also be seen as the first, elemental component of a composition

Above, below and right Villa Mairea, Noormarkku, Finland, 1937–40, Alvar Aalto. In this collage-like composition Aalto combined references to vernacular buildings, orthodox modern architecture and traditional Japanese houses into a compelling synthesis which is unmistakably modern and Finnish.

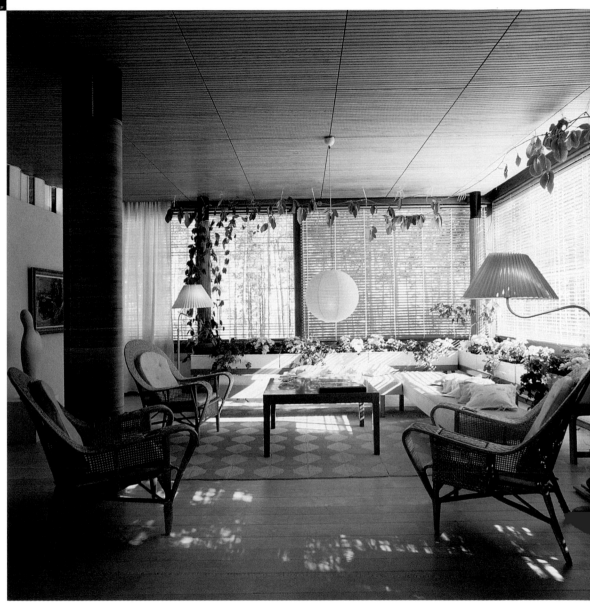

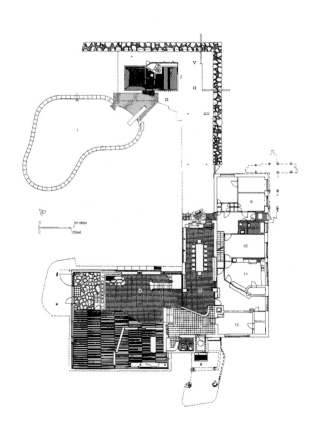

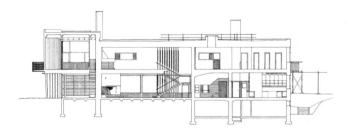

that grows in scale and sophistication around the courtyard, to culminate in Maire's first floor studio. Like the sauna, the studio is clad in wood, but here the boards are subtly moulded, identical to those Aalto designed for the Finnish Pavilion at the 1935 Paris World Fair, intended perhaps as a reminder of Maire's student days in the city. With its grass roof and wooden walls, the sauna seems reassuringly traditional, but the roof is flat and the boards have the sophistication of a Japanese tea-house – Aalto was besotted with Japan, and used to appear in the office in a kimono given him by the Japanese ambassador. Similar complexities occur all through the house. The covered dining terrace, for example recalls a single-storey fragment of a Dom-Ino house, but sports a grass roof on timber boarding and a wooden gutter hollowed from a log.

Internally, Aalto planned a continuous living space to meld modern open plan with the traditional *tupa* emulated by Gallen-Kallela and Saarinen. In the *tupa*, spaces were differentiated by poles at ceiling level, but in the Villa Mairea Aalto used a change of level to separate the entrance area. Also, the floor finishes become progressively more domestic and intimate – from stone through tiles, to timber boarding and rugs. As in a traditional house the focus is the fireplace, which greets you across a long diagonal vista. Where it meets the glass, the white-plastered block is hollowed out by a sinuous curve – nicknamed 'Aalto's ear' in the office – which recalls the sculpted forms of wind-driven snow, visible outside for several weeks in most years.

A regular grid of columns runs through the living space, but the black-painted circular steel columns are rendered unique by being variously doubled or trebled, wrapped with rattan singly or in pairs, clad with birch-wood strips or – in the library – made of concrete instead. His aim, Aalto said, was 'to avoid all artificial architectural rhythms', and in place of the 'clear structure' of Mies we are presented with a system that refuses to be seen as a grid. The presiding metaphor is the forest, emblem of Finnish identity and freedom, and it is reinforced by the detailed articulation. The rattan-wrapped columns, for example, are abstract representations of pine trees, whose dark bark peels to reveal a golden core. The library is separated from the living space by an undulating glazed screen in which glass alternates with solid, curved panels: with low sun or artificial light spilling through, it reminds you of sunlight through trees. And, to add another subtlety, the twin-sectioned white column supporting the studio can be seen as a metaphoric birch tree at the edge of the 'pine-forest' within – the inclined half is structurally redundant, and was only included at Maire's insistence after the engineer asked for it to be omitted.

In the Villa Mairea, Aalto collaged together fragments designed to bring to mind traditional Finnish buildings, memories of nature and more exotic sources. Japan is the most obvious, but also his beloved Italy – the white surfaces are again lime-washed brickwork, not render – and even Hollywood in the racily modern swimming pool. The spaces are all designed with the human subject as their centre: the main living area no longer has a dominant structure of its own, but seems to open and close, restructuring itself around you as you move through the space. It was a brilliant response to his clients' demand for a house both Finnish and modern, and nothing produced in Europe before the war came close to rivalling its inventive transformation of modern architecture to respond to

Above Villa Mairea, Noormarkku, Finland, 1937–40, Alvar Aalto. The interior unfolds as an abstraction of the Finnish pine forest, with black-painted steel columns wrapped in rattan or clad with birch strips, and the entrance area and main staircase screened by vertical poles.

specific cultural traditions. When, after the war, he came to embody his personal vision of life close to nature Aalto again turned to collage-like techniques to conjure up a slightly different set of associations.

Aalto Summer House Muuratsalo, Finland, 1953, Alvar Aalto

Aalto's summer house was built in 1953 as a gift for his new wife Elissa (he had lost his first wife, Aino, to cancer in 1949), on land given to him by the grateful client for his recently completed masterpiece, Säynätsalo Town Hall. The site was on the nearby island of Muuratsalo, at that time accessible only by boat, and the L-shaped house frames a small square courtyard, from whose corner a slender tail of timber buildings and fenced enclosures runs into the forest, each element angling and adjusting itself to the site – the foundations are made of logs positioned according to the rocks. The courtyard is the set-piece. At its centre is a square barbecue pit – square within square within square – and facing the living room the wall breaks completely to open a long view down the lake. In the other wall, at high level, a large opening is screened by white timber slats that rhyme with the trees. The walls themselves are a richly textured patchwork of bricks, tiles and climbing plants. Aalto described them as 'experimental' and said it was vital for him to test materials in the harsh northern climate before imposing them on his clients.

The 'experiments' were part of an unsuccessful ruse to avoid tax by claiming the house as a business expense, but the real innovation was aesthetic, not technical, and again Aalto's intentions are revealed by the details. Next to the living room door is a blue-tiled 'window', complete with wooden lintel; elsewhere, patches of brickwork suggest openings that have been closed up. 'I always have a journey to Italy in mind', he once remarked, and here, beside a Finnish lake, Aalto created his own Italian fantasy, a private piazzetta, patched and pre-weathered to inscribe time and the elements into the place and to defy the shock of the new. It is difficult to imagine anything further in substance or spirit from the seamless surfaces of the International style.

The summer house has offered many Nordic architects a unique opportunity to escape not only the city but also the expectations of their day-to-day professional life. When he built his at Stennäs in 1937, Aalto's friend and mentor Gunnar Asplund turned resolutely towards the vernacular. Although at first glance it might appear simple to the point of being cottagey, it was in fact a deceptively refined design. One notes, for example, the asymmetry of the main roof, which subtly adjusts both to the site and to the needs of the spaces within, and the artful crank in plan that pivots around the cavernous fireplace to realign the main room in recognition of the view.

Few summer houses better express the widely felt Nordic ideal of retreating to nature for physical and spiritual refreshment than that built by the Norwegian Knut Knutsen. Although he never subscribed to the values of the new architecture, and was known for his commitment to the national traditions of building, Knutsen was a notably inventive designer. During the 1930s he became the focus of opposition to the circle of ardent young Modernists gathered around Arne Korsmo, so when he built his summer house in 1949 on a rocky coastal site at Portør, it came as no surprise that he chose to make it entirely of that most traditional of Norwegian building materials, wood. The result, however, was

Below Summer House, Muuratsalo, Finland, 1953, Alvar Aalto. Built as a wedding gift for his second wife Elissa, Aalto used the summer house as an opportunity to experiment further with architectural collage. The presiding image is the time-worn walls of Italian streets and piazzas, with blue tiles here standing in for the southern sky seen through an empty window opening.

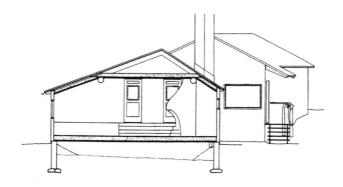

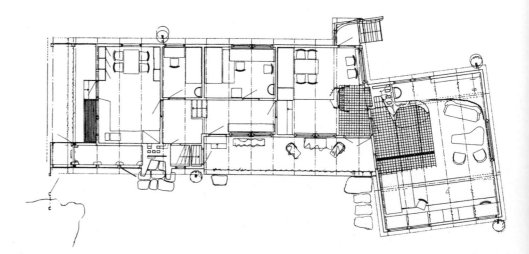

Right and opposite Asplund
Summer House, Stennäs, Sweden,
1937, Gunnar Asplund. The references
to the vernacular are more pervasive
here than in Aalto's Villa Mairea, but
the subtle adjustments to the
topography and views lift the design
far above a simple-minded exercise in
the neo-vernacular.

Above Knutsen Summer House, Portør, Norway, 1949, Knut Knutsen. The architect's sketch captures better than a photograph the essence of his design – folded planes of wood emulating the rocky landscape of the coastal site.

Below Ugalde House, near Barcelona, Spain, 1951, Antonio Coderch. Whitewashed stone walls, the smoothly abstract surfaces of the International Style and a site-adjusted plan combine to create an architecture inseparable from its Mediterranean context.

radical. From a distance the folded planes of the roof, clad in wide, overlapping boards, are almost indistinguishable from the surrounding rocks. Close to, they are revealed as wonderfully irregular, slipping and dipping to link house to landscape, whose rooms in turn jut and deflect as they settle into the terrain. Rediscovered in the 1980s by a new generation of architects, Knutsen's house became an emblem of the burgeoning Norwegian 'green' movement.

Recourse to the vernacular became a favourite strategy for reconnecting the rootless International style to local traditions. Gerrit Rietveld's cleverly asymmetrical Verrijn Stuart summer house in Breukelerveen, The Netherlands, in 1941 projects a relaxed, timeless air, as does the Ugalde House, built by Antonio Coderch on a coastal site at Caldes d'Estrac outside Barcelona in 1951. By combining thick, whitewashed walls, modern transparency and a complex, site-adjusted plan, Coderch achieved a serene power of expression that would influence a new generation of Barcelona architects three decades hence. For those Modernists who did not flee Nazi Germany the vernacular provided a safe dress beneath which spatial adventures could be indulged in private. Thus, for example, in 1937 we find Hugo Häring reinterpreting the Bavarian gabled farmhouse in his Von Prittwitz House at Starnbergersee near Munich, and Hans Scharoun wrapping the still impressively free interior of his house for the painter Oscar Moll in Berlin Grünewald with a folksy exterior.

Flight from Hitler brought several leading Modernists to London in the mid-1930s, among them Walter Gropius, Serge Chermayeff and Marcel Breuer. Chermayeff stayed long enough to build himself a large country house near Halland in Sussex. He submitted the design for planning permission in 1935 and was refused, only to win – a familiar story in England – following an appeal and public inquiry. The house was unmistakably modern, but made almost entirely of timber in deference to its rural location. Far from turning to the vernacular language of barns, however, Chermayeff discreetly but unmistakably evoked the tradition of the English country house. The garden front, with its exposed structure and layered façade is formal, even classical in spirit, while the entrance court is far less self-conscious and given over largely to service rooms. There is a generous, slightly raised terrace that just prevents the lawn lapping right up to the house in the manner of Capability Brown, and from today's perspective the scheme seems to resonate with tradition, whereas to the hapless planning officials at the time it doubtless threatened an alien modernity. What could be more English?

Climates and cultures radically different from those of its origins provoked many of the most original adaptations and transformations of the International style, but we cannot leave Europe without mentioning one of the most singular houses in the world, that of Curzio Malaparte on Capri. A prolific writer in several genres, war correspondent, magazine owner and film maker, Malaparte was also at various times a Fascist, a Communist and a Maoist. He was exiled and imprisoned for his varied but fanatically held convictions, and it was during one of his island exiles that he resolved to build a house on the Bay of Naples. He settled upon the site on Capri in 1937. The scenery, rediscovered by aristocratic nature-lovers early in the century, was outstanding and there was the added advantage that Mussolini's son-in-law, who was also the Italian foreign minister,

Above Chermayeff House, Halland,
England, 1935–7, Serge Chermayeff.
Modern Movement structure acquires an
appropriately classical air on the garden
front as the *emigré* Chermayeff
responds to the English country
house tradition.

Above and opposite Casa
Malaparte, Capri, Italy, 1937–40,
Curzio Malaparte. Spectacularly sited
on a headland on the island of Capri,
Malaparte's house is a platform and
frame for viewing the landscape. In
the sparsely furnished main salon the
fire in the hearth (seen on the right)
burns against a tiny window, uniting
interior and sea, fire and water.

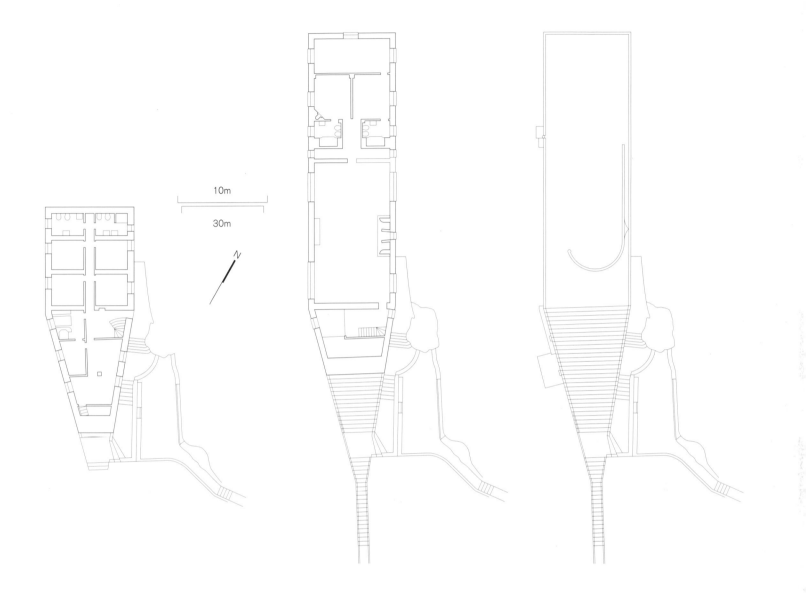

10m

30m

N

holidayed there – and promised to get him a building permit. The site must be among the most breathtaking in the world and to obtain permission to build there Malaparte commissioned a design from the Roman architect Adalberto Libera, to whom the house was attributed for many years. It is now clear that most of what was built was the work of Malaparte himself, supported by his master-mason Adolfo Amitrano.

Casa Malaparte Capri, Italy, 1937–40, Curzio Malaparte

The house grows directly out of the rocky headland, with its roof forming an outdoor terrace, approached via steps that widen as you ascend – they recall those by Michelangelo for the approach to the Campidoglio in Rome, but were modelled on the Church of the Annunciation in Lipari. Malaparte widened the foundations slightly to enable him to construct an axial sequence of rooms, rather than the single-banked corridor Libera envisaged: it seems likely that his model for the planning was the Hellenistic *domus*, examples of which were excavated during the 1930s. To reinforce the Classical atmosphere he formed the main entrance through the steps, modelled on the similarly formed *vomitorium* in a Greek theatre, but this was blocked up before completion, at the mason's insistence, because it risked flooding the interior. Malaparte then moved the entrance to the long flank, which explains, if not excuses, the modest, boxed-in staircase that leads rather inauspiciously to the 15-metre (49-foot) long salon above, leaving the stairs outside to serve only the roof.

The plan is rigorously orthogonal within the site-defined perimeter, neat and familiar so it does not obtrude on what really matters: the landscape, both built – the house as platform – and, supremely, natural. The breathtaking scenery becomes an endless performance to be viewed from the theatrical steps, and from inside every view is stunning, framed and viewed by the simplest of rectangular windows cut in the massive 80-centimetre- (30-inch-) thick walls. 'I didn't construct the house,' Malaparte claimed to have told Field Marshal Rommel, 'but I did construct the landscape'. The only overtly artful touch comes in the main salon, with the small glazed opening in the hearth through which you can see flames flickering in the Mediterranean, fire and water combining in a moment of sublime artistry.

Malaparte furnished the huge salon with white-covered sofas which look almost ethereal beside the slabs of wood on massive, fluted stone or timber columns that he used for tables. The means are minimal and the effect surreal, like a De Chirico painting – Malaparte explained it as an expression of his 'nostalgia' for the prison in which he was confined on Lipari. The house lay empty and sealed for twenty years following its owner's death in 1957. It seems likely that he wanted it to be his personal mausoleum, like the 'flaming red pyramid' of a Roman tomb Amedeo Maiuri claimed, in his *Breviario di Capri* of 1937, to have seen on the Anatolian coast. Whatever its meaning for the creator and owner, Casa Malaparte stands outside time and any conventional narrative of architectural development. The sensibility behind it is, however, unmistakably modern, even if the romantic, rebellious intellectual who created it was dreaming of the confinement of prison and the idealized freedom of the Classical world.

Leaving Europe for Brazil we return to the mainstream, and then quickly swerve into new territory as the genius of the place asserted itself. Modern architecture arrived there in earnest in 1936 when Le Corbusier was enlisted by

...

Lúcio Costa to help his team of recent graduates with the design of the new Ministry of Education building. Another European arrival was Bernard Rudofsky, who was born and trained in Austria before leaving for South America in 1937. He later achieved fame as the advocate of 'architecture without architects'. In 1941 Rudofsky completed an unassumingly modern house in São Paulo in which, predictably in view of his later interests, he turned to the patio-type as a response to the climate – although, due to local regulations, the form was not popular in the city. The house was laid out around a sequence of outdoor living spaces and, seen in plan, inside and outside appear almost interchangeable. The courtyards were heavily planted to provide shade, and deep overhangs supported on slender steel columns created large covered terraces and porches. The planning is modern, with a suite of interconnected living spaces, but spatially unremarkable. What marks the house out is its avoidance of stylistic affectation and wholehearted adaptation to the climate.

Le Corbusier's presence, needless to say, was galvanizing to local architects, above all to Oscar Niemeyer, the most gifted of Costa's team. When Niemeyer designed his own house in Rio de Janeiro in 1942 it was unashamedly conceived as a homage to Le Corbusier. The plot was small so he raised the accommodation on *pilotis* to preserve the continuity of the ground. With reflected light from the brilliant, high sun, the space below the building was credible as a continuation of the garden in a way that was rare in Europe. The house itself was organized around a ramp, which began its journey in the covered garden and ended, somewhat unceremoniously, in a narrow landing outside the bedrooms. The design was more than competent, but gave few hints of the explosive talent already evident in another project Niemeyer designed the same year. This was the Casino, the first of a group of recreational buildings at Pampulha in which the freedom of planning and dynamism of form made Le Corbusier's first moves in that direction look tentative.

The so-called 'Glass House', designed from 1950 to 1951 (and also lived in) by Lina Bo Bardi on a site outside São Paulo, became the social focus of modern architecture in Brazil and a mandatory visit for foreign artists and intellectuals – the architect-visitors included Max Bill, Gio Ponti and Aldo van Eyck. Italian by birth, Lina Bo edited the influential magazine *Domus* during the war before marrying the scholar Pietro Maria Bardi and settling in Brazil. Their house was Miesian in inspiration, perched dramatically above a reserve of Brazilian forest on impossibly slender tubular columns – the great engineer Pier Luigi Nervi assured them it would not have been allowed in Europe (and would not now in Brazil). The vast living room, fully-glazed on three sides, backed up against the bedrooms, which looked into a private court against the blank wall of the servants' wing. At first sight it seems an orthodox International style building, but the atmosphere is subtly different, softened by the sky-blue flooring and columns, the curtains which replace walls, the gentle curve of the roof, and the relaxed cohabitation of antique and modern furniture. Seen in the embrace of the surrounding forest, with its exotic birds and croaking frogs, it strikes visitors as organic, unmistakably feminine and quintessentially Brazilian.

In 1953 Oscar Niemeyer decided to build a new house for himself on a dramatic site in Rio de Janeiro occupying high ground between two towering

Above Courtyard House, São Paulo, Brazil, 1941, Bernard Rudofsky. Although not popular in the city due to local regulations, the courtyard form was ideally adapted to a climate which demanded shady interiors and invited outdoor-living.
Overleaf Glass House, near São Paulo, Brazil, 1950–51, Lina Bo Bardi. Lina Bo's house became both an emblem of the new architecture in Brazil and a social focus of progressive culture. The blue colouring and gently curved roof create sufficient distance from International Style norms to suggest something subtly adapted to the Brazilian context.

Niemeyer House Rio de Janeiro, Brazil, 1953, Oscar Niemeyer

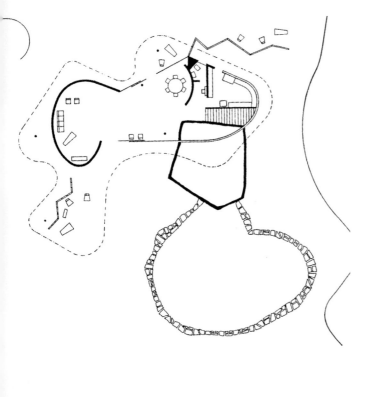

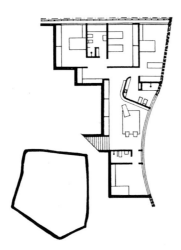

hills, with spectacular views down-slope which he wanted to preserve by ensuring visual continuity through the interior. This suggested large areas of glass shaded by an overhanging roof to ensure transparency and minimal internal divisions, so he consigned the four bedrooms and a sitting space to a lower level, cut into the hill. Its roof was treated as new ground, across which the living spaces and an open terrace were freely disposed – more freely, perhaps, than in any other house that has been considered here.

At first sight the main plan resembles an abstract painting more than a building. A continuous broken line, signifying the roof, meanders apparently at random around some freely arranged curved and straight planes; a shallow arc makes a place for the dining table, evoking memories of Mies's Tugendhat House, and then breaks free to zigzag its way into the landscape (its echo is found on the covered terrace, where a zigzag screen shelters outdoor seating); an irregular pentagon drawn with a thick black line represents a massive, immovable boulder which juts into the free-form swimming pool. Beyond the house, more wriggling lines describe tropical plants – or are they abstract sculptures? – of which the roof, suddenly, seems like a massive enlargement. 'It is not the right angle that attracts me,' Niemeyer explained, 'nor the straight line, hard and inflexible, created by man. What attracts me is the free and sensual curve – the curve that I find in the mountains of my country, in the sinuous course of its rivers, in the body of the beloved woman'.

Niemeyer's house offended some of its earliest European visitors, who found the relationship between the two floors incoherent, and the intensely personal quality arbitrary. But, by rejecting the formal consistency of orthodox modern architecture and responding directly to the site, Niemeyer achieved an unsurpassed integration with the setting. House and garden were unified visually and formally, and the latter was designed by his friend Roberto Burle Marx, a master of the art. All the forms can be read as abstractions of vegetation or rocks, and the large preserved rock outcrop became the pivot of the composition. It links pool to house, supports a roof column, marks the tapering edge of the stairs, and dominates views of the house. As in a Japanese garden, it also stands as a miniature of the hills to either side, which in turn are integrated into the space like living murals – the abstract spatial continuity of early modern architecture here became palpable and intensely habitable. Niemeyer pushed the *plan libre* to new extremes of freedom, but for all its suave sophistication his house also conjures up the atmosphere of a primitive shelter: as a vision of an earthly paradise it has few rivals.

A similar vision was realized, using very different architectural means, by the Mexican Luis Barragán, who was renowned almost as much for his gardens as for his buildings. Born in Guadalajara in 1902, he trained as an engineer but almost immediately made the move into architecture, completing a couple of dozen Spanish Colonial style projects in his native city over the next decade. He travelled to Europe in 1931 and 1932, where he met Le Corbusier and assimilated the ideas espoused in *L'Esprit Nouveau*. Eager to practise the new architecture on his return, he moved to Mexico City, where he rapidly completed some thirty projects in an accomplished and markedly anonymous version of the

Above, right and opposite.
Niemeyer House, Rio de Janeiro,
Brazil, 1953, Oscar Niemeyer. By
radically separating the lower,
bedroom, floor from the living level,
Niemeyer achieved an unprecedented
freedom of planning and a total
integration of house, garden
(designed by Roberto Burle Marx)
and landscape.

Above, right and opposite

Barragán House and Studio, Mexico
City, Mexico, 1947, Luis Barragán.
Designed as a refuge from the tumult
of the city, Barragán's house deploys
simple architectural means – cubic
volumes, planes of colour, stone floors
– to elemental effect, not least in the
almost surreal roof-garden.

International Style. Then, in 1940, he informed his clients and friends that he was retiring from commercial practice, acquired a large estate and developed a house for himself. Externally it still bore the marks of the International style, however the organization was based not on an open plan but on rooms inside and, just as important, outside, in the interlinked walled gardens. Seven years later, he built a second house on a site nearby, which he continued to work on throughout his life. It became his living laboratory, and in the process grew into one of the century's great dwellings.

Barragán House and Studio Mexico City, Mexico, 1947, Luis Barragán

Externally the Barragán House and Studio are stark and unremarkable, an anonymous presence in its unpretentious neighbourhood. But as soon as you open the door the ambience is unique. It owes something to Spanish Colonial architecture, much more to the vivid colours of traditional Mexican building and, in the preference for geometric clarity, to the International Style. But the whole is new and timeless. The walls are framed in concrete and filled with concrete blocks; most are roughly plastered and brilliantly coloured, their intensity and rough textures enhanced by indirect lighting. The only other materials you see are large pine beams, wide floorboards and volcanic rock paving and steps. The living room faces a main garden contained by ivy-clad walls, like a captive slice of jungle intended to bring the pleasures of wild nature into the house. You look into the garden through a vast sheet of glass divided by a thin cruciform mullion. This religious note is entirely deliberate, adding a mystical quality to the boundary between interior and garden, where nature was allowed free rein – Barragán chose to introduce no objects, nor to interfere in the processes of growth and decay.

From the hall a granite staircase supported by a yellow wall connects to the bedrooms, and from the upper floor a small staircase leads up to the roof garden – an abstract world now open only to the sky (he raised the walls higher in 1954 to block out Mexico City's growing skyline). It clearly owed something to Le Corbusier, and is contained by vividly coloured walls – cream and terracotta, scarlet and purple – of varying heights, interspersed with tall blocks of plain cement render. In a light less intense than Mexico's it would easily turn to kitsch and in photographs it can look slightly lurid, but this is misleading. According to the Portuguese architect Alvaro Siza: 'The photographs show vivid, pure colours – the colours one finds in any Mexico City street, or in a Mayan ruin – but of my visit to Barragán's house, the colour I remember is gold.'

Octavio Paz, the Nobel Prize-winning novelist, has written that the 'Mexican searches for the silence of closed worlds', and in what has become the world's most populous city Barragán's house was designed as a defence. 'The walls create silence', he said, and sheltered by them he could face life. Deeply Catholic, Barragán believed beauty has a redemptive quality and that a stoical acceptance of solitude was part of our fate. His house was also inextricably bound up with ideas on time: with the luxury of 'wasting' time in contemplative inaction; with surfaces that register the passage of time through the development of patina – unlike those of the International Style, unchanging and timeless; and finally with the ability of the house to evolve through time in response to his needs – the cross of redemption in the window, for example, was one of his last interventions. A bastion against the tumult of modern life, Barragán's house was more like a life

Below and opposite Jaoul Houses, Neuilly-sur-Seine, France, 1954, Le Corbusier. Like the *béton brut* of the Marseilles Unité, the exterior of the Jaoul Houses signalled the new, tougher sensibility of Le Corbusier's post-war work. Internally, however, they are marvellously inviting: punctuated by sculptural built-in furniture and bursts of brilliant colour, the spaces unfold freely along and across the shallow vaults.

Top Villa Sarabhai, Ahmedabad, India, 1951–6, Le Corbusier. The vaulted Monol-type was combined with materials such as handmade bricks to create a modern Indian vernacular.

Jaoul Houses Neuilly-sur-Seine, France, 1954, Le Corbusier

lived than a design: it offers a compelling critique of the belief that a true dwelling can be reduced to either an industrial product or an unchanging work of art.

Le Corbusier's post-war houses continued the move towards rougher, natural materials and the muscular, sculpturally expressive forms of the Unité at Marseilles. In 1951, in a pair of houses at Neuilly-sur-Seine on the edge of Paris – close to the Cook and Stein houses – he returned to the vaulted structure of the Weekend House of 1935. The Jaoul Houses, as they were called, were composed of a narrow and a wide band of space, with shallow Catalan vaults of rough concrete forming the suspended floors and roofs. Internally and externally, the finishes were deliberately crude and tough – roughly pointed brickwork, tiles, board-marked concrete – but the spaces were rendered enticingly habitable by a revetment of plaster and timber.

On their completion in 1954 the Jaoul Houses divided even Le Corbusier's most fervent admirers, some of whom seemed to have forgotten the Weekend House and must have ignored or not taken seriously the eulogies of peasant building that peppered his writings of the 1940s. They provoked a celebrated debate in England. Peter Smithson thought they were perfectly poised 'on the knife edge of peasantism', whereas James Stirling, in an influential article for *The Architectural Review* entitled 'From Garches to Jaoul', criticized them as a dangerous retreat from the polemical vigour of what the Smithsons later christened the 'Heroic Period' of the 1920s. But when, in the same year that his article appeared, Stirling came to design a group of flats at Ham Common the influence of the Jaoul Houses was obvious, as it was in many buildings of the late 1950s and 1960s.

Following an invitation in 1951 to plan Chandigarh, the new capital of the Punjab, Le Corbusier received several private commissions in India. They included two for houses in Ahmedabad, centre of the textile industry. In them he brought the Monol and Citrohan/Dom-Ino types to a new peak of spatial refinement. Handmade sun-dried bricks and rough concrete were the modern vernacular of India and for the first of the houses, for Manorama Sarabhai, his wife and their extended family, Le Corbusier opted for the vaulted Monol type. The main body of the house is ten bays wide, and the interior expands laterally through large gaps in the supporting brick walls to form a deep, freely spreading space. Rectangular and free-form timber boxes, housing bathrooms and other service spaces, sit below the concrete beams, frequently bridging the spatial units to establish a counterpoint to the dominant grain.

The open ends of the house are oriented towards the prevailing winds to ventilate the interior naturally, with the glazing and infill panels set well back to provide shading and form generous covered porches. The roof, accessible from a small upper storey, was grassed and planted to become, Le Corbusier said, 'a magnificent garden of lawn and charming flowers'. To cope with the heavy storms brought by the monsoon winds it was provided with a system of concrete channels: water from the first floor disgorges through large gargoyles, while that from the upper level plunges dramatically down an enormous chute, like a children's slide, into a pool. To the Indian architect Charles Correa, the Sarabhai House was a masterly response to the needs of an extended family, 'as complex, as amorphous, and as open-ended as a Banyan tree'.

Above Villa Shodhan, Ahmedabad, India, 1952–6, Le Corbusier. Adapted to the Indian climate, the vision of the modern house as a continuous, three-dimensional field of space shielded by *brises-soleil* found a compelling new form.

At first sight the Villa Shodhan, the second house, forms a complete contrast: upright, four-square and permeable, it is a descendant of the Dom-Ino type explored at length in the 1920s. In keeping with his new, robust manner and in response to the climate, concrete piers have replaced spindly *pilotis*, large areas of solid wall alternate with deep *brises-soleil* and porches, and the roof garden has given way to a shady parasol. The composition exploits the freedom of the *plan libre*, although the majority of the spatial divisions follow the lines of the structural grid. In this respect it resembles the Sarabhai House, but whereas there the space expands only horizontally, here it is fully three-dimensional. Alan Colquhoun has remarked that the Corbusian free plan was won at the expense of a paralysis of the section, with space sandwiched between the floor slabs. Here we see Le Corbusier attempting to free the section through the complex interlocking of single-, double- and triple-height spaces to create an interior through which both the eye and the air can move freely.

Like the Unité at Marseilles, Le Corbusier's post-war houses make clear that his belief in a machine-age utopia had given way to a concern for a timeless, elemental relationship with nature. Deeply moved by the experience of India, he wrote about the 'possibility of getting in touch with the essential joys of Hindu principles: a brotherhood of relationships between the cosmos and all living things'. Although they were not always cast in such heroic terms, architectural expressions of affinity with nature have been a recurring theme in modern architecture, as they were two decades later for a young and then unknown South African architect, Stanley Saitowitz.

We noted in Chapter 2 that a strong group of young Modernists flourished in South Africa. They built several fine houses in a post-Corbusian style but the most talented among them, Rex Martienssen, died tragically young in 1942 and after the war the impetus was lost. The darkening political climate was not conducive to further development but in the 1970s Saitowitz – who now works in

Halfway House Transvaal, South Africa, 1976, Stanley Saitowitz

San Francisco – designed a house that beautifully illustrates the meeting of global and local cultures we have been exploring. It is located, somewhat confusingly, at Halfway House (which I will use as its name), on six acres of savannah on the high veld in the Transvaal.

Saitowitz's ideas – which he characterizes as 'geological architecture' – were informed by studying the homes of the native N'debele people. Made from the earth on which they stand, the houses are loosely gathered to form a settlement defined by walls and thresholds. Freshly painted, the mud walls bloom in the spring, only to erode in the summer rains, and then be remade by the occupants each winter: their architecture, like their agriculture, is inseparable from the natural rhythms of the seasons, and their houses are more like a process than a product.

Halfway House is sited in the shelter of a cluster of rocks, against which a circle was marked on the ground; within it, the contours were heightened by terracing and planted with alternating strains of grass. Close to the rocks the terraces sweep up to form a series of arched roofs, which are then staggered to allow light to pour in at high level through the gaps. Echoing the roofs, the straight, parallel terrace walls turn into semi-circles which ripple out from the bathroom, growing in scale, to celebrate – Saitowitz explained – the curves of the

Above and right Halfway House, Transvaal, South Africa, 1976 Stanley Saitowitz. Lightweight, seemingly improvised, the design is a response to the rocky outcrops and towering clouds of the high veld and creates a richly habitable place in the open landscape.

Magney House Bingi Point, Australia, 1984, Glenn Murcutt

Magney House, completed in 1984 on Bingi Point, New South Wales, represents a lyrical peak in the development of Murcutt's favourite house-type, a long metal pavilion with, ideally, an en-suite sequence of rooms. It sits on 33 hectares (82 acres) of bare, almost tree-less coastal land, where the clients had camped regularly and wanted a house that would preserve a sense of relaxation. The linear plan is oriented east-west and organized around central living and dining areas, with the parents' bedroom at one end, and two for children or visitors at the other. Along the southern (sunless) frontage is a narrow band of service spaces – kitchens, toilets, showers, and so on – and next to them a longitudinal open passage which turns into a closed corridor only where needed to separate the children's/guest bedrooms.

The section, with its sinuous, asymmetrical gull-wing roof, directly echoes the plan and was developed in response to the prevailing winds and solar penetration. The southerly elevation is solid brick up to 2.1 metres (7 feet), above which a sloping glass clerestory is cantilevered out with pivoting wooden slats, in the horizontal gap between wall and glass, to allow for cross-ventilation in summer. The north elevation is fully glazed, with continuous external louvres in front of sliding doors and a roof overhang – restrained by elegant diagonal ties – to exclude high sun from the clerestory. Louvres and doors can all open to give the occupants the feeling of sitting outdoors. Seen from close to, the house is an exquisitely made object; at a distance, it is reduced to an evanescent silver slash in the landscape, as if to obey the Aboriginal injunction to 'touch this earth lightly'.

The love of clarity of construction evident in Murcutt's houses has been a recurring theme in English architecture. William Morris, we may recall, ascribed ethical value to 'truth to materials' and his favourite building was a medieval tithe barn at Great Coxwell, Gloucestershire, a majestic work of pure construction. A similar commitment informs the work of Edward Cullinan, who traces many of his architectural values back to the Arts and Crafts movement. Cullinan's love of how buildings are made manifested itself in a desire to build as well as design. This led, as he observed, to 'a mode of construction and expression that uses a severely limited range of available materials, puts a stress on "placed together" joints and junctions, has materials mastering and oversailing one another and avoids the partial sophistication of "flushness" and hidden detailing.' In his own house, built in 1963 in a mews in London's Camden Town, Cullinan turned these principles into a language of great subtlety and power. Built between two party walls, two-storeys high to the north, one-storey to the south, the house has a cave-like base of London stock bricks containing bedrooms and a bathroom, above which an open-plan, timber-framed eyrie is layered over and between concrete columns and beams. To the rear of the tiny plot a single garage was somehow squeezed in. Its roof became a terrace, accessible from the inside via a timber deck and steps from the living room, and from the outside by narrow steps and an ingenious ramp which wrapped up and around the back of the garage under the foliage of a sycamore tree – a miniature but authentic *promenade architecturale.*

In the work of the German architect Walter Segal, who settled in London in 1936, an interest in self-building led to the development of a readily assembled timber-building system based on the American balloon-frame. He tried it out on

Below and opposite Magney House, Bingi Point, New South Wales, Australia, 1984, Glenn Murcutt. Combining his favourite linear plan-type with a suavely curvilinear roof, Murcutt creates a statement of great elegance and clarity, its under-stated formality a perfect foil to the relaxed life of holidays by the sea.

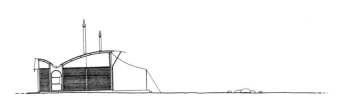

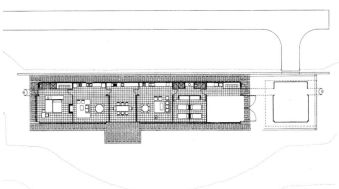

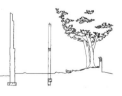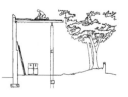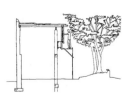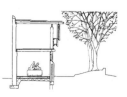

himself in 1963, building the 'Little House' in his back garden. Then, eventually, after many false dawns, in 1976 the council of the London borough of Lewisham approved – by one vote – a proposal to set up a self-build housing scheme for people on their housing waiting list. It took almost three more years for work to begin on site, and by mid-1980 fourteen unique council houses were ready for occupation. 'He taught us to think for ourselves', said one of the builder-residents, 'and gave us such confidence when we finished our houses we felt we could go on to do anything we set our minds to – he literally changed our lives'. In *Eupalinos or the Architect* the poet Paul Valéry has his architect observe that, 'By dint of constructing. . . I truly believe that I have constructed myself'. The houses and lives of Cullinan and Segal testify to the power of this belief.

The love of clear construction was combined with a passion for landscape in arguably the finest English house built in the 1960s, Creek Vean by Norman Foster and Richard Rogers, then practising with their wives Wendy and Sue as Team 4. Hugging the contours of a Cornish headland and opening to the views through splayed rooms, the plan is spilt into two wings by a grass-covered staircase. Inspired by Aalto's example at Säynätsalo Town Hall, its straight steps appear organically curved in perspective, like natural contours, due to the irregular geometry. Cornwall had long been a favourite haunt of English Modernists and a colony of artists had flourished in St Ives since the 1930s. The house contained many examples of their work – by Ben Nicholson, Barbara Hepworth and Patrick Heron, among others – which evoked the spirit of modernity and place that drew artists to this unique peninsula. Externally, the bare concrete-block surfaces are softened by vegetation spilling down from the roofs. Inside, the crisply geometric spaces unfold like an inner landscape beneath a sinuous roof, epitomizing a liberating functionalism which, by reducing things to essentials and inscribing itself into the landscape, heightens our awareness of the ever-changing nuances of a local light of unsurpassed clarity.

As an expression of a new machine for civilization, the International Style aspired to a global relevance predicated on unending economic growth. Culturally, as we have seen, these ideals were being questioned as early as the 1930s, but in the commercial sphere they went unchallenged and by the 1960s Miesian steel-and-glass towers were the dominant emblem of multinational corporate power. It took the oil crisis of the 1970s to make businesses look seriously at the energy consequences of large areas of glass, which were often unsuited to the climate and necessitated air-conditioning for comfort. But in most of the houses we have examined in this chapter efforts were made to respond to the climate, and in some – those by Barragán and Murcutt, for example – it was a major determinant of their design. In the work of the English architect Ralph Erskine, who has lived in Sweden all his professional life, climatic considerations were of overwhelming importance well before worries about global warming forced them into every architect's consciousness.

Erskine's convictions were partly born out of necessity when he built a tiny house near Stockholm – known as 'The Box' – for himself and his wife in 1942. It consisted of only two spaces, kitchen and living room, in which the bed doubled as a sofa and could be lifted up to the ceiling to free the space for work. The

Creek Vean Pill Creek, Cornwall, England, 1966, Team 4

Above Walters Way Self-build Housing, Lewisham, England, 1976–85, Walter Segal. This group of fourteen houses was built by their residents using the 'Segal System' of timber construction. Ecologically ahead of its time, it allowed for the possibility of the houses being taken apart and their components re-used.
Opposite and below Cullinan House, London, England, 1963, Edward Cullinan. This self-built house is organized as a timber 'nest' of living space above a brick 'cave' of bedrooms, and detailed to simplify and celebrate the process of construction.

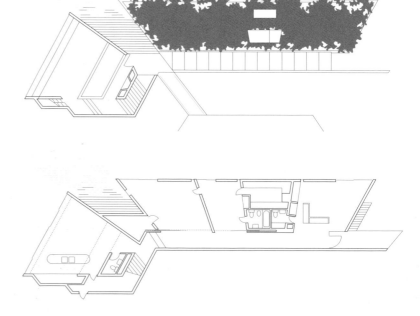

Above right and opposite Creek Vean, Pill Creek, Cornwall, England, 1966, Team 4. Tucked tightly into a steep headland and engulfed in plants, the house makes the most of the Cornish landscape and light by opening to the views and sky through splayed reflecting walls and a linear roof-light.

only water was from a well, the only heat from a log fire. Along the north elevation Erskine placed a hollowed-out 'thick wall' for storage, from which his desk folded down and against which, under cover outside, logs were stacked to increase the insulation. To the south, the living room's full-height glazing captured winter sun, but was saved from overheating in summer by the oversailing roof.

Erskine's fascination with climate assumed more dramatic form in the Villa Ström, built near Stockholm in 1961. The house sits on a steep slope and is entered at high level, from where the spaces spiral down, around the central fireplace, growing in volume in a manner reminiscent of Adolf Loos's *Raumplan* as much as modern 'flowing space'. The form is cubic, to minimize the external envelope, and the balconies are freestanding structures to prevent thermal transmission through their exposed surfaces. On the roof, angled plates reflect the low sun into the heart of the house through roof lights, the light spilling down over the hearth. Energy from sun, fire and wind was central to Erskine's conception of a building, and as we shall see, in the era of global warming many of the 'passive' energy-control ideas he pioneered have become part of the language of architecture.

Can Lis Porto Petro, Majorca, Spain, 1973, Jørn Utzon

No house better sums up the issues we have considered in this chapter than Can Lis, the home Jørn Utzon built for himself and his wife Lis on Majorca in 1973. As befits its Mediterranean setting, Can Lis has classical roots – 'crystal clear forms on a site-adjusted base', as Utzon puts it. But the architect's openness to the possibilities of the site, the use of locally available materials, and the creative collaboration with the masons who built it, lend the composition a suppleness and ease that are more often to be found in a vernacular building. Sited on a long strip of land running between a narrow, pine-roofed road and a precipitous 20-metre- (66-foot-) high cliff, it consists of a series of small buildings and walled patios. Each is adjusted to the site and to the horizon, and there are tapering gaps between them to allow glimpses through to the sea. You enter via a generous covered porch beneath which, in a gesture of welcome as much symbolic as practical, stands a tiled bench. Open the plain wooden door and you are greeted by a crescent moon-shaped opening through which you glimpse the slender, twisted trunk of a young pine silhouetted against the blazing light – the moon was inspired by nothing more exotic than the name of the road, Media Luna, Half Moon.

After this magical moment of arrival you are drawn into the golden light of a nine-square plan, colonnaded court, from where you face the sea on a stone platform which steps down towards a low wall. It feels timeless, ancient as the ruins of a Greek *stoa*. The kitchen and dining room line the rear wall, and under one of the colonnades is another stone bench and a table over which is draped a tiled 'cloth'. Retracing your steps you pass under cover into a small court and from there into the living room. As high as it is deep and receding upwards into shade, it is articulated by a free-standing column into a square sitting space and narrow, L-shaped passage. Roughly at the centre of the square Utzon put three unequal tables – sectors of an implied polygon – and around them an almost semi-circular couch, also of stone with blue tiled nosings and white cushions. Large enough to gather the whole family in its embrace before the spectacle of Nature, the couch is a permanent emblem of the values he holds most dear.

Above Erskine House ('The Box'), Lissma, Sweden, 1942, Ralph Erskine. With its concern for the minutiae of living, fully-glazed south-facing living space and solid north wall insulated by storage inside and stacked logs outside, this tiny house exemplifies the principles which inform Erskine's later work.

Opposite Villa Ström, near Stockholm, Sweden, 1961, Ralph Erskine. Minimizing heat losses and maximizing exposure to sun and daylight generated the cubic form, light reflectors and free-standing balconies of this climate-responsive house.

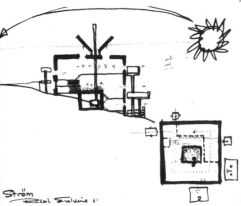

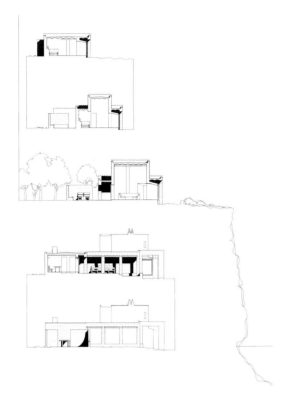

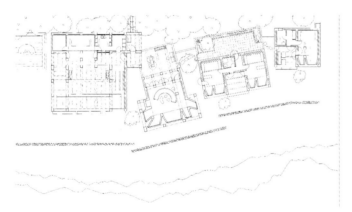

From the seat you view the world through windows large enough to stand in, with deep reveals and soffits angled inwards and downwards to direct your gaze towards the meeting of sea and sky. In mid-afternoon a slice of sun, so distinct you feel you could pick it up, falls on the floor to the left, through a small glazed opening – too rudimentary to call a 'window' – placed high in the west wall. Minutes later, a diagonal slash of wall above the windows is dusted with light, intensifying for a few precious minutes into a stone-dissolving shaft only to recede, leaving a glowing patch of light to linger in the opening as a reminder of the sun's daily visit.

If the Villa Savoye remains, after almost three-quarters of a century, the most compelling vision of the early Modernist dream of a new way of living, serviced by machines and detached from the particularities of place, Can Lis represents a high point of that other face of Modernism, pioneered by Le Corbusier in the wake of a second world war, which sought to renew a declining Western civilization through recourse to the primordial. It is a measure of the architect's artistry that Can Lis feels as natural as the sun, stone and sea whose intercourse it celebrates.

Above and opposite Can Lis, Porto Petro, Majorca, Spain, 1973, Jørn Utzon. Built on a dramatic cliff-top site Utzon's vacation/retirement home uses the readily available building materials of Majorca to create a house imbued with the spirit of the Mediterranean, ancient as Mycenae yet unmistakably modern in its abstraction and acute sensitivity to place.

Taliesin East Spring Green, Wisconsin, USA, 1911, Frank Lloyd Wright

Above and opposite Taliesin East, Spring Green, Wisconsin, USA, 1911, Frank Lloyd Wright. Intended to be 'of, not on, the hill', Wright's home and studio was designed to grow out of the landscape as naturally as the rock strata it emulated.

America's greatest monuments are the work of Nature, not Man, and the canonical American houses are all rural, not urban – the southern plantation house, Jefferson's Monticello, Thoreau's hut by Walden Pond, Frank Lloyd Wright's Fallingwater. When asked to explain his approach to architecture Wright said, 'I was born an American child of the ground and of space'. To Wright, as to many Americans, the family house occupying its own plot of land was an emblem of freedom and the basis of American democracy, for which he invented the word Usonia. The frontier might no longer be there in reality, but the frontier spirit, determined to push ever-outwards into open space and virgin land, was still alive in the imagination, finding its ultimate expression in the twentieth century in putting men on the moon. Asked by clients how far out of the city they should look for land, Wright advised them to go 'ten times as far as you think you ought to go' because the future, he was convinced, lay in decentralization and re-establishing contact with the earth. And when he said a natural house should 'grow out of the ground' on which it stood, he meant it quite literally: all Wright's great houses were driven by his desire to derive their architecture from the land.

The Prairie houses were Wright's first attempt to design a natural house, although as we have seen their relationship to the landscape was abstract rather than direct. Their influence is still very much apparent in Taliesin East, the home and studio Wright built for himself in 1911 in Wisconsin, but there the buildings are inseparable from the terrain. The siting was critical: the house is wrapped around a hill, of which it becomes the brow – Wright had Welsh ancestry and Taliesin is an old Welsh word meaning 'shining brow'. The house is no longer 'on the hill', he said, but 'of the hill', and after studying the rock strata visible in the landscape he took the 'outcropping ledges in the façades of the hills' as the model for his stonework. All traces of ornament were expunged, leaving Nature to provide the decoration – 'icicles by invitation might beautify the eaves', he suggested; the 'sweeping, soft air of the rain' would make 'music on the roofs'; and entire walls of glazed doors could 'open to the breezes of summer and become like an open camp'.

Wright's aspirations were rooted in the Romantic tradition that figured so strongly in nineteenth-century American thought, and as such are hardly new. What was new, and so radically new that it takes some effort to see through its seeming naturalness, is the way he gave formal expression to the idea of uniting architecture and nature. The richly layered timbers and rubble stone walls of Greene and Greene's Gamble House shared a similar ambition, but are still eminently recognizable as a 'house' and a 'terrace', whereas in Taliesin, as Neil Levine has suggested, 'the piers and parapets of stone, the planes of plaster, and the lines of shingled roof are experienced primarily as . . . shapes disengaged from any figurative role'. By collapsing the familiar image of a house Wright was able to rid himself of all traces of traditional styles, freeing his architecture to take Nature as its model. Traditional houses might be articulated to link to their sites, but Wright's would now appear to grow out of the site, as he put it, 'like the rocks and trees'. The walls of Taliesin were not calculated to *look like* an outcrop, but *made as if they were* outcrops, seemingly as natural as strata exposed by millennia of erosion.

The aspirations first realized at Taliesin informed all Wright's later work, to a

Above La Miniatura (Millard House),
Pasadena, California, USA, 1922–3,
Frank Lloyd Wright. Built of specially
designed concrete 'textile blocks', La
Miniatura was Wright's first attempt to
design a house which blossomed from
the landscape of Southern California.

La Miniatura Pasadena, California, USA, 1922–3, Frank Lloyd Wright

greater or lesser extent, beginning with a series of houses in California designed in the 1920s. These include the monumental Hollyhock House and four others built using a 'textile-block' construction system invented in 1906. The first and most delicate of the latter was built for Alice Millard, a former client from the Prairie Style period who was now widowed and wanted to run her rare book and antique business from home. The budget was tight and the client small – hence the name Wright gave the house, La Miniatura. He persuaded her to buy a cheap 'unbuildable' site in a small ravine, which had two beautiful eucalyptus trees and struck him as typically Californian. The plan consists of two interlocking squares; the one nearer the road contains the entrance loggia and a garage, while to the rear is a three-storey cubic volume. At ground level are the servant's room, kitchen and dining room, which opens onto a terrace overlooking a small pond. Above are a double-height living room and guest room, and on the top floor Mrs Millard's bedroom, also double height, with a balcony overlooking the living room and a door leading onto a terrace on the garage roof.

With his textile-block system Wright aimed, as he put it, to 'take that despised outcast of the building industry – the concrete block' and 'make it live as a thing of beauty – textured like the trees'. For the Millard House he designed three units: a plain one, used mainly for solid internal partitions; a cross-shaped pattern, which could be embossed or perforated, and left permeable for screen walls or sealed by casting in glass; and a type with a square boss on its face and U-shaped channels in its sides, which used back-to-back to form piers. The 40-centimetre (16-inch) square grid of the blocks controlled all the vertical and horizontal dimensions – even those you cannot see, like the spacing of the floor joists. The square motifs in the blocks established additional controlling dimensions for details like mullions and transoms. They appeared to extend outwards in all four directions, permeating the surfaces and making clear the meaning of 'textile' block: the spaces are woven as a continuous three-dimensional fabric, supressing, so as not to disturb the system, the reinforced concrete columns and beams that were structurally necessary.

'Standardization was the soul of the machine,' Wright explained, 'and here I was the Weaver taking it as a principle, knitting a great future for it.' Several of Wright's key ideas have been persuasively linked to the nineteenth-century German architect Gottfried Semper, whose theory of the 'Four Elements' (earthwork, hearth, framework/roof and lightweight enclosure) were widely discussed in Chicago in the 1890s. They are clearly legible in the Prairie houses and it seems likely that in developing the weaving analogy Wright had in mind Semper's discussion of textiles as one of the earliest forms of enclosure, and of the transposition of ideas from one medium to another. If the Greeks could emulate timber construction in stone, why could he not 'weave' in concrete? Externally, Wright's exquisite perspective looking down on the house beside its pond stressed graphically the link to the eucalyptus trees. But to my eyes the blocks do not seem so much to be 'textured like the trees' as studded with flowers, like those other beguiling images of earthly paradise, Persian carpets. What is unmistakable is the pervasive organic quality, the feeling that the house has blossomed from its site, like plants luxuriating in the sun. The Millard House

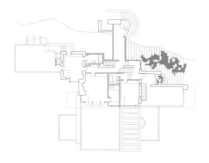

Fallingwater Bear Run, Pennsylvania, USA, 1935–9, Frank Lloyd Wright

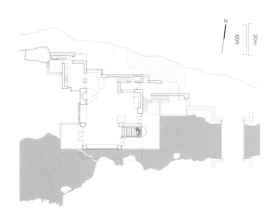

was a convincing beginning to Wright's search for 'a distinctly genuine expression of California', and in later and larger designs in the series he went on to break up the block-like character and develop the plans along out-reaching diagonals.

Among twentieth-century buildings Fallingwater, built at Bear Run in north-west Pennsylvania in 1935–9, is probably second only to Sydney Opera House in public recognition. The clients were Edgar and Liliane Kaufmann, owners of the Kaufmann department store in nearby Pittsburgh. They were introduced to Wright through their son, Edgar Jr, who had started work the previous year as an apprentice at the Taliesin Fellowship, Wright's combined office and school. They decided to commission a 'forest retreat' on their 650-hectare (1600-acre) estate in the Allegheny Mountains, and the idea of building a house 'to the music of the stream' occurred to Wright on his first visit. It took nine months to mature and the first time he touched paper was during the two hours it took his client to drive from Milwaukee to Taliesin, after Kaufmann had 'phoned ahead to ask if it would be all right to come and see the drawings'. The design was living in his mind and the plans and sections Wright hastily set down defined all its essential features. He named it 'Fallingwater' just before Kaufmann arrived.

The house was structured as a series of reinforced concrete trays, cantilevered from a rock ledge next to the stream and supported by orthogonally arranged load-bearing walls and piers. They were of local stone, specially quarried nearby and laid, like those at Taliesin, in irregularly coursed horizontal beds, the thinner of which project to form narrow ledges: the result is indeed more like eroded sedimentary rock than a conventional wall. The plan is organized around a 'great room' which, as in the Prairie houses, moves from entrance and hearth to glazed screens and open terraces – towards which you gravitate, drawn by the sound of falling water. The hearth is the surface of an enormous boulder, which emerges through the shiny flagstone floor like a rock in a stream. It had added significance for the Kaufmanns, having been Edgar's favourite resting-spot before the house was built.

The terraces cantilever dramatically more than 5 metres (16 feet) out over the stream below – seen from the bridge as you approach the effect of suspension in space is staggering – and the main room not only opens out but up, through a glazed concrete trellis, and down, through a sliding glass hatch onto a concrete staircase, hung by steel bars and descending to the stream. Wright thought it might be possible to deepen the stream for swimming at this point, but the stair was as much an excuse to create the symbolically necessary connection. Above and to the rear of the living room, the bedrooms pinwheel around the large chimney, each a miniature of the space you have left, with its own fire and floating terrace.

Wright described the house as 'an extension of the cliff' and anchored it back with a concrete trellis that continues the plane of the first-floor tray through the rear stone wall. One of the beams forms a semi-circle to wrap around the trunk of a tree, emphasizing the integration with nature. Framed and contrasted, the ridges on the tree's bark are echoed in the striated surfaces of the stones behind. Like all the exposed concrete, the beams are painted a pale peach-cream. Wright originally wanted to coat them with gold leaf, and when even this

Above, left and opposite
Fallingwater, Bear Run, Pennsylvania, USA, 1935–9, Frank Lloyd Wright. Designed 'to the music of the stream', Fallingwater was a structural and compositional tour de force which represented a lyrical peak in Wright's search for the 'Natural House'.

most enthusiastic of clients deemed that too expensive he explored aluminium as an alternative. Then he experimented with a paint containing mica flakes, which he thought would be more sympathetic to the stone. The choice of finish was critical, as the concrete trays are almost all one sees on approaching the house through the woods. Wright's intentions are clarified by an observation Lewis Mumford made shortly after the house was completed: 'The stones represent, as it were, the earth theme; the concrete slabs are the water theme'. Wright always thought of concrete as a fluid material – of which the spiralling Guggenheim Museum in New York became the ultimate expression – and detailed it, as here, with rounded edges and corners. He wanted the surfaces to come alive by both responding to, and evoking, the light flashing from the running water or flickering through the foliage. Gold leaf would also have given the illusion, he said, of the glisten of water on dying autumnal leaves.

Throughout his life Wright was fascinated by natural processes, especially the large-scale ones revealed by geology. He thought of stone as the 'basic material of our planet' which reveals the laws of 'cosmic change', and whereas Taliesin had been an essentially static expression of the relative permanence of geologic features – in terms of human time – Fallingwater was an image of flux. At one end of the timescale the structure and volumes of this extraordinarily dynamic composition evoke the processes of transformation and erosion that affect rocks. At the other, by heightening our awareness of the ever-changing forest light and sounds of moving water, they provide a vivid reminder that life is perpetual flux.

Unlike Wright's earlier work, Fallingwater was sufficiently Modern to satisfy MOMA's criteria and in 1938 they gave it a one-building exhibition, emphasizing the apparent links to the International Style. The similarities were, however, superficial. Developments in Europe surely contributed to the elimination of ornament and a greater freedom in planning, but Wright's work never followed a set of stylistic formulae and was grounded in unchanging principles whose expression could vary dramatically according to the demands of the site, climate and materials. This was made abundantly clear in the project on which he began work in 1937, his winter home and studio in the desert near Phoenix, which he named Taliesin West. The plan was based on the earlier design, but overlaid with a diagonal geometry that rendered it dynamic, and established – partly by luck, partly by judgement – alignments to major features in the surrounding landscape. The building was anchored to the desert not so much by careful siting as by calculated orientation.

Taliesin West Scottsdale, Arizona, USA, 1937–8, Frank Lloyd Wright

At one level, like its namesake in Wisconsin, Taliesin West can be interpreted as a response to the physical landscape. The battered walls, made of what Wright called 'desert rubble stone', echo the surrounding mountains, which he described as 'spotted like the leopard's skin', and to reinforce the link their surfaces are grooved horizontally to suggest the erosion patterns found in desert canyons. But just as clearly, the forms were intended to recall the site's cultural history. Characteristic Toltec-Mayan profiles are evoked and, in places, the forms bring to mind a wide-bellied basket or jar. Visitors were given pointers in this direction by the petroglyph stone that greeted their arrival and by large jars placed at key points around the complex. The latter recalled the idea, expressed by the Chinese philosopher Lao-

Above Taliesin West, Scottsdale, Arizona, USA, 1937–8, Frank Lloyd Wright. In his new winter home and studio, Wright combined the now familiar 'geological' response to the landscape with an interest in the traces of the desert site's archaeological history.
Opposite Fallingwater, Bear Run, Pennsylvania, USA, 1935–9, Frank Lloyd Wright. Light and and space seem to cascade through the trellis and staircase, which leads down from the living room to a plunge pool in the stream.

Tzu and frequently reiterated by Wright, that the reality of architecture is the 'space within'. In this context their significance was increased by the possibility, which intrigued Wright, that the earliest buildings in the desert might have been made in imitation of baskets or jars.

The long duration of archaeological and geological time was emphasized by the comparatively ephemeral nature of the roofs, canvas supported by rough-sawn redwood trusses, which Wright envisaged being replaced cyclically as the Fellowship made its annual migration from Taliesin East to West. Externally, the structural system resulted in a jagged profile, with thin, boldly projecting timber trusses alternating with stepped layers of canvas. The jagged, almost aggressive profile, was again a response to the landscape because, as Wright observed, 'in all this astounding desert there is not one hard undotted line to be seen'. Spatially, the contrasts are similarly extreme: the 30-metre (98-foot) long drafting room, originally open along one side, evoked the spirit of a tent, while other spaces were cave-like enclosures cut into the sloping ground.

When Taliesin West was built, Phoenix was little more than a large town of 65,000 inhabitants and the road that passed the site had not even been paved. Reaching it became a pilgrimage, and over the twenty years before his death Wright refined the spiral processional route around the site, framing a distant view here, adding another petroglyph there. Its logic had more to do with the positioning of ancient temples than functional site planning. He liked to quote his wife's observation that it 'looked like something we had been excavating, not building', and to his friend Elizabeth Gordon, editor of *House Beautiful*, the massive walls seemed 'as if they had been cast in place 100,000 years ago'. In his search for permanence and monumentality Wright anticipated the major shift in architecture precipitated by the Second World War, which was typified in Europe by the later work of Le Corbusier, and with suburban sprawl now lapping around its edges Taliesin West's challenge to what Wright saw as the all too time-bound 'degeneracy' of modern civilization seems both urgent and tragic.

Before considering Wright's smaller Usonian houses, it is worth comparing Taliesin West with another seminal desert house. It was built, like Fallingwater, for Edgar J. Kaufmann but known as the Desert House because Kaufmann never openly acknowledged ownership while Wright was alive, lest the latter be offended that it was by his former assistant, Richard Neutra. The plan, with its three wings pinwheeling out from a central fire, was clearly indebted to Wright, but whereas Wright chose to emulate the desert's textures and colours, Neutra opted for an abstract architecture of floating planes and reflective surfaces 'to make the rocks more rocky', as he put it. Around the house he created a 'natural' garden of indigenous rocks and cacti, anticipating ideas promoted in magazines in the 1950s as appropriate to the Californian climate and landscape. Here, as so often later, until worries about water shortages and the future of the planet began to change attitudes, it was contrasted with a verdant oasis of neatly mown lawn around the large, rectangular swimming pool. Neutra's vision, echoed in the work of a new generation of architects, helped to define the modern Californian lifestyle. In the post-war climate of growing optimism about the material pleasures being unleashed by the world's most powerful economy, Wright's heroic vision of life in

Below and opposite Kaufmann Desert House, Palm Springs, California, USA, 1946–7, Richard Neutra. The intense sun and clear forms of the desert proved an ideal foil to the crisp planes and flowing space of modern architecture, and in this house – one of many he built after the war – Neutra crystallized an influential image of a new expression of house and garden for Southern California.

Kaufman Desert House Palm Springs, California, USA, 1946–7, Richard Neutra

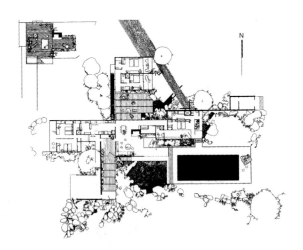

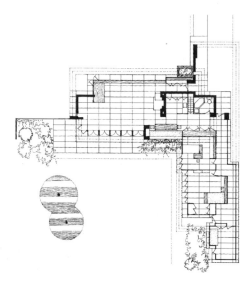

Jacobs House Madison, Wisconsin, USA, 1936, Frank Lloyd Wright

the desert might just as well have been on another planet.

During the late 1920s Wright developed a vision of the city based on 'Ruralism', in direct opposition to Le Corbusier's *Urbanisme*. Both were responses to the car, but where Le Corbusier envisaged vast apartment blocks in a continuous green park criss-crossed by elevated highways, Wright proposed an agrarian alternative, an endless but radically restructured suburbia. The basic unit was a 4-square-mile module, derived from the Jefferson grid of the Louisiana Purchase and intended to function as a semi-autonomous community. He devised new systems of finance to eliminate land speculation and envisaged each American citizen claiming their birthright of a house on an acre of land. He designed prototype houses for a variety of income levels and called the most basic 'Usonians'. In 1934, with work hard to come by in the Depression, he put his apprentices to work on a vast model of a square-mile section of his ideal city, exhibited the following year in New York, Pittsburgh and Washington D.C. to considerable press interest.

In 1936 Wright had his first chance to build a Usonian house. At 116 square metres (1250 square feet) the Jacobs House, built for a journalist/author and his wife in Madison, Wisconsin, is a small three-bedroom home by American standards. Wright despised the convention of placing a dwelling in the centre of its plot on a tiny lawn, like a plantation house in severely reduced circumstances, and instead developed an L-shaped plan to frame the garden. The house was positioned close to the boundary, with its back to the street and only the high-level windows to the bedroom corridor visible to public gaze. At the heart of the plan was the kitchen – Wright soon started calling it the workplace – from which Mrs Jacobs could command the house like a captain on the bridge of a ship. The dining and living areas formed part of a continuous living space, articulated by solid brick piers and surrounded by long runs of book-shelving and a screen of glazed opening doors. The bathroom was placed next to the kitchen to minimize service runs, and the three bedrooms ran off in a staggered tail of accommodation served by a one-sided corridor. Outside, the car was left by the door under the shelter of a carport – a Wright invention.

To keep down costs, Wright developed a highly efficient construction system for the Usonian house. Masonry was concentrated around the service core and kept to the minimum needed for load bearing and wind bracing. The other walls were either glazed or of a board-and-batten sandwich panel of extreme thinness – in long runs, bookshelves were actually needed for structural stiffening. The stripes of the battens provided a vertical module, while horizontally the houses were laid out on a 60 x 120-centimetre (2 x 4-foot) module, to suit the sizes of plywood and other sheet materials. This grid was marked in the painted concrete floor slab as a perpetual reminder of the underlying discipline. The overhanging roof prevented unwanted solar gain in summer, but allowed the low summer sun in to warm the interior. The brick walls and floor – into which heating pipes were embedded – acted as a 'thermal flywheel', releasing the heat absorbed during the day as free warmth in the evening. Wright's use of underfloor heating was novel, inspired, he said, by Japanese and Korean examples. The principle, of course, goes back to the Romans and had been revived in England in 1907 by Arthur

Above and opposite Jacobs House, Madison, Wisconsin, USA, 1936, Frank Lloyd Wright. The first of Wright's numerous 'Usonian' houses, it was built using a highly economical construction system. The L-shaped plan pivots around the hearth and kitchen, presenting almost blank walls to the outside and opening to the garden which its wings reach out to enclose.

Henry Barker, who used piped hot water in the walls of churches and houses: Wright may well have known of Barker's books.

Wright's drawings make it clear that he thought of the garden as the most important 'room' in the Jacobs House. In organic architecture, he said, 'we have no longer an outside and an inside as two separate things. Now the outside may come inside, and the inside may and does go outside'. He rejected air-conditioning because it cut us off from the natural climate and his vision of 'The Natural House' – the title of a 1954 book – envisaged direct contact with nature as vital to physical and mental health. 'Whether people are fully conscious of this or not, they actually derive countenance and sustenance from the "atmosphere" of the things they live in or with. They are rooted in them just as a plant is in the soil'. The Usonian House was ecological and energy-efficient before its time.

The January 1938 issue of *Architectural Forum* was devoted to Wright's solution to the 'small house problem' and he presented the Jacobs House in pragmatic terms. He made no claims about its beauty, but stressed the practical, cost-saving benefits of his methods – by using his paying apprentices as general contractors he managed to drag the costs down even further, building some houses for as little as $1500. He built numerous Usonians, developing a series of superbly resolved plan types and often startling his clients by giving their small homes his personal attention. Wright's reputation as one of the foremost architects of the twentieth or any other century rests on his major houses and a handful of public buildings, but in light of our current concerns few designs in this book seem more prescient, or pertinent to the new century, than his modestly-sized Usonians.

Wright was by no means alone in evincing a concern for energy efficiency in the 1930s because in part it was a response to government calls during the Depression to reduce costs and speed up residential construction. In 1932 the Royal Institute of British Architects had published what proved to be an influential manual, showing how to track the sun's movement across a building's elevations, and illustrated a device called a heliodon, developed to model this motion. The Chicago practice of Keck and Keck began designing houses to trap solar energy during the 1930s and a project like their Kellett House, built in Wenasha, Wisconsin in 1939, shows a mature understanding of the principles involved. To the north, its curving elevation – designed to maximize views of Lake Winnebago – has minimal glazing, while to the south a two-storey solarium allowed morning and low winter sun into the core to heat the house. The glazing was protected from high summer sun by a deep, visor-like roof, and the overhang was lightened visually by rectangular openings designed primarily to relieve wind pressure. The roof retained water in summer to reduce solar transmission, and in winter could be drained to avoid booming noises from the sound of cracking ice. While building a house in Madison, across town from the Jacobs House, William Keck visited Wright at Taliesin and was particularly intrigued by his ideas on underfloor heating, incorporating them in the Kellett and many later houses. When *House Beautiful* published an article on the Kellett House in 1942 it appeared under the title, 'What Houses will be Like after the War'.

In 1920, six years before completing the Lovell Beach House (see p.54), Rudolf Schindler was working in California on Wright's Hollyhock House. In

Opposite Kellett House, Wenasha, Wisconsin, USA, 1939, Keck and Keck. Opening to the sun and to views over Lake Winnebago, the Kellett House was amongst the first to be designed using modern 'passive solar' techniques. The overhanging, visor-like roof protects the glazing from high summer sun, and has holes to provide relief from wind pressure.

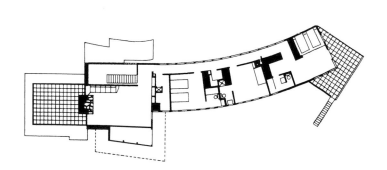

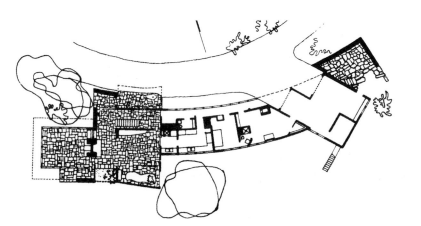

Schindler-Chace House Los Angeles, California, USA, 1921–2, Rudolf Schindler

Above Dodge House, Los Angeles, California, USA, 1915–16, Irving Gill. Although often linked to the abstraction of the International Style, the cubic forms and white rendered surfaces of Gill's houses grew out of the local Spanish Mission Style and became a model for others seeking a regional style for California.

response to the benign climate, the basic idea for the house was, as Aline Barnsdall put it, that it should be as much 'outside as inside'. It was organized around a courtyard, and the main bedroom – which Schindler detailed – was conceived as a tent-like space hovering over the trees. The other important influence on Schindler's ideas was Irving Gill who, like Wright, originally hailed from Chicago. Inspired by the local Spanish mission buildings, Gill built several cubic, whitewashed, flat-roofed, asymmetrical houses – such as the Dodge House of 1915–16 – which were totally devoid of ornamentation. They were seen as proto-Modern by Pevsner and others, but are better understood as a local flowering of Arts and Crafts principles than as unwitting 'anticipations' of what came later.

All these early influences, filtered through the floating world of Japan, can be discerned in Schindler's first and finest building, a double house built for himself, his wife and their friends Clyde and Marian Chace on North Kings Road, West Hollywood, from 1921 to 1922. The inspiration sprang from a camping and horse-riding trip the Schindlers took in Yosemite Valley: they wanted a house as open to nature as a tent. After teaming up with the Chaces, they decided that each couple should have an L-shaped wing with, as they explained in a letter to Pauline Schindler's parents, who were to lend most of the funds, 'large studio rooms – with concrete walls on three sides, the front open (glass) to the outdoors – a real California scheme. On the roof two "sleeping baskets" are provided – for open-air sleeping – with temporary covers for rainy nights'. The open garden fronts were fitted with large sliding doors, above which two cantilevered beams supported an overhanging roof, sliding light fittings and movable partitions. The varied roof levels, rooftop sleeping baskets, and close integration between the rooms and patios produced a complex, three-dimensional interlocking of house and garden which anticipated the relaxed Californian lifestyle that emerged after 1945. Schindler went on to develop a formal language based on wood framing and stucco, producing a steady stream of fine domestic projects into the early 1950s. But none, save the Lovell Beach House, rivalled the clarity and poetry of the Schindler-Chace houses.

Wright's Hollyhock House also played a decisive role in the life of Harwell Hamilton Harris. He visited the house in 1925, while still a sculpture student, and discovered, he later said, 'sculpture on a completely different scale'. It was a Road-to-Damascus experience. He decided to become an architect, and the sense of privacy, sculptural form and love of nature he encountered in Wright would inform all his work. He visited the Schindler-Chace house in 1928, where he met Schindler and a toga-clad Dione Neutra – who, with her husband Richard, had replaced the Chaces four years earlier. When Neutra himself arrived he promptly offered Harris a job – as assistant on the Lovell Health House (see pp.54–5), which would prove to be the finest American example of the International Style. By 1939 when Mr and Mrs Lee Blair, directors at the Walt Disney Studios, came to commission a house from Harris he was beginning to experiment with wood in a way that would in turn influence Neutra and Schindler and contribute to the formation of the so-called 'Redwood school' of California modernists. The Blairs' site was precipitously steep and their brief modest, just one bedroom, a small studio, and living space. Harris's response was as simple as

Above and right Schindler-Chace House, Los Angeles, California, USA, 1921–2, Rudolf Schindler. Melding influences from the emerging modern architecture of Europe, Irving Gill, Wright and Japan, this was the first house to capture a vision of the relaxed California lifestyle which would be the ideal for many after 1945.

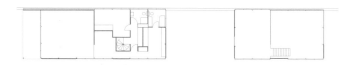

5m

15ft

Opposite, top Blair House, Los
Angeles, California, USA, 1939, Harwell
Hamilton Harris. Designed for two
directors at the Walt Disney Studios,
this small house stepped dramatically
down its steep site in the Hollywood
Hills. Harris's bold use of timber proved
a major influence on the California
'Redwood School' after the war.
Opposite and below Eames House,
Los Angeles, California, USA, 1949,
Charles and Ray Eames. The most
widely influential of the Case Study
Houses promoted by John Entenza
through his magazine *Arts and
Architecture*, the Eames House, with
its enviably relaxed use of industrial
building technology, came to epitomize
the new Californian architecture
and lifestyle.

Eames House Los Angeles, California, USA, 1949, Charles and Ray Eames

it was elegant. He disposed the three elements of accommodation on separate
floors, the rear edge resting on the ground, and the front on the rear of the floor
below, whose roof became a terrace. He used grass matting, plywood walls and
Celotex ceilings throughout, and each room had a wall of glass opening into a
garden or terrace. Low furniture, mostly by Aalto, was sparsely scattered to
enhance the feeling of space.

Harris had published in 1935, as a list of nine dos and don'ts, the principles on
which the Blair House and others were based. His article appeared in *California
Arts and Architecture*, and three years later another of his clients, John Entenza,
became editor of the magazine. Entenza, who had been working for MGM, set
about transforming the magazine from an unadventurous regional publisher of
homes, gardens and theatre reviews into a leading vehicle for progressive ideas.
Articles on serious modern architecture started appearing. 'California' was
dropped from the title in 1943 and in the same year he ran a competition for a
worker's house entitled 'Design for Postwar Living'. Then, in January 1945, he
launched the 'Case Study House Program' to promote new housing in which
social and aesthetic ideals and innovation went hand in hand. In place of
'speculation in the form of talk and reams of paper', said Entenza, he would show
real houses built for real clients, and mostly by young architects using innovative
materials. It would make his magazine one of the most influential in the world.

Entenza's programme came to worldwide fame in 1949 with the
completion in Los Angeles of Case Study House # 8 by, and for,
Charles and Ray Eames. The couple were already renowned as
the designers of what the architect Eliot Noyes described in *Arts and
Architecture* as the 'most important group of furniture ever developed in this
country'. The Eames House was designed in 1945, in partnership with Eero
Saarinen, but when the materials arrived on site in the autumn of 1948 Charles
Eames radically altered his ideas. The delicate, cubic house of glass and steel
that resulted was made using standard lattice beams and window sections, and
seemed to be as 'natural' to them as Wright's houses were to their very different,
organic materials. Taut and neat, it was bathed in sunlight filtered by a stand of
mature eucalyptus trees and filled with exquisite furniture, plants and items from
the Eames's ever-growing collection.

The Eames House consists of two two-storey pavilions ranged against a 60-
metre (200-foot) long retaining wall. The house itself is eight bays long, the last
of which is open on two sides (each bay is 2.25 metres/7 feet wide by 6
metres/20 feet deep); a first-floor sleeping loft covers part of the volume. An
open courtyard, four bays wide, separates the house from the five-bay studio.
Both house and studio are enclosed by slender black steel-framed industrial
window sections, horizontally proportioned like Japanese *shoji* screens. Much of
the exterior is glazed, with a mixture of glass from clear to translucent, and the
regularity is further broken by cross-braces, white or primary-coloured infill panels
and occasional subdivisions within the large modules. Inside, the ribbed underside
of the ceiling is exposed and painted white, as are all the steel beams, and a
spiral stair with slender plywood treads leads up to the sleeping loft, where *shoji*-
like panels can be slid across the glazed wall to modify the light. What makes the
space magical is the light: sunshine, bathing or dappling the floor; even daylight,

Above Case Study House #16,
Los Angeles, California, USA, 1952–3,
Craig Ellwood. The first of Ellwood's
three Case Study houses was
conceived as a weightless floating
world, seen at its most evanescent at
night when the back-lit translucent
screens to the bedroom courts
transform it into a shimmering field
of light.

Opposite Bass House, Los Angeles,
California, USA, 1958, Buff, Straub
and Hensman. The twentieth of the
Case Study houses and atypical in its
use of a timber frame, barrel-vaulted
living space, and highly site-specific
design – it was built around the
mature Italian Stone Pine, which has
since had to be cut down.

Case Study House # 22 Los Angeles, California, USA, 1959–60, Pierre Koenig

filtered by the translucent glass; and the ever-changing play of shadows from the eucalyptus on the translucent surfaces, flickering like the brushstrokes in Far Eastern calligraphy.

Dumped on a suburban plot, deprived of its filtered light, and emptied of its artfully arranged contents the Eames House would lose much of its magic. The eucalyptus outside, and the plants, furniture, objects and decorations inside, are as much part of the architecture as the fabric of the building. The house represented, as Entenza put it, 'an attempt to state an idea rather than a fixed architectural pattern'. In this it was in striking contrast, as we shall see, to the steel and glass houses being built at the same time on the East Coast. The consummately artful yet relaxed ordinariness of the Eames House struck a chord with a new generation of designers. Its appeal was augmented by fascination with the increasingly sophisticated American consumer products, from pop-up toasters to automatic dishwashers. Charles and Ray Eames were lauded in magazines around the world, and by the mid 1960s their house was established as one of the iconic achievements of post-war architecture. To his friend Peter Smithson, Charles Eames was 'a natural California Man, using his native resources and know-how – of the film-making, the aircraft and the advertising industries – as others drink water; that is almost without thinking'. With its elegant, all pervasive displays of objects and images from around the world the Eames House was like a showroom. It became a favourite setting for fashion shoots with magazines like *Life* and *Vogue* and was a perfect emblem for the burgeoning consumer society.

The Case Study House Program ran until 1964, by when twenty-seven houses, as well as a few apartments, had been completed. Among the most radical was # 18 (1956–8), the third of Craig Ellwood's contributions designed using a prefabricated steel frame and panel system. The result was about as minimal as architecture can get, wonderfully light and delicate, with paper-thin roof planes floating above the entrance and carport: a later owner transformed it into a Mediterranean-style villa.

Another in the series, Case Study House # 22 (1959–60), the Stahl House by Pierre Koenig, has come to epitomize the glamour of Los Angeles. This is thanks in part to a magnificent night-time photograph by Julius Shulman – whose images did much to promote the Californian vision of modernity – and even more to its use as a location for countless advertising, fashion and film shoots. The house is perched high in the Hollywood Hills and visitors are greeted by a view of more than a hundred square miles of the city laid out temptingly below them like a luxurious carpet. It feels much larger than its 214 square metres (2300 square feet), and it is difficult to grasp that on completion it was regarded as economical, rather than the epitome of luxury it has become. The only solid wall faces the street; behind, all the perimeter is of minimally-framed glass, in sheets up to 6 metres (20 feet) wide, giving the house a 270-degree panorama of the city. The plan is L-shaped, with a core of services in the corner, bedrooms in one wing and an open-plan kitchen-dining-living space in the other. In the embrace of the wings are a small terrace and the obligatory swimming pool. Like Mies van der Rohe, Koenig worked, as Reyner Banham aptly put it, by 'elegant omission' and the house seems to float

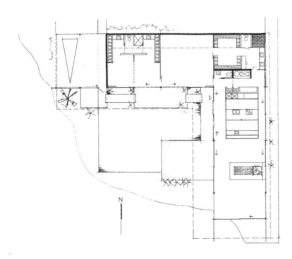

Above and opposite Case Study House #22 (Stahl House), Los Angeles, California, USA, 1959–60, Pierre Koenig. Dramatically cantilevered out from its site high in the Hollywood Hills and more luxurious than earlier Case Study designs, the Stahl House came to epitomize the freedom and glamour of Southern California.

effortlessly on air. In architecture the appearance of ease is usually hard-won and here the cantilevered wing sits on 75-centimetre (30-inch) deep concrete beams supported by up to 10.5-metre (35-foot) deep concrete caissons. The Stahl family have lived happily in their house for over thirty years, but contrary to predictions in magazines at the time its compelling expression of the Southern Californian version of the good life did not herald the arrival of steel as an important material in mainstream housing.

The Case Study Houses are the best known and most ambitious of many efforts to promote modern ways of living in the aftermath of the Second World War. In 1945 the editors of New York's *Architectural Forum* magazine published a book entitled, *Tomorrow's House: How to Plan your Post-war Home Now*. It explained, room by room, how superior a modern, functionally planned house was to the tired 'period' styles and was illustrated almost entirely by modern, if not always strictly Modern, examples. The following year MOMA brought out *If You Want to Build a House* by Elizabeth B. Mock which, not surprisingly, was more forthright in its promotion of Modern design for modern living. 'Light and space work together and they have much more to do with our feeling of well-being than is generally granted,' Mock explained, adding that, the 'advantages of freedom in space and generous uniform light are peculiar to modern architecture'. There was a small but steadily growing market for individually designed modern houses but, with a single and singular exception, volume house-builders failed to respond to the many calls. The exception was Joseph Eichler and he operated, not surprisingly, in California.

Eichler was born in 1900 in New York, and migrated with his parents to San Francisco in the 1920s. In 1942, he moved his own young family into a rented house designed by Frank Lloyd Wright and fell in love with modern architecture. After discovering simple post-and-beam construction in 1947 through the work of Earl 'Flat-top' (after his houses' flat-roofs) Smith, he decided to set up his own house-building company. Two years later the first recognizable 'Eichler House' was built to designs by Bob Anshen. Over the next eighteen years, before his main business went bankrupt in 1967 due to the rising cost of materials and the demand for air-conditioning (which his designs could not economically accommodate), Eichler built over 10,000 houses in the Bay Area and what we now know as Silicon Valley. The standard formula was simple: a blank elevation to the street; rear and, depending on the site, side walls of glass; fenced gardens; post-and-beam roofs, typically with a shallow pitch to a central ridge; boarded ceilings and, as in Wright's Usonians, radiant-heated concrete floors. It is said that by the mid-1950s every self-respecting Bay Area resident could spot an Eichler, a level of recognition no other speculatively built house has ever enjoyed, and by 1972 when the influential *Sunset* magazine, gospel of the California lifestyle, surveyed its readers, over 60 percent were found to own an Eichler home.

I know of no mass-built modern houses to compare with the quality or popularity of Eichler's. They exemplified the new relaxed lifestyles that flourished in California's benign coastal climate, which was rarely too hot or too cold and sufficiently dry to prevent insects becoming a nuisance, still less a threat. In the 1950s the West retained something of the frontier spirit, and in California social freedom came to be identified with living in an open-plan house with glass walls

Opposite The houses built in the San Francisco Bay Area by Joseph Eichler, such as this typical example designed by architect A. Quincy Jones, made the new architecture available to large numbers of middle-class Californians – some 10,000 of these and similar houses were sold during the 1950s and 1960s.

Above Breuer House, New Canaan, Connecticut, USA, 1947, Marcel Breuer. The combination of a masonry base surmounted by a cantilevered timber-clad first floor proved widely influential, and was typical of the less doctrinaire modernism practised by Gropius, Breuer and other European *emigrés* after settling on the East Coast of the USA.

Above and below Demonstration house, Museum of Modern Art, New York, USA, 1949, Marcel Breuer. Built as part of MOMA's campaign to promote modern architecture, the butterfly-roof form (probably derived from a little known project by Le Corbusier) was widely imitated.

that fused inside and out. The dream of a Modern house affordable by the majority had finally become a reality, and an active Eichler network still flourishes in California, with its own magazine, website and advice on maintaining and improving the homes.

Seen from California, the East Coast of America was a foreign country, and modern architecture was different there. The Ivy League universities, home to several distinguished schools of architecture based on Beaux-Arts principles, encouraged an academic attitude that was the antithesis of the freewheeling 'can-do' approach which drove innovation in the West. When, in 1937, Walter Gropius accepted an offer to direct the department of architecture at Harvard, where he was joined by Marcel Breuer, it was seen as an important victory for the Modern cause. The following year the university invited Sigfried Giedion, secretary of CIAM, to give the Charles Eliot Norton lectures, which were published in 1941 as the massively influential book, *Space, Time and Architecture: The Growth of a New Tradition*. Harvard produced a stream of graduates trained in modern architecture, but in many essentials the academic tradition persisted and Gropius's belief in teamwork and anonymity increasingly resulted in banality rather than hard-won simplicity.

Breuer left Harvard for practice in New York in 1946 and the following year built his own house in New Canaan, Connecticut. Its timber-clad box cantilevered from a masonry lower floor with a very shallow pitched roof was elegant and polite, as was the showhouse he built in the garden of the Museum of Modern Art in 1949. As the officially sanctioned face of modern architecture in the East this proved very popular, and its distinctive butterfly roof was widely imitated. It might well have been inspired by Le Corbusier's Errazuriz House project in Chile of 1930, but whereas there the roof was locked into the structure of the house, following the slope of the ramp and responding to the views, in Breuer's it was reduced to a decorative motif with scant relationship to the spatial organization.

1949 also saw the completion of Philip Johnson's Glass House. The historian/critic had become an architect and disciple of Mies van der Rohe, and during the following half century would undergo several dramatic stylistic reincarnations. Johnson's was the first all-glass house to be completed, but it was based on a 1945 design by Mies – who was now head of architecture at the Illinois Institute of Architecture in Chicago – for Dr Edith Farnsworth, though her house was not built until 1951. The site of the Farnsworth House at Plano, Illinois, was prone to flooding so Mies raised the ground floor by 1.5 metres (5 feet), slinging rectangular floor and roof planes between eight H-section columns. Both beams and columns are oversized according to conventional structural requirements, the former to ensure that the planes remained perfectly level, with no trace of sag, and the columns to suit the size Mies deemed correct visually.

A broad flight of steps leads up to a third rectangular plane, hovering above the ground on stubby columns, from where identical steps rise onto a covered terrace at the end of the fully-glazed volume. Inside is a freestanding, primavera wood-veneered core containing two bathrooms, a galley kitchen and a fireplace. Privacy was afforded by shantung silk curtains, and as in the Tugendhat House, Mies's own furniture was intended to be laid out in perfect islands on cream-coloured rugs. Inside and out, the floors are of travertine and the detailing

Farnsworth House Plano, Illinois, USA, 1946–51, Ludwig Mies van der Rohe

Below and overleaf Farnsworth House, Plano, Illinois, USA, 1946–51, Ludwig Mies van der Rohe. The combination of exquisite materials, visually (if not always technically) flawless detailing, and an open plan divided only by the free-standing service core represented the apotheosis of Mies's less-is-more aesthetic.

minimal and meticulous. The paving is perfectly flat with open joints for drainage, and the columns are welded to the face of the beams, with all traces of work removed by grinding the welds flat and painting the steel white. When tapped, the steelwork rings like a tuning fork.

Edith Farnsworth was single. A successful nephrologist, she met Mies at a party and mentioned that she was thinking of building a weekend house; he naturally offered his services. They became good friends, but probably nothing more (contrary to popular assumptions), and she was won over to Mies's vision of architecture. As the project progressed, however, she realized that he saw her as a patron rather than client, a means to execute his unyielding less-is-more vision of the Modern house. With tradesmen questioning the wisdom of some of Mies's plumbing and electrical arrangements and the costs reaching almost double the $40,000 estimate – already a lot of money for a house of this size – Dr Farnsworth became increasingly distressed and put the matter in the hands of her lawyer, prompting Mies to countersue for his fees.

After a long legal battle Mies eventually won an out-of-court settlement, but the legal case was as nothing compared to the fight in the press. In interviews Farnsworth made her house sound completely uninhabitable – though she chose to remain there for twenty years – and it became the focus of a campaign against the vices of the new Modern aesthetic and the 'self-chosen elite who are trying to tell us what we should like and how we should live', as an article in the April 1953 issue of *House Beautiful* put it. Dr Farnsworth found the lack of an enclosed bedroom unsettling, and disliked the fact that while her guests had a separate bathroom they were expected to sleep on a sofa or a mattress on the floor. She tried to tame Mies's rigorous geometry by furnishing the house with family heirlooms rather than Mies's designs, but eventually gave up the struggle and in 1971 sold it to Peter Palumbo, a developer and Mies enthusiast who lived in London. Palumbo installed the furniture Mies intended, and happily used the house as a vacation home for his young family, responding enthusiastically to its aesthetic qualities. The sight of lime tree leaves silhouetted on the silk curtains by the dawn sun, he says, 'is a scene no Japanese print could capture to greater effect'.

In the architectural world the reception of the Farnsworth House echoed Palumbo's enthusiasm, and it was widely regarded as the ultimate expression of the open plan and of Mies's ideal of *beinahe nichts*, 'almost nothing'. Palumbo recalls that Mies told him he would prefer him not to hang pictures on the house's primavera core, adding, 'I give you the space, it's open plan, you do what you like'. But of course the architect was being disingenuous. The difficulty with Mies's version of the open plan was that its 'freedom' could quickly become a new kind of tyranny, every bit as demanding – and to Farnsworth, intimidating – as the *Gesamtkunstwerken* of an architect like Josef Hoffmann. Where Le Corbusier designed light, easily moved furniture, and was happy to mix classic old styles with new designs in an interior, Mies's work was deliberately heavy and intended to be installed like sculptures by the architect-curator. Where Mies's designs of the 1920s had been dynamic, asymmetrical and quintessentially Modern, those of the post-war period were destined to be static, symmetrical and

Glass House New Canaan, Connecticut, USA, 1949, Philip Johnson

essentially neo-classical in spirit. The Farnsworth House, with its frozen perfection and hidden symmetries, marked the point at which the die was cast.

Philip Johnson's Glass House, although inspired by Mies's design, looked to his commercial projects in Chicago for guidance in detailing the steelwork. It sits like a diminutive temple at the centre of a terraced lawn, with the columns at the corners to form a static, closed box. In place of the rectangular primavera core he used a cylinder of brick containing a hearth and bathroom: to spectators gazing in from outside it might almost be a parody of the all-American home. Introducing the project in 1950 Johnson said, 'Perhaps if there is ever to be "decoration" in our architecture it may come from the manipulation of stock structural elements such as these', and went on to suggest that the more playful use of structure might develop into a 'mannerist' phase like that which followed Renaissance Classicism. Trained as a historian, he thought in terms of style; living as a gay man, he never dreamt of proposing his house as a model for the American family; and being the heir to a substantial fortune, he had the resources to indulge his architectural fantasies. Johnson almost immediately complemented the Glass House with a guest house in which a glass living pavilion sat over a masonry bunker containing the sleeping accommodation and bathrooms. He remodelled the austere base in 1953, turning it into a camp stage set with a palatial bedroom, canopied like a fantasy from the Arabian Nights.

In retrospect, Johnson's Glass House looks less like the Modern masterpiece it was declared at the time, and more like a commentary upon the nature of modernity. For Johnson, the radical, innovative drive that inspired early Modern architecture and was still thriving on the West Coast seemed altogether too earnest. He opted for the knowing manipulation of a chosen vocabulary or set of stylistic tropes. Throughout his long, multi-faceted career Philip Johnson has had an uncanny knack for anticipating, and often catalyzing, a new trend. The East Coast soon polarized between an academic, anti-historicist Functionalism, promoted by Gropius and his colleagues at Harvard, and a concern for a 'New Monumentality', of which the Glass House can be seen as the first, perhaps unwitting, manifesto. Johnson's later public buildings were prime exemplars of this new trend, and Yale University, under the chairmanship of George Howe, the academic focus.

The most gifted and original architect to emerge on the East Coast after 1945 was Louis Kahn. He was a late starter and from 1950 to 1951, after twenty years in practice, much of them spent building public housing projects and some as an assistant to George Howe, he took a mid-career break as resident architect at the American School in Rome. He travelled the Mediterranean, experiencing Greek, Roman and Egyptian architecture for the first time. Overwhelmed by what he had seen, he returned to America determined to rethink his art from the ground up. He rediscovered the room as the basis of architecture; he divided accommodation between 'served' and 'servant' spaces – a kitchen serves a dining room, a pantry the kitchen, and so on; and he took absolutely nothing for granted. To Kahn, cutting holes in walls to make windows violated the wall's integrity. He sought ways of generating forms from a rigorous inner spatial and constructional logic, playing with repeating units or cells and trying to find a basis for every

Above Sheats Residence, Los
Angeles, California, USA, 1963,
remodelled for Jim Goldstein, 1969,
John Lautner. As if to outdo Pierre
Koenig's similarly dramatic Stahl
House also in Los Angeles, the glass
walls of the master bedroom can be
retracted at the touch of a button.
Opposite Malin Residence
('Chemosphere'), Los Angeles, USA,
1960, John Lautner. Perched
precariously on an 'unbuildable' site in
the Hollywood Hills, the Chemosphere
became an instant emblem of the
West Coast's can-do mentality.

took the form of a logarithmic spiral rising from the ground and coiling itself around a steel pole from which the roof, floors and stairs were suspended. 'Floors' is not quite the right word, however. Goff called them 'living area bowls': there are five, and they are dish-shaped, fabricated from welded steel bars and – yes! – clad in gold carpet. Curtains provided the only form of privacy and furniture was built-in: the beds, for example, were sunk into the bowls to lie flush with the floor. The kitchen and bathroom were tucked into the masonry core – which became like one of Kahn's servant spaces – and the entire house was a conservatory for plants and birds. As an expression of the clients' way of life the Bavinger House was as inventive and persuasive as anything we have considered. The freedom to live how you want, unconstrained by government regulation and the tyranny of accepted rules of taste, remains central to the mid-Western version of the American Dream. In Bruce Goff this rugged individualism found its poet.

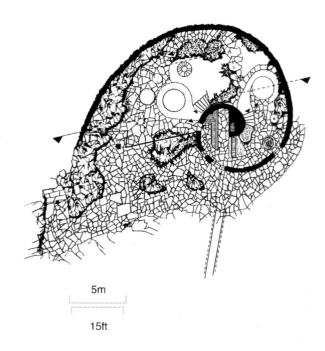

5m

15ft

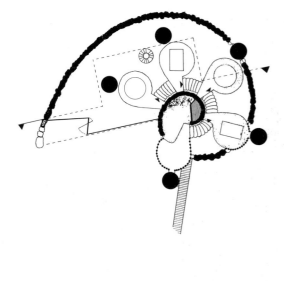

Opposite and above Bavinger House, Oklahoma City, Oklahoma, USA, 1949, Bruce Goff. Built for a young art professor, his ceramicist wife and their new-born son, the Bavinger House was planned as a continuous, open-plan spiral of space in which tropical plants, birds, fish and the young family could co-exist in a unique symbiosis.

scandinavian modern

A young girl stands with her back to us, hands linked casually behind her neck, blonde hair and bare skin glowing in the low sun. She is at the edge of what appears to be a pond formed from run-off gathered around the base of a rock outcrop, and looks back to a single-storey house, a door invitingly ajar and windows flung open to the sun and air. The pond is actually a small swimming pool and this artfully composed idyll – in Europe, one of the most widely reproduced images of the immediate post-war period – illustrates the house and garden of the architect Sven Markelius, director of city planning in Stockholm. It was built in 1945 and the design was more innovative than it appears. The walls were made from a novel prefabricated timber system of Markelius's own design; the roof trusses bore only on the perimeter walls to allow complete freedom in positioning partitions; and it was heated using hot air distributed through floor grilles.

Markelius House Kevinge, Sweden, 1945, Sven Markelius

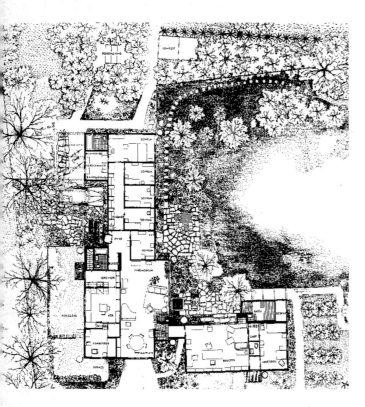

Visually, however, it wore its technical innovations lightly. Timber boarding painted with traditional dull yellow oil paint has replaced the smooth white surfaces of Functionalism, of which Markelius had been a distinguished exponent. But what was radically new was the fusion of the house with a seemingly natural garden in the heart of suburban Kevinge, not in the depths of the countryside. Markelius's daughter, the photograph tells us, is completely at home in this sylvan world, and what is presented is a compelling image of the free, modern life that awaits her and her generation.

The presentation plan is just as revealing as the photograph. Inside the house Markelius drew every piece of furniture, not in some ideal arrangement, as in a Mies design, but to convey a sense of habitation. The house, we can see, is organized around a large, informal room where the family eat, relax and listen to the piano. Outside, everything is described in even more exhaustive detail, from the car, two bicycles and child's tricycle under the generous entrance canopy, through the meticulously rendered paved surfaces, to individual shrubs and trees. As an image of the good life its message is as clear as the photograph: in the aftermath of the Second World War, life is going to be lived close to nature in a more informal way. Enter the house and we find a world of white walls, floors scattered with rugs, a fair-face (no applied finish) brick fireplace and a mixture of traditional-looking wicker chairs and unostentatious contemporary wooden furniture. The missionary zeal of the Heroic Period has gone. The machine must still be put to use – the structure is, after all, prefabricated – but it no longer demands an overtly machine-age style, nor precludes the use of natural materials – of wooden rather than steel furniture. Ideas anticipated in the work of Aalto and others in the 1930s are poised to dominate the mainstream.

Markelius's house was one of several built in the late 1940s and early 1950s in which a new way of living was given architectural expression, in a style now known as Scandinavian Modern. This was the European counterpart to the so-called Contemporary style of post-war California, with which it shared many similarities in terms of both lifestyle and design. Its influence would similarly be felt worldwide, most directly through the wooden furniture that became almost ubiquitous in the Western world during the late 1950s and '60s. Like most styles offered for popular consumption through magazines, Scandinavian Modern is a distillation of ideas drawn from disparate sources. It did not spring up overnight,

Above and opposite Markelius House, Kevinge, Sweden, 1945, Sven Markelius. System-built yet reassuringly traditional in feeling, Markelius's house and its natural-seeming garden exemplified the ideals of the 'softened' modernism of post-war Swedish architecture.

but can be readily traced to the vision of an unpretentious family life, with children at its centre and filled with sunlight and fresh air, projected so successfully half a century earlier by Carl and Karin Larsson. And these values in turn were very much in evidence at the event that marked the official launch of Functionalism in the Nordic countries: the hugely popular 1930 Stockholm Exhibition, co-ordinated and partly designed by Gunnar Asplund.

Like the Weissenhof in Stuttgart the Stockholm Exhibition presented fully furnished model houses and apartments to an amazed public, but unlike Stuttgart it was never intended to leave a permanent legacy of buildings. This enabled Asplund to design it as a festive market place for new ideas. Sigfried Giedion declared that there had been 'no exhibition to rival this one for overall effect' and in his newspaper reviews Alvar Aalto caught its mood perfectly. 'The exhibition speaks out for joyful and spontaneous everyday life,' he wrote, and 'consistently propagates a healthy and unpretentious lifestyle based on economic realities. . . the deliberate social message that the Stockholm Exhibition is intended to convey is expressed in the architectural language of pure, spontaneous joy. There is a festive elegance, but also a childlike lack of inhibition about it all. . . This is not a composition of glass, stone, and steel, as a visitor who despises functionalism might imagine; it is a composition of houses, flags, floodlights, flowers, fireworks, happy people, and clean tablecloths.'

In an influential article entitled 'The New Empiricism: Sweden's Latest Style', published in 1947, the British *Architectural Review* welcomed the new developments, but recognized that a house like Markelius's might easily be mistaken for 'local builder's bungalow style'. They stressed its technical innovations and quoted Sven Backström to explain for those readers who might be troubled by the apparent rejection of the 'objectivity' of 1930s Functionalism that the new style was an attempt to extend its rationality by bringing to bear the insights of the science of psychology. 'Today we have reached the point where all the elusive psychological factors have again begun to engage our attention,' explained Backström. 'To interpret such a programme as a reaction and a return to something that is past and to pastiches is definitely to misunderstand the development of architecture in this country.'

In Sweden Markelius's house was followed by several others in which the now familiar Scandinavian style was crystallized. The Ränangen House, built in Djursholm near Stockholm in 1951 by Leonie and Charles-Edouard Geisendorf, offered a relaxed combination of brickwork and full-height glazing panels, several with vertical, grey-stained boarding to one side or below the window to fill out the panel. Internally, the fire sat to one side of a large fair-face brick wall, and slight changes of ceiling plane – variously finished in plaster or narrow timber boarding – marked places of rest and transition. Stig Ancker's summer house in Halland, completed two years later, also epitomized the new approach. Externally it is a simple cubic composition of white-painted blockwork walls, with a low-pitch interlocking tiled roof and dark-stained window frames and timber-boarded doors. Inside it has boarded walls, floors and ceilings, with simple, modern-looking kitchen furniture and colourfully striped woven rugs on the floor. Interiors like this would feature in countless interior design magazines.

Ränangen House Djursholm, Sweden, 1951, Leonie and Charles-Edouard Geisendorf

Opposite Ränangen House, Djursholm, Sweden, 1951, Leonie and Charles-Edouard Geisendorf. With its relaxed combination of natural materials, clean planar surfaces and large windows, the design and furnishing of the Ränangen House epitomized the essence of what would later be known as the 'Scandinavian Modern' style.

As with its Californian counterpart, the influence of Japan was crucial to the emergence of what we now think of as quintessentially Scandinavian. When Alvar Aalto's library in Viipuri opened in 1935 Gustaf Strengell wrote that, 'the interiors of the building display Japanese characteristics in many places. Observe the pale, light colouring which give the rooms not just their charming airy quality but actually a scent. Quite particularly the Japanese streak appears in the choice of pale wood only – birch, pine, beech – for the panelling and furnishings, and it is even more striking in the treatment of smooth surfaces: in true Japanese manner, they are not treated at all, but "left in their natural state", which is both attractive to the eye and pleasing to the touch.' As we have seen, Aalto also made extensive use of lime-washed brickwork and timber boarding in his own house and studio, also completed in 1935. In the same year, in his lecture entitled 'Rationalism and Man', he argued that a truly rational architecture must extend to psychological issues. In essence, the elements of Scandinavian Modern were formulated in the 1930s, but it took a decade and a world war for them to enter the mainstream.

The new manner was not, however, without its critics. In the Göth House of 1950 in Uppsala, designed by two young architects Bengt Edman and Lennart Holm, for example, we see an altogether tougher architecture of severely cubic form. It has unrelieved brick walls in which the internal partitions register as vertical zips in the joint pattern and a ribbon window sits below an exposed steel lintel. The architects shared an office with Gunnar Asplund's son Hans who commented, with a hint of sarcasm, that they were 'Neo-Brutalists'. He repeated the term to some English architect-friends who took it back home where it was adapted by Alison and Peter Smithson and others who styled themselves exponents of New Brutalism. The phrase caught on. It was intended as a riposte to what its proponents saw as the abandonment of rigorous architectural standards by an older generation eager to embrace the 'softened modernism' of the New Empiricism – which the editors of *The Architectural Review* allied to the English Picturesque tradition and suburbia. New Brutalism, the Smithsons declared, was 'an ethic not an aesthetic'.

Extolling traditional Japanese architecture as the manifestation of 'a general conception of Life, a sort of reverence for the natural world and, from that, for the materials of the built world,' the Smithsons saw architecture 'as the direct result of a way of life'. They were therefore more interested in peasant dwelling forms than past architectural styles. Equally, by placing 'reverence for materials' at the centre of the New Brutalist ethic they were trying to return architecture to the intellectual heart of the Modern Movement. Despite its avowedly broad scope, New Brutalism became identified stylistically with an architecture of massive plasticity and coarse surfaces – exemplified by Le Corbusier's Unité at Marseilles and his Jaoul houses, which were appropriated as early and representative examples. But when the Smithsons came to design a house (1955–6) for an engineer at Ove Arup, Derek Sugden, and his wife Jean, they attempted to give contemporary expression to the English way of life rather than dogmatically use a specific formal language. Indeed, this would have been difficult given that the planning constraints on the site on the edge of Watford dictated secondhand London stock bricks, a tiled roof and standard steel windows.

Above, below and right Ancker Summer House, Halland, Sweden, 1953, Stig Ancker. Austere, white-painted blockwork walls frame interiors epitomizing the new sense of domesticity exemplified by light timber-boarded floors, woven rugs and simple, unpretentious fittings.

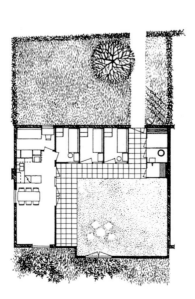

Below and opposite Utzon House, Hellebaek, Denmark, 1952, Jørn Utzon. Sited like a dam at the head of a small valley, Utzon's house melded influences from Mies van der Rohe, Wright's Usonians and Japan with native Danish brick-building traditions to create an architecture of unmistakable authority.

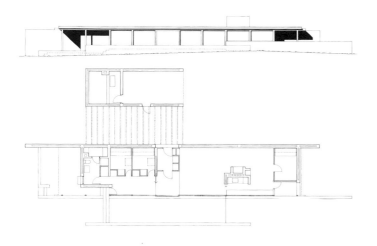

Utzon House Hellebaek, Denmark, 1952, Jørn Utzon

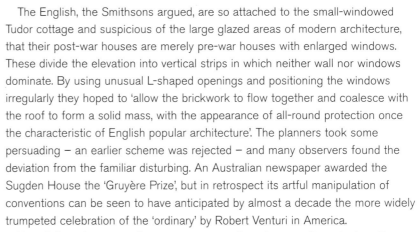

The English, the Smithsons argued, are so attached to the small-windowed Tudor cottage and suspicious of the large glazed areas of modern architecture, that their post-war houses are merely pre-war houses with enlarged windows. These divide the elevation into vertical strips in which neither wall nor windows dominate. By using unusual L-shaped openings and positioning the windows irregularly they hoped to 'allow the brickwork to flow together and coalesce with the roof to form a solid mass, with the appearance of all-round protection once the characteristic of English popular architecture'. The planners took some persuading – an earlier scheme was rejected – and many observers found the deviation from the familiar disturbing. An Australian newspaper awarded the Sugden House the 'Gruyère Prize', but in retrospect its artful manipulation of conventions can be seen to have anticipated by almost a decade the more widely trumpeted celebration of the 'ordinary' by Robert Venturi in America.

Not all Scandinavian architecture was as softened – or soft-centred, as its critics saw it – as the Swedish version. In Denmark several of the best known houses could, with little difficulty, have been aligned with the declared values of New Brutalism, if not always with the forms through which they were expressed. Again, Japan played a vital role. Tetsuro Yoshida's book *Das Japanische Wohnhaus*, published in 1935, proved a revelation with its detailed cultural and technical explanations of the Japanese house. Cast in terms that would appeal to Functionalists, it explained the close relationship to the climate and way of life and emphasized how the houses were built using a 'kit' of standard components. 1935 also saw the construction of the Zui-Ki-Tei teahouse in the grounds of the Ethnographic Museum in Stockholm, which was documented in detail in the leading Swedish journal *Byggmästaren*. As Sweden was neutral during the war, it became a place of refuge for architects from other Scandinavian countries, who naturally took the opportunity to see the Zui-Ki-Tei at first hand. Its influence was felt throughout the Nordic states, but nowhere as keenly as in Denmark, and nowhere more originally than in the work of the most talented member of the post-war generation of architects, the Dane Jørn Utzon (whose house on Majorca, Can Lis, we considered in Chapter 4, pages 124–7).

Utzon spent three years working in Stockholm during the war and in 1949 won a scholarship to travel to Mexico and the United States, where he spent a week with Frank Lloyd Wright at Taliesin East and met Mies van der Rohe in Chicago. In 1952, when he came to build his own house on a large wooded plot at Hellebaek in northern Zealand, he managed to meld a series of influences – those of Wright's Usonian houses, Mies's Farnsworth House and of Japanese architecture – into a distinctive, original whole. The house was sited at the head of a shallow valley across which he threw up a solid wall, like a dam, against the north winds and, in its shelter, a low brick platform. The rigour is unyielding. The wall is broken only once, by the main entrance, and as a consequence the study and children's bedrooms have only roof lights – in protest, his young daughter tried to scrape her own tiny opening in the wall.

Spatially, the house unfolds in layers between parallel wall-planes and around a service core. Internally, the boarding on the partitions stops short of the ceiling and floor, to allow the roof and floor planes to float visually, and the doors are full

which the living and dining areas address through full-height glazing. The lake becomes the focus of living, *in* the house, but *with* nature.

The Middlebøe house found no imitators, but Utzon's Hellebaek house, on the other hand, was widely emulated around Copenhagen. 1956 saw the completion of a one-family house in Søllerød by Børge Glahn and Ole Helweg and of his own house by Bertel Udsen. The former was directly derived from Utzon's design, but lost the spatial subtlety of the original by developing it into a more compartmentalized, L-shaped plan, while Udsen's was more successful in retaining the planar layering of the space by allowing the scheme to develop either side of the 'closed' wall. In Erik Chr. Sørensen's own house, completed in Jaegersborg in 1955, the debts to Japan are more obvious than those to Utzon, although the handling of out-reaching brick walls probably owed something to him. The plan was organized around a sequence of courtyards in which Danish versions of the natural garden were displayed to full effect.

A similar continuity between inside and out is evident in one of the most accomplished houses of the period, built in 1958 by Halldor Gunnløgsson for himself at Rungsted Strandvej looking out over Øre Sound north of Copenhagen. The open plan unfolds between two unbroken flank walls, with the spaces, column-and-beam structure and window divisions conforming strictly to a 2 x 2 metre (6.5 x 6.5 foot) module. Deep beams span between the flank walls, along each window wall and down the centre of the 8-metre- (26-foot-) wide plan, supported by columns at 4-metre (13-foot) centres. Above them, evenly spaced roof beams establish a counterpoint to the module, and cantilever at each end to protect the terraces. Between the beams the ceiling is boarded flush with its underside and the pine is left in its natural colour to contrast with the dark-stained structural elements. The flank walls and chimneys are plastered and painted white, and the floors finished with bright grey Swedish marble. Timber decks, flush with the internal floor, run along each edge, one looking out to sea, the other into a large terrace garden. The meticulously controlled interior, in which Miesian and Japanese ideals are fused, is perfectly complemented by Poul Kjærholm's furniture, epitomising the Danish sense of *quality*. This was a word used frequently to convey not only the understated elegance and refinement for which Danish design in the 1950s became renowned, but also an appropriate balance between form and material, production and cost, innovation and tradition. Danish design in its heyday exemplified the informality and freedom of the Scandinavian lifestyle, while retaining an underlying classical discipline which largely disappeared in Sweden after 1945.

No architect better epitomized these qualities than Arne Jacobsen who, having been a pioneer of Functionalism, re-established his position as a leading Danish architect with a group of houses in Søholm, designed in 1950 and completed over the next five years. Threaded between the mature trees of an old estate, the houses were cranked at 45 degrees to the road to optimize their exposure to the sun and to the views across Strandvej to Øre Sound. In plan, the more eye-catching of the two house-types is intricate yet surprisingly compact, with all the living spaces, bar one bedroom above the garage, ranged between cross-walls placed 4 metres (13 feet) apart. Jacobsen's houses were widely admired but, being so specific to their site, not easily emulated.

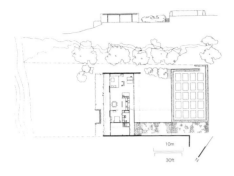

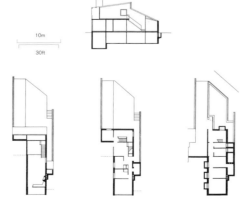

Above Gunnløgson House, Rungsted, Strandvej, Denmark, 1958, Halldor Gunnløgson. The structural clarity, Miesian planning, natural materials and understated detailing of this fine house exemplify the classical virtues of Danish architecture.
Left Link-houses, Søholm, Copenhagen, Denmark, 1950–55, Arne Jacobsen. Ingeniously organized in plan and section, this influential group of houses was designed to make the most of a difficult site which enjoyed views across the coast road to Øre Sound.

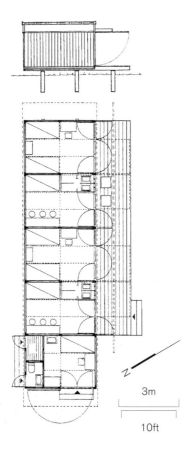

3m

10ft

sequences of courtyard houses there was to be a communal building with dining room, lounge and a small hotel for guests. The scheme was completed in 1965, well after Utzon left to work full-time in Sydney on the Opera House, but before leaving he established the principles to be followed in designing the walls of the individual courtyards. The builder's tender included an allowance for a standard number of bricks, and each wall was to be individually designed by one of Utzon's assistants sitting in the courtyard and determining by eye – according to possible views, exposure, overlooking, orientation, etc – an appropriate configuration. Utzon's inspiration was a lecture he had heard in Stockholm, in which Alvar Aalto proposed a branch of flowering cherry as a model for a housing scheme – each flower the same, yet each unique, according to its relationship to its neighbours, the sun, wind, and so on.

Something similar had been attempted in the Kingo houses, but too many identical walls were repeated: at Fredensborg the result is masterly. The gently undulating greensward framed by a continuous built fabric feels as timeless as the Islamic and medieval European settlements that were its ultimate inspiration. The balance between privacy and community, repetition and variety, is finely struck, and just as important as the designed variation of the private courtyards is the individuality that comes from Utzon's boldness in fitting the houses to the sloping land. Some, at the ends of the long terraces, stand almost 3 metres (10 feet) out of the ground. They are given no special treatment, such as a window overlooking the farmland beyond, and confront the open landscape with unbroken walls of brickwork up to 7 metres (23 feet) high. The result suggests a small city-wall. It is breached only once, and the view down between the gable ends, across the grass to the terraces beyond, seems, for a moment, like a glimpse of Umbria.

Utzon's courtyard houses were widely admired and emulated in Denmark. The Ved Stampedammen courtyard houses in Usserød, completed in 1965 by Frederiksen, Hammer, Moldenhawer and Paulsen for example, were modelled directly on the Kingo project but executed in the white-painted brick style that originated in the private houses of the 1950s and was widely adopted in the 1960s. In a terrace of houses in Overrød, completed in 1963, Bertel Udsen framed the houses with bold, L-shaped walls and emulated the 'city-wall' appearance Utzon achieved, while the terraced houses in Carlsminderpark in Søllerød, by Henrik Iversen and Harald Plum, echo Utzon's formal language, including the distinctive chimneys.

The summer house continued to provide Scandinavian architects with outstanding opportunities for experimentation, and again Japanese influence was very much to the fore. Just how varied were the outcomes of the continuing fascination with the Japanese house can be seen by examining contrasting examples. The first, designed in 1957 by Vilhelm Wohlert (renowned for the Japanese-inspired Louisiana Museum, designed with Jørgen Bo) was a guest annex at the great physicist Niels Bohr's summer residence. Wohlert's design adapts the openness and seasonal flexibility of traditional Japanese architecture to the Nordic climate and in plan is simplicity itself. Two double and two single rooms are placed in line, entered directly from the outside via a south-facing deck, with a separate nanny's room entered from the short, west-facing end.

Above Fredensborg Housing, Fredensborg, Denmark, 1962–5, Jørn Utzon. The continuous fabric of yellow brick walls and tiled roofs, punctuated by the cubic chimneys, has a unity reminiscent of medieval settlements, and successfully accommodated a rich variety of private worlds within the dwellings and courtyards.

Opposite Nils Bohr summer house (guest annex), Tisvilde, Denmark, 1957, Vilhelm Wohlert. Built for the inventor of Quantum Theory, this annex to his summer-house changed from a secretive black box in winter to an open belvedere in summer.

Above Kaapeli, Lingonsö, Finland, 1969, Kaija and Heikki Siren. This private 'chapel' for nature-worship, which forms part of the Sirens' summer-house, evokes memories of ancient Japanese Shinto shrines like those periodically re-built at Ise.

Opposite, bottom Span houses, Ham Common, Surrey, England, 1956, Eric Lyons. The landscaped public space and combinations of tile-hanging, timber-boarding and render reflected Scandinavian influence in the most innovative speculatively built modern housing on offer in England.

In the winter it is completely sealed, a mysterious black-stained wooden box with only a clerestory to hint at the possibility of habitation. Shutters at each end and a pair in the middle swing open to reveal glazed doors with broad, white-painted frames. They can be fixed open at 90 degrees to subdivide the terrace, providing privacy and shelter, or turned inwards to leave the sun terrace completely open. The large window shutters, painted black outside and white inside, can be lifted up into a horizontal position to form a sun roof, and the windows then fold away to open the interior completely.

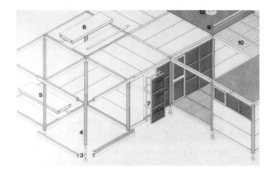

Above 'Moduli' summer-house system, Finland, 1969, Gullichsen and Pallasmaa. Miesian discipline combines with the Finnish love of natural materials in this elegant system-built house.

During the 1960s many leading Finnish architects again became preoccupied with industrialization, and in 1967 Arno Ruusuvuori was commissioned by the well known fashion and fabric company Marimekko to design an experimental summer house using simple prefabricated components. The result was simple but strikingly elegant, a long, thin box with a covered porch linking house to sauna. It was emulated two years later by two young architects, Kristian Gullichsen (son of the family who built the Villa Mairea) and Juhani Pallasmaa, in the industrialized summer house system they named 'Moduli'. In total contrast, and also completed in 1969, is the sitting room Kaija and Heikki Siren added to their summer residence at Lingonsö. The site is an isolated island of rock and the fully glazed space is framed with four substantial hand-hewn columns, cut to receive similarly robust beams. With its elevated, cantilevered floor and projecting roof it almost recalls a rudimentary Greek temple, but the ultimate inspiration was Japanese – the Japan of the sixth century Ise Shrine, rebuilt almost every twenty years since, not of Edo period modularization which inspired Ruusuvuori and the younger generation.

Kaapeli Lingonsö, Finland, 1969, Kaija and Heikki Siren

Designing it as a space from which to contemplate nature, the Sirens named their new room Kaapeli – 'Chapel'. At first sight the contrast with the Moduli system could hardly be more complete, but in much of the best Scandinavian architecture the two poles – organic/mechanical, craft-made/machine-made – can both be discerned. In the Villa Mairea, we may recall, Aalto used steel columns but wrapped them with rattan, both as a reference to nature and to humanize the industrial product, rendering it warm and tactile. Similarly, although the Siren's Kaapeli is conspicuously handmade, its geometry and tectonic expression are rigorous, utterly devoid of the sentimentality so often associated with the handcrafted. Similarly, too, the Moduli system uses wood, not steel or aluminium, and even as austerely systematic a design as this retains those links to nature that are widely seen as the essence of the Scandinavian contribution to modern architecture. Nowhere, arguably, did the Scandinavian influence receive a greater welcome from architects and a progressive section of the public than in England, and it is with two English examples that we will conclude our discussion.

The continuing reluctance of English popular taste to come to terms with modern architecture was much discussed in the architectural press. By the mid 1950s, however, in the wake of the 1951 Festival of Britain, education by the BBC and women's magazines, and the arrival of such exotic continental delights as espresso bars, there was a small but tangible demand for more modern houses. The need was most famously met by Span Builders and their architect Eric Lyons. Span advertised in *The Observer* and *The Sunday Times*, which were

Turn End Haddenham, England, 1967, Peter Aldington

Above, below and opposite Turn
End, Haddenham, England, 1963–7,
Peter Aldington. Melding forms and
materials drawn from the local
vernacular with Continental – not least
Scandinavian – influences, Peter
Aldington created a marvellously
habitable group of three houses
which fit seamlessly into a small
English village.

read almost exclusively by literate professionals. They built initially in salubrious
outer London suburbs such as Richmond, Twickenham and Blackheath, and
Lyons often worked in the teeth of opposition from amenity societies and local
planners to whom the houses still seemed dangerously modern. To describe the
Span style as overtly Scandinavian would be misleading, but the relaxed
combination of brick cross-walls, tile hanging, weather-boarding and large areas
of glazing was an English version of the easy-going 'New Empiricism' that found
such a receptive audience in Britain. Internally, the house plans daringly opened
up the familiar semi-detached house-type, offering a continuous ground floor with
living room to the front and dining/kitchen to the rear. Even more innovative, and
clearly marked by Scandinavian examples, was the creation of a continuous, richly
planted public landscape, beautifully scaled to the houses. The elimination of
front gardens was unheard of in private housing in the UK at the time, but it
became a main selling feature in Span's advertisements.

A smaller shared landscape also formed part of the remarkable
group of three houses – known as Turn End – created by Peter
Aldington in Haddenham. The site was acquired in 1963 and the
houses completed in 1967. Aldington still lives in the largest of them, more land
has been acquired, and under his care the garden has evolved into an exquisite,
quintessentially English setting. He conceived the houses as a series of walled
enclosures and when asked to cite the influences on his work named his student
heroes – Mies, Wright and Le Corbusier. Their impress is apparent in the open-
plan, loft-cum-gallery, built-in seating and Jaoul-like toughness of the masonry.
But the ambience is far closer to some of the Scandinavian examples we have
examined, and details such as the split roof section with high-level glazing, close-
spaced mullions and tile-capped chimneys immediately recall Jacobsen's Søholm
houses and the detailing of Aalto and Utzon.

Stylistically, these houses did not set out to be radically innovative. What makes
them exemplary is the way in which English picturesque and vernacular traditions
are combined with the tougher, evolving language of modern architecture and
then fitted into a traditional village. By preserving existing buildings, using local
materials and details – such as the distinctive lime-rendered and tile-topped walls
– and planning the three houses as an intricate, interlocking composition,
Aldington achieved an organic unity that is a riposte to the all too familiar pattern
of treating each house in a development in splendid isolation from its neighbours.
But finally what makes them unique is the magical, seamless unity of interior and
exterior, house and garden. Few houses built in Britain in the twentieth century
can rival them as richly habitable places to live.

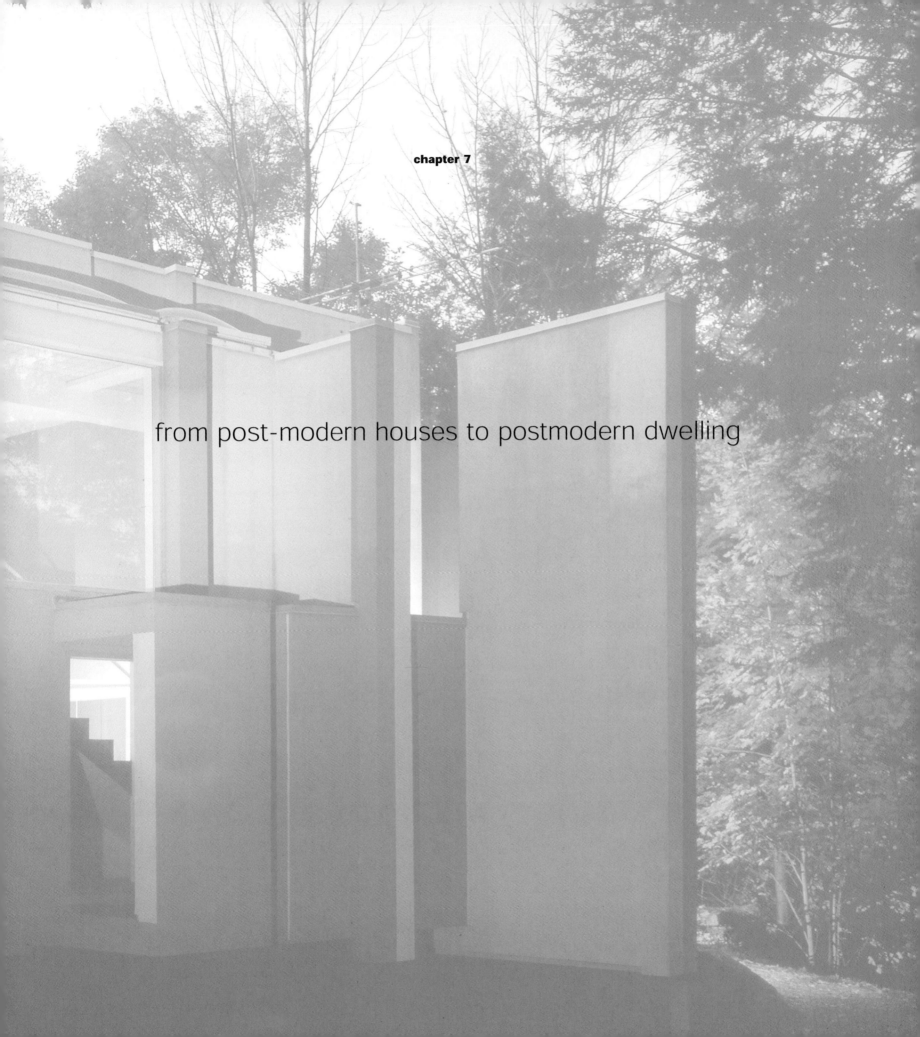

from post-modern houses to postmodern dwelling

In 1966 the Museum of Modern Art in New York published the first of its 'Papers on Architecture'. Entitled *Complexity and Contradiction in Architecture*, and written by the Philadelphia architect Robert Venturi, it was later seen to mark the arrival of Post-Modernism though the style was only christened a decade or so later by Charles Jencks. By the now ubiquitous term 'Post-Modern' Jencks meant an architecture that rejected the central assumptions of modern architecture – abstraction, spatial continuity, truth to materials, etc – and addressed itself primarily to issues of communication and style. Architecture was seen as a language that, by drawing on historic styles, popular culture and its own more recent past, could communicate with a variety of audiences. The term postmodern – no capitals, and with the hyphen now increasingly commonly dropped – gradually came into use to describe a more far-reaching cultural phenomenon which one of its leading theorists, Jean-François Lyotard, argues began with the transition to the so-called post-industrial age towards the end of the 1950s. In this chapter we will begin by looking at Post-Modern houses in the narrower, stylistic sense, and then move on to consider broader issues centred around the ideas of 'dwelling' and 'place'.

Vanna Venturi House Chestnut Hill, Pennsylvania, USA, 1962–4, Robert Venturi

The house Robert Venturi built for his mother Vanna Venturi in Philadelphia's leafy suburb of Chestnut Hill (1962–4) is the first emblematic building of Post-Modernism. At a glance the front elevation resembles the classic child's drawing of 'house': gabled and symmetrical, with a big central chimney, a door in the middle and windows either side. Look again and you find it is anything but simple. The gable is split down the middle, the fissure coming to rest on an expressed lintel though which is drawn the line of an arch. The windows are all different but linked by a rudimentary stringcourse. To the left are large and small squares, to the right a miniature Corbusian ribbon window which slides into the corner and destabilizes the sense of solidity that the rest of the façade might seem designed to evoke.

Walk round to the back and symmetry is again asserted – by the overall form, emphasized by a lunette window at high level – and then denied by three different openings whose form clearly has more to with the internal requirements. This is what Venturi meant by 'complexity and contradiction'; it is also an example of what Jencks later called 'double-coding', the pernicious idea that buildings should communicate high-brow aesthetic meanings to the architecturally literate, and simpler, familiar messages for the man-in-the-street. The literate, for example, were meant to 'spot' that the split gable might be a knowing reference to Luigi Moretti's apartments on the Via Parioli in Rome, illustrated on page 29 of Venturi's book, or to various Mannerist villas – Mannerism being one of his favourite styles.

The complexities of Venturi's architecture are by no means skin deep. In plan, symmetry was asserted and then 'accommodated' (he used the word in a particular sense) to the functional requirements. The kitchen balances a bedroom, but not exactly, and the chimney and stair battle for supremacy at the centre of the composition. The stair is wider at its bottom than at the top, as befits the transition from 'public' downstairs to 'private' upstairs, and cleverly sliced by an angled wall which eases open the entrance porch to make room for the double entrance doors. At three of the four corners, recesses and a covered veranda

Above and opposite Vanna Venturi House, Chestnut Hill, Pennsylvania, USA, 1962–4, Robert Venturi. The house Venturi designed for his mother exemplified his ideas on 'complexity and contradiction in architecture' and was later hailed as one of the first manifestos of Post-Modern design. Although deliberately house-like, the gabled front elevation plays games with symmetry reminiscent of Le Corbusier's Villa Stein at Garches.

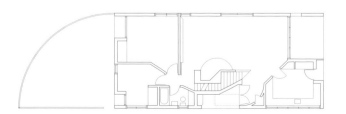

reveal the thinness of the walls, turning the front and rear elevations into screens – an effect reinforced by the parapets in which they terminate.

The Vanna Venturi house was undeniably clever, and Venturi proved to be one of the most artful planners of his generation, drawing ideas as freely from Le Corbusier and Aalto as from historical architecture. He became increasingly obsessed with architecture as imagery, however, and later took his students to Las Vegas to study the casinos and roadside signs as 'an architecture of communication'. The book *Learning from Las Vegas* appeared in 1972 and in it Venturi, his wife Denise Scott-Brown and colleague Steve Izenour indulged in a High Camp reverie of the city's relentless kitsch. Buildings, they declared, could be considered either Ducks or Decorated Sheds. The former, named after a Long Island restaurant in the shape of a duck, included all form-follows-function buildings which try to communicate though manipulating the form of the entire building, while the latter encompassed fancy, communicative façades or signs that screened some cheap building to the rear. It was a deeply cynical reduction, but epitomized a growing fascination with the idea of architecture as a language operating through culturally determined codes rather than the abstract properties of space, form and structure – an idea explored at length in Charles Jencks's influential 1977 book *The Language of Post-Modern Architecture*.

Jencks dated the 'death of modern architecture' with oft-quoted precision: it passed away, he declared, on 'July 15, 1972 at 3.32pm' when several slab-blocks of Minoru Yamasaki's Pruitt-Igoe development, a twenty-year-old, award-winning public housing project in St-Louis, Missouri, were dynamited. Like many other critics and theorists in the 1970s Jencks borrowed ideas from the linguistic theories of Saussure, Chomsky and others. Through their preoccupation with space and structure, he argued, Modernist architects had neglected vital semantic and symbolic aspects of architecture and thereby cut themselves off from the wider culture. Jencks's advocacy of style, language and meaning was to lead architects in startlingly disparate directions. Venturi, Charles Moore, Robert Stern and Michael Graves, all prolific house builders, moved inexorably towards increasingly self-conscious re-uses of historic styles, whereas others – most famously the New York Five – treated the architecture of the Heroic Period, the 1920s, as a stylistic resource.

Trubek and Wislocki Houses Nantucket, Massachusetts, USA, 1971–2, Robert Venturi

Venturi's Trubek and Wislocki houses of 1971–2 on Nantucket, Massachusetts, are clearly derived from the Shingle-style houses for which the island is renowned, but at the same time allude to other, more distant architectures. Their placement, turning towards each other as if in conversation, was, according to Venturi, influenced by the Greek temples at Selinus. The larger house boasts a Palladian gable to suggest a grander scale, but is then deflated by having its corner sliced diagonally in deference to the direction of approach. As in his mother's house, what seems at first familiar, even conventional, turns out to be complex. Thus, for example, on one house the veranda is 'conventional', added to the rear of the house, in the other it cuts into the volume in a thoroughly Modernist way. The windows, similarly, are commonplace sashes eccentrically distributed in response to internal requirements. The idea is given a different spin in the Tucker House of 1975, in Katonah, New York, which exaggerates almost to the point of caricature the familiar form of 'house'. The pyramidal roof is like a giant hat, and its profile is repeated inside to frame the fireplace. Venturi's explanation for the tapering, tower-like form was, however, refreshingly straightforward: it looked better among the aspens, and involved cutting down fewer trees.

The architect Robert Stern was one of the first to recognize Venturi's talents, giving him pride of place in the 1965 edition of the Yale architecture journal, *Perspecta*, which he edited while still a student. Stern has always regarded himself as an adapter rather than inventor, an informed eclectic content to work with the ideas of others, variously refining, exaggerating and distorting their forms. His Wiseman House (1965–7), a year-round vacation home in Montauk, New York, is patently indebted to the Vanna Venturi House, in both plan and elevation, but it plays games with the prototype. The front elevation has been expanded laterally to address the distant views by means of diagonal corners to create a bigger scale, and the lunette window has been vastly enlarged to make a huge arch – part window, part open frame – defining the edge of a roof-top terrace.

Venturi's Brant House of 1971, in Bermuda, likewise appears to have been an inspiration for Stern's much larger house of 1974–6 in Westchester County, New York, which turned the idea of the screen wall used by Venturi into a leitmotif of the whole composition. A curving screen sweeps across half the entrance front, framing the entrance and sheltering a private outdoor space for the servants, while to the rear a symmetrical, bowed screen wall reduces the apparent length of the elevation and provides solar protection. It is echoed inside, in the form of the symmetrical wall framing the kitchen, one of several examples of what Stern describes as 'formal interventions which are assembled by the observer as he moves through the spaces'; these are encountered on promenades that culminate in open vistas across the garden. If this sounds suspiciously like a description of a 1920s villa by Le Corbusier it is hardly surprising, because the Corbusian syntax is also much in evidence here. The shallow, S-shaped wall dividing the two servants' bedrooms is surely a knowing reference to the almost identical partition of the maid's room in the Cook House, thus a clue to the ultimate inspiration behind Stern's repeated layering of space. The walls, of cream-coloured stucco with two narrow terracotta stripes forming a rudimentary cornice, are intended, Stern says, to remind us of Tuscan villas, Fallingwater and 1930s Hollywood, but the prevailing influence is unmistakably Art Deco. Rambling and picturesque, the house is a large-scale exercise in the decorative use of space and surfaces; skilful in its way, but by comparison with the Corbusian models on which it drew, slack and devoid of a strong controlling idea.

During the late 1970s and 1980s Stern's work became more overtly derivative of past styles. A large house in Llewellyn Park, New Jersey emulated French Classicism externally while inside it mixed traditional rooms and flowing spaces; another at King's Point, New York played games with broken symmetry but was cast in a more consistently Classical manner. The Shingle style that had inspired Stern's first house in Montauk was followed more closely in the Bozzi House at East Hampton, New York, of 1983. This appears to be a faithful rendition of a house that might have been designed a century earlier, but on closer inspection it turns out to question many of the underlying assumptions of the style. The

Overleaf Trubeck and Wislocki Houses, Nantucket, Massachusetts, USA, 1971–2, Venturi and Rauch. Ordinary at first sight, but replete with artful deviations from vernacular norms on closer inspection, these small houses dominate the landscape like Greek temples conversing silently across space.

Above and opposite Private
House, Westchester County, New
York, USA, 1974–6, Robert Stern. Art
Deco colours and styling combine with
Corbusian spatial layering in this
rambling, picturesque composition.

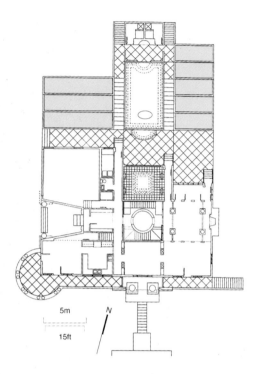

Plocek House Warren, New Jersey, USA, 1976–82, Michael Graves

Above and opposite Plocek
House, Warren, New Jersey, USA,
1976–82, Michael Graves. Cross-axial
planning and broken symmetries
confirm an underlying Classical
discipline, which is overlaid by an
eclectic range of details, from the
cubic corner windows to entrances
reminiscent of Egyptian pylons.

chimney is detached at one end of the composition, not integral to it as a spatial
and social focus; the porch is Classical and added on, not cut out of the main
volume as was usual in the classic Shingle style houses; the eyebrow dormer-
windows are a familiar feature of East Hampton Shingle style houses, but Stern's
are apparently unrelated to the rest of the composition and deeper than usual,
more like applied features than delicate incisions into the roof covering propped
open by slivers of glass; the gridded screen on the west elevation is borrowed
from William Ralph Emerson's Hemenway House of 1883, but whereas there the
corner is marked by a thicker post, Stern neither registers the different structural
condition nor closes the corner visually.

Vincent Scully, we may recall, identified in the Shingle style a feeling of organic
wholeness in the way the richly articulated masses were 'indicative of plastic
volumes within'. In Stern's reworking of the style that wholeness is consistently
denied; he does not aim at formal or spatial coherence but strings together forms
and spaces calculated, as Gavin Macrae-Gibson has argued, to bring back
memories of Atlantic resorts and traditional summers by the sea. Stern's method
is scenographic rather than architectonic: no longer able to believe in the
possibility of building a better world, the Bozzi House invites us to inhabit images
of a past one.

Michael Graves began his career as a member of the self-styled New York
Five, who achieved widespread recognition with a manifesto-like compilation of
their work published in 1975 as *Five Architects*. The book was square and white.
The cover featured only the architects' surnames in block letters and the work it
contained was avowedly modern – pure 'White' as opposed to the eclectic 'Grey'
of Venturi and his ilk. Graves was then the master of what were popularly dubbed
'Cubist kitchens', highly-worked – or over-worked, according to your taste –
essays in post-Corbusian abstraction tacked onto unsuspecting houses around
Princeton University where he taught. Graves made a rapid transition to an overtly
Post-Modern style, however, and his Government Building in
Portland, Oregon, of 1980–82 became the public flagship of the
movement. In the Plocek House, designed in 1976 and
completed in 1982 on a steep, wooded site in Waren, New Jersey, the future
direction of his work was clear.

Like Palladio's Villa Madama, which provided a model, the plan is organized
around two axes; they begin with tapering entrances at different levels, cross in a
circular hall carved out of what Graves calls the 'stair column', and then move on.
The long axis terminates in a mural entitled *Archaic Landscape*, painted by
Graves above the large fireplace, while the cross axis disappears through the
library window to end nowhere in particular, thanks to the client's failure to build
the projected keystone-shaped pool house. The plan is composed of traditional
rooms, some wholly contained by walls, others defined by perforated screens, and
abounds in symmetries and sub-symmetries.

Externally, the modelling is intended to suggest the traditional Classical
tripartite division into *piano rustica, piano nobile* and *corona aedificii* but
Graves's Classicism is far from orthodox. The stair column which begins as a
circular void at the ground floor emerges above as a freestanding cylindrical
drum, and then blossoms into a conical, wood-framed 'capital' below a skylight

which allows light into the centre of the house. The windows are mostly square rather than upright and on either side of the main entrance two eminently Modernist projecting cubes of glass dissolve the corner, only to rest on rudimentary cylindrical columns. The side entrance, on the other hand, recalls Egyptian pylons and might almost be contrived to intimidate rather than welcome. You enter through a tall, narrow slot which expands into a keystone-shaped void; this was intended to be projected into the garden as the unbuilt pool house but it is now somewhat forlorn, an unconsummated example of Post-Modern wit.

Unlike later, more stylistically earnest Post-Modern Classicism, the Plocek House simulates thickness and mass but does not seriously attempt to convince you its walls are solid and heavy. You hardly need to tap them to know that they are hollow, that slender timber framing rather than masonry lies behind the rendered surface. Despite this, the gap between material substance and visual effect is disturbing. The house offers itself as a commentary on the world rather than as a piece of it, a feeling reinforced inside by the built-in cabinetry, furniture, lamps and rugs, all designed by Graves, which contrive to give it the air of a film set rather than somewhere palpably real. The effect is hardly coincidental, for Graves's work epitomizes the values of our media-dominated world. Permanence, for so long a hallmark of architecture, is here a product of the building's appearance, of the Classical language it deploys, not of its material substance. Post-Modernism was always meant to be ironic in its use of past styles, but the real irony is that less than twenty years after its completion Graves's return to the supposedly timeless language of Classicism should already seem so old fashioned, like last month's hit record or last season's fashions.

During the late 1970s and early 1980s Charles Jencks seemed able to discover or invent a new style every few months, disseminated as special issues of *Architectural Design* magazine with such titles as 'Post-Modern Classicism', 'Free-Style Classicism', 'Abstract Representation' and 'Late-Modern Architecture'. Jencks put his money where his mouth was by teaming up with the English architect Terry Farrell to convert and extend a London villa into his own 'Thematic House', published in 1985 in the glossy, overweening book *Symbolic Architecture*. By then, however, the tide was turning against the superficial pillaging of architectural history for forms and 'meanings', and whereas *The Language of Post-Modern Architecture* reportedly sold over 100,000 copies, *Symbolic Architecture* was destined to linger in the publisher's warehouse for years to come.

The term Post-Modern in architecture increasingly came to be identified with witty, ironic or in other ways unorthodox interpretations of Classical architecture, and its brief time in the limelight had more to do with media and marketing than with lasting architectural quality. But as Jencks rightly pointed out, the term could equally well apply to the New York Five. The two most important members of this group were Richard Meier, who based his work on a self-conscious reworking of Le Corbusier's 1920s villas – which, by the end of his life, Le Corbusier himself reportedly came to dislike; and Peter Eisenman, who treated architecture as a self-referential language. Eisenman was inspired to a lesser extent by Le Corbusier and more by the layered structures of Giuseppe Terragni and plastic energy of De Stijl.

Smith House Darien, Connecticut, USA, 1965, Richard Meier

The Smith House of 1965 exemplifies Meier's early work. It sits on a magnificent half hectare (one-and-a-half acre) site overlooking Long Island Sound, set back from the rocky shoreline among trees. Spatially the house is divided into two zones: a three-storey block of cellular rooms and, in front, a triple-height volume stratified but not compartmentalized by three platforms. Structurally, the rooms are enclosed by timber-framed walls with pierced openings, and the open zone is demarcated by columns and beams, permitting large areas of glass. The contrast is further heightened by placing an enclosed stair in one corner of the cellular zone and an open outdoor stair diagonally opposite to provide alternative links between floors.

Anyone receptive to the abstract language of modern architecture can hardly fail to find this white beacon of modernity set amid pristine nature aesthetically appealing. Meier's version of the Corbusian language is thoughtfully worked out and skilfully deployed, but it is also almost completely lacking in the tension and subtlety that made its model so potent. By the 1960s the dream of universality represented by the architecture of the Heroic Period was widely realized to be no longer tenable, and Meier's choice is, therefore, stylistic. Whereas the Modern Movement aspired to a twentieth-century vernacular, Meier offers a particular 'modern style' as his selling feature in the increasingly global marketplace. It proved a shrewd choice and he built a substantial career — museums, university buildings, corporate headquarters, a city hall — on the basis of a few years of Le Corbusier's endlessly inventive career: no matter that the language became mannered and stretched beyond its capacity, it *sold*.

The most original thinker presented in *Five Architects* was Peter Eisenman. He called his contributions 'Cardboard Architecture' and presented two projects, the laconically named House I and House II. Whereas most Post-Modernists concentrated on language as a semantic system he turned to syntax, to the grammatical and other structures that make linguistic communication possible. Emulating the 'generative grammars' of Noam Chomsky, Eisenman derived his houses from transformational rules that were purely formal in their operation. An initial set of what he called 'formal conditions' — an array of grids, planes and volumes — was variously shifted, translated and rotated to generate bewilderingly complex structures from which he could distil a sequence of habitable spaces. 'Such a logical structure of space,' said Eisenman, 'aims not to comment on the country house as a cultural symbol but to be neutral with respect to its existing social meanings.' Like the Minimalist sculptures of Sol Lewitt and Donald Judd produced around the same time, early Eisenman houses were hermetic, autonomous works: their form bore no relation to their site, nor did their organization spring from the pattern of activities they might house.

For Eisenman, however, House I and House II, and two further projects that followed them, still 'contained many preconceptions which upon reflection seemed to me to be culturally conditioned'. In particular, he felt they had been designed from the outside in rather than from the centre out, a process that would enable him to challenge the whole idea of 'façade'. In House VI, completed in 1975 for the photographer Dick Frank and his wife Suzanne, an architectural historian, Eisenman set about inverting these preconceptions about the nature of architecture. He again used

House VI West Cornwall, Connecticut, USA, 1972–5, Peter Eisenman

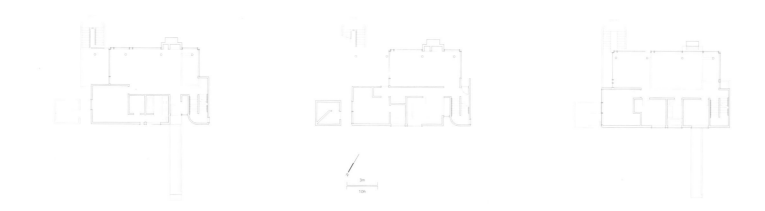

Above, left and right House VI, West Cornwall, Connecticut, USA, 1972–5, Peter Eisenman. In his self-styled 'cardboard architecture' Eisenman subjected the planar language of Modernism to complex formal transformations using rules which he likened to the syntax of a natural language.

Opposite Smith House, Darien, Connecticut, USA, 1965, Richard Meier. Often magnificently sited, as here, Meier's houses are seductive essays in the manner of Le Corbusier's Twenties villas.

'diagrammed transformations' but saw the house not as an end product of the process, but as a record of it. The resulting solids and voids, columns and planes, were not a resolved composition, but an invitation to the mind to reorder them, and in the process question their 'meaning'. The house is permeated by vertical and horizontal slots, some glazed, some open, which seem to imply the existence of a 'virtual house' of absent columns and beams to be perceived in parallel with the real, physical one. And as if to reinforce this reading, each has its own staircase: a green one which connects the two floors, and a red one which goes nowhere and merely hangs in space as a 'sign' – like an anti-stair escaped from an Escher engraving.

Both clients and critics were responsive to House VI's visual and intellectual pleasures. Suzanne Frank described the 'series of slots, beams, and columns that unfold when viewed from the bedroom' as 'an effect as spellbinding as the movement of bits of glass on mirrors in a kaleidoscope'; the sociologist Robert Gutman recalled the first glimpse of the house as 'literally breathtaking – one of the superb visual experiences of modern design'; and Kenneth Frampton declared it 'canonical' on account of its 'dense orchestration of impacted form, comprised simultaneously and to the same degree of planes, transparencies, volumes and masses'. As a home, even a vacation home, however, it proved problematic. A column makes conversation around the dining table difficult: even after 'mental relocation' it remains insistently present. A window in the floor of what became the master bedroom required the clients to sleep in separate beds; guests had to cross the master bedroom to reach the bathroom; the kitchen worktops were too high to work at comfortably except when seated on a stool – a great inconvenience for Dick Frank who photographs food and is a keen cook; and views of the beautiful site from the living spaces were largely cut off by solid planes.

In 1988 the Franks decided to renovate their thirteen-year-old house. It was leaking – Eisenman, they said, was somewhat cavalier about details such as roof-flashings – and they had had enough of sleeping in separate beds and putting up with the other idiosyncrasies. The renovation took four years and, like the saga of the Farnsworth House, became something of a *cause célèbre*. Eisenman declared the house had lost its edge, but finally seemed to be reconciled to its new life. In the intervening years, as his work developed in new directions, he had also become clearer about the wider implications of his ideas. The novelist William Gass hinted at them when he wrote as follows about House VI: 'The world of this house was Copernican. Its spaces did not flow from me as though I were their source and centre. Its surfaces were not the limits of my sight and movement, places for paintings, shepherds of privacy, backgrounds for my furniture. Nor did the floor exist to support my rugs or serve to assure me, always, that I was safe on the hard and even earth.' Eisenman and a growing coterie of New York intellectuals based their work on the theory that in the wake of the Holocaust and Hiroshima it was no longer possible to sustain the classical, Western belief in the centrality of human values. The task of architecture, therefore, was to 'de-centre' the human subject: in House VI the owners finally chose to re-centre parts of the house around their needs.

In Europe, the most searching manifestation of Post-Modernism was the so-

Above House at Ballyweelin, County Sligo, Ireland, 1983, O'Donnell and Tuomey. Although rooted in Irish Classicism and immediately at home in the landscape, the design reflects contemporary debates about the tectonic virtues of 'Doricism', notably in the exposed roof structure above the terrace which looks out to the sea.
Opposite Casa Rotonda, Stabio, Switzerland, 1981, Mario Botta. Split down a central axis and oriented to the four points of the compass, the cylindrical house ignores its suburban neighbours to address the wider landscape.

called neo-Rationalist movement associated with the Italians Aldo Rossi and Giorgio Grassi, the German Oswald Mathias Ungers, and the Luxemburg-born brothers Rob and Leon Krier. Their preoccupation was with restructuring the city, using traditional urban blocks and house types to create a fabric for monumental public buildings. The individual house did not loom large in their concerns, but their ideas were widely influential, not least in the Ticino, the Italian-speaking canton of Switzerland where Mario Botta produced a string of distinctive houses in the late 1970s and '80s. Botta's houses typically have strong, closed forms cut with bold openings and are planned symmetrically about a central axis. They are invariably built of concrete block which contrasts with delicate glass and steel windows, roof lights and stairs — the stairs sometimes designed to flex slightly under load to emphasize the solidity of the walls.

Casa Rotonda Stabio, Switzerland, 1981, Mario Botta

Casa Rotonda in Stabio, completed in 1981, is typical of Botta's early work. Aligned to the four points of the compass it stands in defiant isolation, a riposte to the amorphous suburban sprawl around it. The openings are scaled to the horizons and calculated to cut out views of the immediate surroundings and direct attention to untouched landscapes further afield. On the street side the walls step open on either side of the stair to make space for two cars. This allows the stair to stand free in a blockwork tower, whose curved top corbels out to meet the larger cylinder of the house — and in the process suggests a rudimentary column and capital. The reference is entirely conscious, but in no sense is it an applied motif, still less a Post-Modern joke. Botta saw his work as an attempt to propose a 'a new equilibrium between man and his surroundings' and to 'recapture the initial values from which the dwelling was made'.

Similar motives inspired a house at Ballyweelin in County Sligo, Ireland, built by O'Donnell and Tuomey in 1983. The language is gently Classical — almost the vernacular in Ireland — and the simple form, oriented towards the view, contains a subtle sequence of spaces in which changes of level and ceiling height describe rooms of varying importance. The organization is axial, but never simplistically symmetrical, and the fireplace breaks the enfilade to divert you onto the terrace to view the ocean.

Stylistic Post-Modernism in Europe was led by design rather than architecture, above all by the work of Ettore Sottsass Jr and the Alchymia studio he founded with Andrea Branzi, Alessandro Mendini and others in 1976. Their brilliantly coloured and often wilfully dysfunctional forms were later turned into marketable products under the name Memphis. In the mid-1980s Sottsass turned his attention increasingly to architecture and produced a string of houses composed from almost toy-like elements — triangular, gutter-less roofs, cubes and chunky columns. They did not, however, gain comparable international recognition.

In Norway Jan Digerud and Jon Lundberg came, ephemerally, to international notice with two houses in Kongsvinger (1971–3) and Jessheim (1979–81). The distinguished historian and theorist Christian Norberg-Schulz felt able to praise them as an 'important, enriching contribution to Norwegian wooden architecture' but in retrospect the houses appear to be little more than clumsy reworkings of American examples, the planning lacking Venturi's subtlety and the elevations ponderous and overloaded with motifs. In Denmark, an overtly Venturi-inspired

New House Sussex, England, 1986, John Outram

Opposite New House, Sussex, England, 1986, John Outram. Although unmistakably classical in inspiration, the monumental exterior is strikingly inventive formally and constructionally, and harbours a richly articulated sequence of spaces, many of which enjoy outstanding views over open countryside.

house was built as early as 1965 near Jeeling by Ole Ramsgaard Thomsen, and four years later the leading Swedish architect Peter Celsing built a self-conscious exercise in historically-referenced complexities and contradictions for himself in Drottningholm.

Despite the superficially Post-Modern features of his work, the English architect and self-professed Classicist, John Outram, rejects being classified as 'post' anything. His Classicism is of a singularly unorthodox and inventive kind and like most innovative, practising architects, he does not think of his work as belonging to, still less reviving, a particular style, but as a contribution to the ever-expanding language of Architecture. Outram delights in Classicism's other, and to many architects, uncomfortable side: the polychrome colours, primitivism and mixed-up iconography that were rediscovered in the eighteenth century, much to the embarrassment of many later, dryly correct Neo-Classicists. Relishing the physicality and substance of Classical buildings he could never be satisfied by the timber-frame and stucco versions built across the Atlantic, but he has no worries about mixing traditional and synthetic materials – which he likes to invent. Wherever possible, the colours are integral to the materials rather than applied to their surfaces, and his office is scattered with samples of specially coloured concretes with strange aggregates. Outram's designs are guided by what he calls 'generative fictions', personal narratives about the idea of Arcadia and the reconciliation of human culture and nature through Classical mimesis.

'New House', so named to preserve its owner's privacy, was completed in 1986 in the county of Sussex in southern England. It occupies a large estate, replete with lake, 1200 deer and a neo-Gothic orangery, to which it is attached. The plan is a traditional H-shape, with an entry court on one side and a south-facing terrace on the other. The terrace, and the living and dining rooms which frame two sides of it, enjoy fine views down to the lake, and the entire plan sits on a square base like a vast, vestigial stylobate, gridded and elaborately paved, with 'absent' columns marked by circular insets. The structure is of steel set within hollow, 90-centimetre- (3-foot-) square columns which house services. They are clad in banded layers of precast concrete, which Outram thinks of as like geological strata: sedimentation and the action of water are a recurring theme in the choice and finishes of the materials. The base of each column has an exposed pebble aggregate; above it is a narrower band, acid-etched to reveal a crushed limestone aggregate with its marine fossils; most of the shaft is then clad in what he calls 'blitz-crete', concrete ground down to reveal large pieces of brick in the aggregate. The capitals are cubes out of which a sphere surfaces as if through water: made of black concrete, and with black marble aggregate, they are lacquered to look permanently wet and variously house rainwater overflows and floodlights. Between the capitals, not on them, are green lintel beams and arches, and below them the infill-walls are faced in travertine banded with brick.

Inside this massive-looking frame the interior is surprisingly light and airy. The richness of colours and materials, and attention to detail, are breathtaking and endlessly inventive: pink and yellow plywood ceilings, for example, sit happily with luxuriously inlaid wooden doors and stone floors. The shallow dome of the library brings to mind England's most inventive interpreter of Classicism, Sir John Soane,

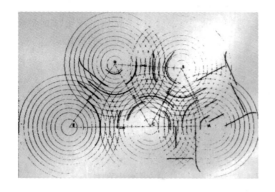

but in no sense does the design feel derivative. It is Classical, certainly, but a thoroughly modern Classicism designed, as Outram explained, in 'direct response to the saturated greens and dense colours that glow in southern England's cool, dim, stormy light with its shafts of brilliant sunlight.' For Outram, soaked in the traditions of his discipline, architecture has a 10,000-year history which 'like the heritage of the rainforests is the best place to find the "cure" to all our ills'. His work is not an attempt to pillage the past in search of forms with which to construct an artificial present, but rather to extend a living past into the future.

Stylistic Post-Modernism enjoyed greater success in commercial than residential architecture, and despite the vast amount of publicity and critical attention it attracted proved to be a surprisingly short-lived episode. The broader critique of modern architecture, recognized retrospectively as postmodern, had a more lasting impact. It focussed initially on the idea of 'place', which we used in discussing the regional adaptations of modernism in Chapter 4, and on the role of architecture in enabling us to 'dwell' in the world. Some of the key ideas were first articulated in short, poetic texts by Aldo van Eyck. In 1962, for example, he wrote that 'it is not merely what space sets out to effect in human terms, that gives it place, but what it is able to gather and transmit. . . what you should try to accomplish is built meaning. So get close to the meaning and build'. Christian Norberg-Schulz provided the most sustained body of theory for this approach, drawing on disparate intellectual sources. Initially he explored existential philosophy and Gestalt psychology, and later the German phenomenologist Martin Heidegger, whose ideas became almost ubiquitous in architectural literature during the 1980s, following the belated discovery of his essay *Bauen, Wohnen, Denken* (Building, dwelling, thinking), originally given at a 1951 conference on 'Man and Space' in Darmstadt.

As its title suggests, Norberg-Schulz's 1971 book *Existence, Space and Architecture* was framed as a challenge to the 'naïve realism', as he put it, of Giedion's *Space, Time and Architecture*. Far from being simply an abstract continuum in which we happen to exist, Norberg-Schulz argued, space as we experience and live it is concrete, compounded of things 'out there' in the environment and 'in here' in our heads. Contrary, for example, to the uniform three-dimensionality of the Schröder House or Eisenman's House VI, space – whether up and down, front and back, even left and right – is qualitatively different. Floors and ceilings may be designed abstractly as planes, but we experience them as above and below us, which brings to our perceptions a range of associations and expectations, not least with the earth and sky. To feel at home in the world, Norberg-Schulz argued, the environment needs to have an 'imageable structure' which offers rich possibilities of identification, enabling us to *dwell*, to belong to a place. Building has traditionally been one of the principal means by which we take possession of part of the world. Understood in these terms the 'meaning' of architecture is not, as Jencks framed it, a problem of communication or language, but of giving spatial form to a way of life in a particular location and culture.

Norberg-Schulz illustrated his ideas on 'existential space' – the precursor to 'place' in his writing – with Casa Andreis of 1964–7, by the Italian architect Paolo Portoghesi. The design can be seen as a commentary on the orthogonal planar

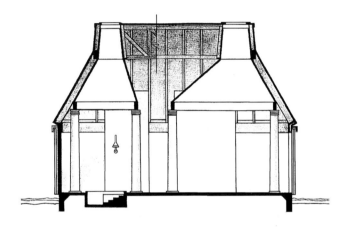

Moore House Orinda, California, USA, 1962, Charles Moore

structures of De Stijl. In place of abstract flat planes, the walls are generated from grids of circles drawn around a series of centres external to the house, establishing a more concrete interplay between building and site and creating a multiplicity of specific 'places' both within the house and in the landscape around it. The walls themselves are concrete, incised with vertical grooves to emphasize their rising movement, a feeling reinforced by the polished aluminium tubes applied to their ends to reflect ground and sky. The design was too idiosyncratic to have a wide impact, however, and it was in the USA, largely independent of European theorizing, that the place-making approach was most extensively realized in the design of houses. The protagonists were Charles Moore, Donlyn Lyndon and Gerald Allen, whose 1974 book *The Place of Houses* was aimed, like those produced just after the Second World War, at potential clients who might want a custom-built house.

The Place of Houses is profusely illustrated with a catholic collection of examples, ancient and modern, including many of the authors' own designs. Its key messages are all present in two small Californian houses by Moore: the Bonham House of 1961 and his own in Orinda completed the following year. Situated in a redwood forest in Santa Cruz County, the diminutive Bonham House makes up in importance what it lacks in stature by asserting its presence among this lofty company of trees with a huge, industrial-looking steel window, as high as the 4.2-metre- (13-feet-) square living space behind it is deep. The main space is supplemented by what Moore called 'saddlebags' (we met them in Bernard Maybeck's Guty Hyde Chick House, which could have been an inspiration) on opposite sides, one containing the kitchen and bathroom, the other a dining alcove. The floor sinks down into that necessity of Californian life, the conversation pit – here gathered around the stove – and rises via narrow, winding steps to the sleeping deck above it. A raised level around the perimeter doubles as display space and seating for the parties that were one of the main reasons why its owner wanted a weekend retreat.

The volume is open and continuous but transformed into a multiplicity of places by the numerous changes in level and light. The same multiplicity-in-unity is achieved, using different architectural means, in the highly personal version of the Californian good life Moore built for himself in Orinda in 1962. The site lies in one of the valleys behind San Francisco, filled with golden grass for most of the year and dotted with Live Oaks. The house is sited in the middle of a roughly circular lawn made by a previous owner in anticipation of building there and, as if in response, the plan is square and open. The roof is pyramidal, but asymmetrically pitched to allow for a roof light along the ridge, and the simplicity of the resulting form evokes an archetypal hut.

The interior is articulated by two square aedicules – miniature shelters consisting of four columns and a white-painted, lopsided pyramidal ceiling, which rises to the roof light. The roof has dark-stained rafters and boarding and is dimly lit by the remaining section of roof light, so that columns and bright light combine to define two distinct places – and imply others around them – within the continuum of the house. The first becomes the main sitting area; the second, and smaller, an oversized sunken bath, 'a celebration of the act of bathing here

liberated from the cramped conventional bathroom', as Moore described it. All four corners can be dissolved by sliding open glazed or solid barn doors. Like a Japanese house this one can be transformed according to season, but unlike a Modernist house there is not, Moore pointed out, 'an imperceptible merging of inside and out, rather the excitement of a boundary that can be leaned out over'.

The Orinda house manifested Moore's lifestyle and taste in detail as well as overall organization. The columns were selected, not designed: with classical entasis and rudimentary capitals, they were recycled from an old factory and then 'lovingly scraped, washed, and painted at their capitals'. The perimeter walls are layered to provide niches in which some of the fruits of his collecting are displayed, as if in a miniature museum: a little self-conscious for some tastes, perhaps, but clearly suited to his. And that is one of the central messages of *The Place of Houses.* Contrary to the exhortations of the 1920s to develop a shared modern lifestyle, Moore and his colleagues extolled the merits of the house as an expression of individual personality: 'You bind together the goods and trappings of your life together with your dreams to make a place that is your own'. Theirs was explicitly and unashamedly a theory of architecture for the consumer society, but sadly while Moore's early work offered the promise of something light and inventive, it quickly degenerated into a cardboard Classicism of no lasting interest.

Moore's early work exerted a considerable influence in America, however, and a house like that which Eugene Kupper completed in 1979 for the singer-songwriter Harry Nilsson and his wife Una would be almost unthinkable without it. Organized around a long, colonnaded spine it consists of a richly layered bunch of places, to borrow Aldo van Eyck's definition of a house, defined by different levels according to the sloping site and variously coloured to respond to different qualities of light. True to the principle of making the house as personal as possible, the nave-like spine is intended as an allusion to Una's Irish Catholic upbringing, but it ends ironically in a bath adjacent to a pulpit-like outdoor platform. The house can equally well be read as a theatre or hillside castle: through the playful manipulation of familiar symbols it invites many interpretations, and insists on none.

Cornford House Cambridge, England, 1967, Colin St. John Wilson

At first sight the Cornford House in Cambridge, designed by Colin St. John Wilson and completed in 1967, appears to belong to a completely different world to the Nilssons' theatrical showpiece. Look again, however, and you notice that it is also informed by a place-making sensibility. This can be seen both in plan – the square rooms defined by a combination of walls and freestanding columns have an obvious affinity with the aedicules at Moore's Orinda house – and in the subtle interplay of opposites: heavy brick against light timber; outside against inside, mediated by clearly articulated 'inbetween realms' (another Aldo van Eyck term); and shared/communal versus individual/private spaces. The similarities are not coincidental: Wilson came into direct contact with the new American thinking in 1960 through a teaching appointment at Yale, where Moore later became chairman, and through his colleague C. J. Long, who studied there as a postgraduate.

Illustrating a house like St. John Wilson's in a chapter on postmodernism may seem strange, because it so clearly belongs to the search for new possibilities

Above and opposite Cornford House, Cambridge, England, 1967, Colin St John Wilson. Although firmly rooted in the tectonic and compositional disciplines of modern architecture, this house reflects the interest in place-making central to the post-war European critique of the Modernist orthodoxy.

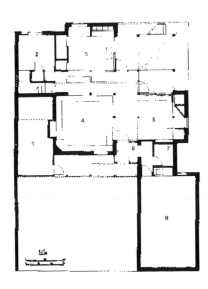

Above Private Residence, Lake
Berryessa, California, USA, 1990,
Christopher Alexander. Built using
'pattern languages' rather than
conventionally designed, this rambling,
site-inflected house attempts to
recapture what Alexander believes are
the timeless, humane values ignored
by what he has called the 'giant scam'
of modern architecture.

House on Cinnamon Hill Lunuganga, Sri Lanka, 1994, Geoffrey Bawa

within modern architecture, free of International style clothing, but firmly committed to the broader values of the Modern Movement. But if a specifically 'Modern' architecture is to be identified as that which embodied the dream of a universal, machine-age style applicable in all climates and cultures, then almost everything of interest since 1945 has to be considered postmodern in the broad sense of the term. Such niceties of historiography are, however, of little concern to practising architects and life itself has a happy knack of turning apparent trends upside down. How many of those in the 1970s who confidently proclaimed the death of modern architecture would have predicted that the 1990s would witness a worldwide resurgence of interest in exploring and extending the twentieth century's most radical body of ideas, Modernism?

To Christopher Alexander, debating the relative merits of Modernism and Post-Modernism was supremely irrelevant because in his view the 'invented series of conceptions about space and volume and style' which underpin both are a 'giant scam. . . not connected to real human feelings, but only the artificially constructed aesthetic rules of a design intelligentsia.' Although trained as an architect, and a long-term professor of architecture at the University of California at Berkeley, Alexander has always marched to a different drummer. In the 1960s he was a leading advocate of systematic design methods, and then in 1978 he launched a comprehensive alternative theory of architecture with the book *The Timeless Way of Building*, a heady mixture of pseudo-scientific analysis, misty-eyed reverie at the delights of the ordinary, and ancient Oriental wisdom.

Alexander believes that beautiful, humane buildings of all periods and cultures are governed by intricate relationships among their parts and with the environment, which he attempts to describe using what he calls 'patterns'. He had published 253 examples the previous year in the book *A Pattern Language* and his ultimate aim was to empower people to become their own architects and builders. Central to Alexander's method is his conviction that many 'design' problems can only be solved working on site and in the process of building, not on a drawing board. While his solutions were too radical to be widely embraced, his critique raised issues that go back to the Arts and Crafts movement and will continue to resurface in our post-industrial economies.

Architects, hardly surprisingly, did not care to be told their ideas were not only unnecessary but often inimical to the task of making beautiful places, and when Alexander stopped theorizing and started building, the results, to most architects' eyes, only confirmed their doubts. The rambling, site-inflected plan of the residence on Lake Berryessa, California is typical of the loose, additive structures that generally emerge from working with pattern languages, and the formal resolution, with its vague memories of Classicism, is altogether less persuasive than the similarly site-responsive, but conventionally designed house on the Cinnamon Hill in Lunuganga, Sri Lanka, which Geoffrey Bawa completed in 1994. Bawa shares Alexander's belief that designs should be improvisations on site rather than premeditated exercises in abstract ideas: he produced only one drawing as the house emerged from inside out, configured in response to the site and in close harmony with nature. Both the bedrooms incorporate antique windows positioned to frame magnificent views of the lake and their en-suite bathrooms are roofless, ceiled by foliage and with living tree roots as towel rails. It hardly matters whether you describe such a house as post- or pre-modern: it is manifestly a wonderful place to dwell, achieving that timelessness to which Alexander aspires.

Above and left House on Cinnamon Hill, Lunuganga, Sri Lanka, 1994, Geoffrey Bawa. Improvising in response to the site rather than imposing preconceived abstract forms, Bawa here achieves the relaxed, timeless quality that Alexander admires in traditional architecture.

continuity and transformations

Although stylistic Post-Modernism proved to be a short-lived episode, the broader postmodern critique cut deep, rendering untenable the belief in a simple-minded modernity of unending progress and universal truths. Global information and entertainment technologies promoted a climate of pluralism and perpetual change. This led many architects, delighted with the multiplicity of the postmodern world, to explore the formal possibilities of fragmentation as a mirror of unruly vitality, and to use the house as a vehicle for an unprecedented freedom of sculptural expression. Others, believing the task of architecture was to create islands of calm and order amid the all-embracing clamour, pursued reductively abstract forms – often referred to, sometimes misleadingly, as 'minimalist' – or sought to ground their work in local cultures and places to counter the pervasive homogenization of environments and experience.

Modernism may no longer have been tenable as a system of values and beliefs, but predictions of its death as a formal repertoire proved greatly exaggerated, and by the 1990s a widespread neo-modern revival which built on the aesthetic and spatial possibilities first explored in the 1920s was evident worldwide. Core ideas such as spatial continuity and transparency were re-examined and transformed, frequently with a new emphasis on the materiality of the forms, and the issues of place, climate and culture discussed in Chapter 4 provided an ongoing and, in the case of climate, increasingly urgent agenda.

After more than twenty years spent designing competent but unremarkable buildings in and around Los Angeles, Frank Gehry burst onto the international scene in 1978 with one of the most influential house-conversions in architectural history. Struck by how much more exciting timber-framed houses looked during construction than when neatly finished in the owner's preferred 'style', when he

Gehry House Santa Monica, California, USA, 1978, Frank Gehry

came to remodel and extend his own home in Santa Monica, Gehry set about taking it apart to reveal the hidden layers of structure, sheathing and insulation – his methods recall the work of the architect-turned-sculptor Gordon Matta-Clark, famous for slicing timber buildings in two and, in 1972, exhibiting segments of walls in a New York loft-gallery. In Gehry's transformed house, white-painted casement windows suddenly found themselves on inside walls, figural incidents in ad hoc assemblages of timber boards and struts through which, layer upon layer, light filtered into the interior. The extensions, Gehry said, resembled boxes dropped on the old building and then casually frozen in space at odd angles, framed in wood and glass or chain-link fencing and variously clad in raw plywood or metal siding. In the kitchen and dining room, built over the old driveway, you discover an eminently serviceable tarmac floor beneath a forest of angled struts.

Inspired by Californian artist-friends who insisted on the primacy of perception, not concepts, in the shaping of form, Gehry worked intuitively using a kind of architectural *bricolage* – the collage-like technique Picasso invented to make sculptures over sixty years before. His transformed house was immediately interpreted as a challenge to conventional notions of domesticity and a commentary on the chaotic vitality of the sprawling megalopolis of Los Angeles; later, in an authentic postmodern critique, Kurt Forster saw it as an attempt to break out of his identity as a male, Canadian-Jewish immigrant. Gehry pursued this gritty, casual-seeming style in several later projects, but for the Winton Guest

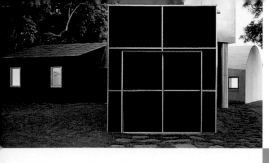

Top Winton Guest House, Wayzata, Minnesota, USA, 1983, Frank Gehry. Like a giant still-life set on the green baize of the lawn, the composition provided a dramatic contrast to the Philip Johnson-designed house for which it became an annex.

Above and left Lawson Westen House, Los Angeles, California, USA, 1988-91, Eric Owen Moss. Where Frank Gehry composes by eye, Moss prefers to use complex 'geometric mappings' to generate deconstructive forms, with results which strike many as apt metaphors for the chaos and vitality of Los Angeles.

House in suburban Wayzata, Minnesota, completed in 1983, he developed a different, equally radical approach. The clients lived in an elegant, Philip Johnson-designed brick box, but needed extra space for their children and visitors. The harsh climate demanded sound construction and, despite choosing Gehry, the Wintons were not interested in anything in his by then celebrated improvisational manner. What he delivered was an architectural still life, a series of objects placed on a lush green lawn, traversed almost imperceptibly, Japanese-style, by irregularly placed stones.

The rooms of the Winton Guest House are attached to the corners of a tall living room, a distorted square with a pyramidal roof, clad in sheet metal and evoking a giant chimney: a parody, almost, of Wright's archetypal dwelling. The hearth is a freestanding brick cube – the same brick as the Johnson house – from which, skewed in plan, rises a square chimney. Detailed with none of the normal concessions to weather, such as copings and cills, nor to gravity – expressed lintels or arches – it resembles a sculptural installation as much as a building. One bedroom is vaulted and covered – roof as well as walls – in limestone, the other in black sheeting, while the kitchen and garage are sheathed in Finnish plywood, and above them a stone-clad sleeping loft stands on a cylindrical metal column. The only reminder of Gehry's earlier manner comes inside, with a fragment of deliberately exposed rough carpentry and chicken wire below the stairs.

In the Winton Guest House Gehry offered a critique of the endlessly repetitive suburbia epitomized for many Americans by Levittown in New Jersey. By breaking the house down into individualized elements, not only did the whole become unique, but each part could assume different meanings for its inhabitants – 'ideas you have liked, places you have liked, bits and pieces of your life that you would like to recall,' as he put it. Treating the individual building as a miniature settlement was hardly new, but the result certainly was, and like Gehry's own house the Winton Guest House can now be seen as an early manifestation of a growing fascination for composing with visually or figuratively charged fragments. A similar sensibility is at work in another Los Angeles architect, Eric Owen Moss, but whereas Gehry works almost entirely by eye, like a traditional sculptor, Moss dissects and reassembles forms on the drawing board or computer screen.

Lawson Westen House Los Angeles, California, USA, 1988–91, Eric Owen Moss

The Lawson Westen House, designed by Moss between 1988 and 1991 and completed two years later, is generated by a series of complex 'geometric mappings' derived from the cylindrical kitchen which is the physical and symbolic heart of the dwelling. The centre of its conical roof is displaced laterally and the cone sliced vertically to make a deck with a view to the Pacific. The parabolic curve created by the cut is pulled down towards the street, creating the curved roof, whose gable end is marked by a strangely angled, cross-mullioned square window; the gable is then 'excavated' to reveal an identical window, conventionally aligned. These products of geometric deconstruction are overlaid by apparently ad hoc elements of structure, revealed or concealed according to taste rather than system, with results that are sculptural rather than tectonic. The garden front, for example, features a boldly projecting section of roof and laminated rafters tied or propped – it is not obvious which – by tubular steel members, one straight, the other

Below Open House Project, Malibu,
California, 1983-90, Coop
Himmelb(l)au. Although unbuilt, this
project was one of the most influential
of the 1980s, capturing more
completely than any of their realized
buildings the lightness and
expressionism of Coop Himmelb(l)au's
deconstructive style.

Open House Project Malibu, California, 1983–90 (unbuilt), Coop Himmelb(l)au

cranked as if fractured, and tied back to the façade with a steel cable.

The formal fragmentation and dissolution encountered in the houses of Gehry and Moss seem especially apt as responses to the chaos and dynamism of Los Angeles, but they were also to be found in the work of a diverse range of architects whose work was rooted in different attitudes, ideas and locales. The convergence was sufficiently striking for critics and magazines to scent a new style and like the International style it was duly christened at New York's MOMA, in the exhibition 'Deconstructivist Architecture' of 1990. The name – quickly reduced to Decon – had in fact been in use for a while and combined allusions to the fashionable school of textual criticism known as deconstruction with the exuberant forms of Russian Constructivism rediscovered in the era of glasnost. The connections between Gehry's intuitive manipulations of form, Peter Eisenman's ever-more esoteric theorizing, and the automatist techniques of the Austrians Wolf Prix and Helmut Swiczinsky – who practised as Coop Himmelb(l)au – were intellectually tenuous, as the MOMA catalogue readily acknowledged, but the fascination with fragmentation did reflect a widespread shift in sensibility.

The most influential Decon project – the Open House at Malibu, by Coop Himmelb(l)au – was never built, although they worked on it for six years, from 1983 to 1990. It began life as a much acclaimed project and following its publication in 1984 the architects were approached by an 81-year-old client who wished to build it. A site was found in 1987, but the client died three years later as construction was beginning; the site and design were marketed through Sotheby's International Realty, but it remains unrealized. Coop Himmelb(l)au was formed in 1968 and is rare among the utopian groups from the late 1960s in retaining its radicalism while also producing convincing mature work. They believe that a work of art should emerge in a moment of automatic self-expression and base their designs on sketches, produced with eyes shut, which they think capture the essence of an idea. The spiky, jagged lines and planes of the Open House are translations into steel and glass of such an original sketch, and generate an exceptionally dynamic form that looks as if it has just touched down from outer space to explore an alien planet.

In place of the orderly, planned world of Modernist dreams, Decon architects offered ecstatic responses to a bewilderingly multifarious world that which seemed to defy systematization. Although new to mainstream architecture, such perspectives had much in common with the techniques of fragmentation, collage and automatism developed in early Modernist art as responses to a world torn apart by war and competing ideologies. Decon buildings, by contrast, were predicated on a world order so apparently stable that it led the historian Francis Fukuyama famously to proclaim 'The End of History': it requires exceedingly sophisticated engineering and a highly developed construction industry to make buildings which can indulge in the luxury of looking as if they are falling apart. For all its radical pretensions Decon quickly became, especially in the USA, the new academy, a manner briefly almost as ubiquitous in schools of architecture as Beaux-Arts classicism had been a century before. Even the best Decon works teetered on the brink of a descent into meaningless, self-indulgent form-making, and the ever nimble Charles Jencks's attempt, in his 1991 book *The Architecture*

of the Jumping Universe, to interpret them as exemplars of the chaotic order revealed by the 'new sciences of complexity' proved less successful than some of his earlier stylistic classifications.

Decon can also be interpreted as an essentially decorative repertoire of devices designed to stimulate jaded senses, and as such inevitably locked into the cycle of excitement, exploitation and rejection typical of a media-culture in which appearance dominates substance. For one of the most influential architects at work in the late twentieth century, the Dutchman Rem Koolhaas, founder of the Office of Metropolitan Architecture (OMA), this was the inescapable condition of the time, to which he responded by exploring architecture as an ironic language of signs. Appropriately, his first major domestic project, the Villa dall'Ava completed in 1991 in the Paris suburb of Saint-Cloud, was commissioned by the publisher of several of France's leading architectural magazines.

At one level the Villa dall'Ava can be read as a commentary on classic Modern houses: the layered organization recalls Mies's Tugendhat House, while Le Corbusier seems to lurk around almost every corner. The open, almost fully glazed ground floor sits on a concrete base clad, like the Villa de Mandrot, in random stone, and the pavilions at each end are ribbon-windowed reminders of the nearby Villa Savoye. A long ramp connects the lower entry level to the top of the base and, as in the Corbusian model, is played off against a spiral stair which links the entrance hall directly to the daughter's bedroom two storeys above. But this is no orthodox *hommage* since Koolhaas takes every opportunity to parody his sources. The front pavilion is supported on a structurally irrational forest of slender columns which jut randomly in all directions, while to the rear the pavilion has a reassuringly familiar *piloti* in one corner, but no apparent means of support in the other.

In defiance of the stuccoed houses all around, Koolhaas clads the bedrooms not with white render but with corrugated metal – blue aluminium to the street, copper to the rear. Finally, on the roof, in place of the Corbusian celebration of the natural delights of *soleil, espace et verdure*, he offers us green Astroturf and a synthetic-blue lap pool, aligned on the Eiffel Tower, which looks as if it has been flown in straight from Hollywood – to the knowing, of course, it recalls Pierre Koenig's seminal Case Study House # 22 (see p. 148). For all its luxury, the roof seems deliberately inhospitable: Astroturf and water form an unbroken plane; there are no inviting ledges or reassuring balustrades; and in place of the Villa Savoye's sinuous, guitar-shaped screen is a potato-shaped fence of orange poly-something-or-other mesh more usually encountered protecting roadworks.

Koolhaas's other major house, completed in 1998 and one of the finest of the decade, is a large private villa on a hillside outside Bordeaux, part of the *jardin anglais* of an old mansion and close to a disused quarry. Shortly before design work began the father of the family who commissioned it was left paralysed following a car crash, unable to walk and barely able to talk. He told Koolhaas, 'This house is my world; please make it as complex as possible,' and in response it was designed on three floors, like a classical villa but with radically contrasting characters. A dramatically cantilevered concrete sleeping bunker is precariously poised over a glass house of Californian clarity and openness, which in turn sits on a travertine-clad

Villa dall'Ava Saint-Cloud, France, 1991, Rem Koolhaas/OMA

Above Villa dall'Ava, Saint-Cloud, France, 1991, Rem Koolhaas/OMA. Like much of Koolhaas's work, the house is an ironic commentary on Modernism – the roof-top swimming pool aligned on the Eiffel Tower is surely a knowing reference to the Surrealist roof-garden of the Bestegui apartment, for which Le Corbusier appropriated the Arc de Triomphe as part of the composition.

House at Bordeaux France, 1998, Rem Koolhaas/OMA

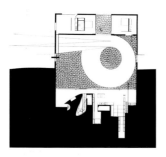

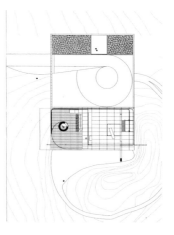

Opposite, below and right House
at Bordeaux, France, 1998, Rem
Koolhaas/OMA. In this tour de force
of a house, a transparent world of
glass is sandwiched between a stone-
clad 'cave' and a dramatically
cantilevered concrete box. Linking
these different worlds is a room-sized
elevator platform for the wheelchair-
bound client.

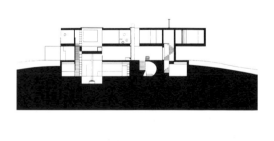

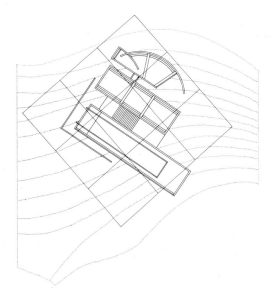

Koshino House Ashiya, Hyogo Prefecture, Japan, 1979–82, Tadao Ando

Above and opposite Koshino
House, Ashiya, Hyogo Prefecture,
Japan, 1979-82, Tadao Ando.
Conceived as a 'bastion of resistance'
against the consumerism which was
sweeping away Japanese traditions,
the interior opens to controlled views
of nature, near and far, celebrating
the passage of the sun and clouds
overhead.

cave-like base. The interlocking of inside and out is more like a Chinese puzzle than an orthodox spatial continuum. Near the centre of the plan is a large, room-sized section of the floor which is a lift-cum-vertical office moving hydraulically between levels to connect kitchen and wine cellar to library and finally bedroom. The house is like a labyrinth, in which you encounter a bewildering array of experiences: the refinement of travertine and lightness and polish of aluminium; cave-like spaces which simulate natural erosion; earth-coloured concrete of determined rawness; and the transparent world sandwiched between. Most surprising, perhaps, is that it seems everywhere to court danger, with unexpected, vertiginous drops: not what regulations normally dictate for someone with severe disabilities, and all the more liberating as a result.

To the Japanese architect Tadao Ando, the chaotic environment of the modern metropolis – and few appear more chaotic than Tokyo or his native Osaka – constitute a threat to both the diversity of regional cultures and to the individual's capacity to develop a stable identity through an inner, personal life. Ando achieved national recognition in the late 1970s following the completion of the Row House Sumiyoshi in Osaka, a reinterpretation of a traditional wooden terraced house which provides a key to all his later work. The house confronts the street with a concrete façade, bare but for a single top-lit recess to one side of which is the entrance door. Beyond lie two, two-storey cubes of accommodation placed either side of an open, similarly proportioned court, across which runs a narrow bridge to connect the upper floors: walking from living to dining room, bedroom to bathroom, involves going outdoors, regardless of the weather. To most Westerners the arrangement appears bizarre, but in Japan it connects with a long tradition of living close to nature. Traditional houses were all but uninsulated, and had a toilet at the bottom of the garden – its chilly delights were the subject of a famous eulogy by the novelist Jun'ichiro Tanizaki.

The Koshino House, completed in 1982 in a national park in Ashiya, Hyogo, brought Ando to worldwide attention as one of the most potent talents of his generation. It consists of two wings linked by an underground passage: a two-storey block containing living room, kitchen-dining room and master bedroom; and a long single-storey block housing a row of six children's bedrooms and two *tatami* rooms for guests. The house is dug into the site and entered at the upper level, from where a narrow stair leads down into the double-height living room. You enter along a wall of unbroken concrete, lit by a continuous slit of glazing between roof and wall through which, at the chosen hour, a raking slice of sun moves across the end wall and then dissolves the blank rear wall in a blaze of light – the performance recalls the living room of Utzon's Can Lis (see p. 124). Two large openings, placed to exclude sight of nearby properties, allow views of the falling ground, trees and distant hills. As in a traditional Japanese house the views are sliced off, partial, inviting the imagination to complete the scene in the mind – very different from the spatial continuity realized by the full-height glazing of Modernist houses.

The handling of openings is but one of several subtle interplays between Western modernism and Japanese tradition typical of Ando's work. Compared with the rambling, echelon form of Classic houses like Katsura, the seventeenth-century imperial villa in Kyoto, the plan looks severely 'rational' – but like a

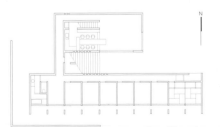

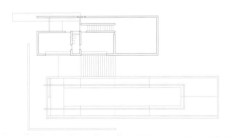

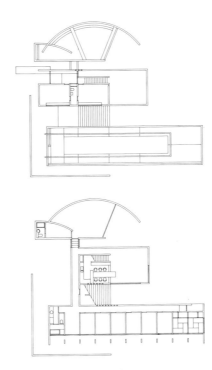

Opposite, above and right
Koshino House, Ashiya, Hyogo
Prefecture, Japan, 1979–82,
extension 1983–4, Tadao Ando.
Designed to complement the
orthogonal world of the original house,
the extension is framed by a quarter-
circular wall and manages the rare
trick of making the new composition
feel as resolved as the original.

Opposite Casa Bernasconi, Carona, Switzerland, 1988-9, Luigi Snozzi. Like all Snozzi's houses, Casa Bernasconi is carefully attuned to the site. The continuous glazing, for example, dramatizes the panorama of distant mountains rather than expressing the double-height living room within.

Right Stone House, Tavole, Italy, Herzog and de Meuron. The concrete frame, which marks the floors and extends as a pergola, signifies the 'global', placeless nature of modern production, and is infilled with local stone which, like the arrangement of non-specific rooms inside, emulates peasant traditions.

Below Hudson House, Navan, Ireland, 1998, O'Donnell and Tuomey. Conceived as an urban fragment, with external circulation between living and sleeping spaces, the house is rendered in concrete which recalls the widely influential work of Tadao Ando.

From aesthetic reduction to minimalism:
Top Ungers House, Cologne, 1995,
O. M. Ungers.
Above and left Skywood House,
Middlesex, England, 1998, Graham
Phillips.
Opposite Gaspar House, Zahora,
Spain, 1991, Campo Baeza.

Above Tallon House, Dublin, Ireland, 1970, Ronnie Tallon. Although clearly inspired by the Farnsworth House, the plan, with bedrooms either side of an open living space, was like that of countless traditional Irish houses.
Below Goulding Studio, Enniskerry, Ireland, 1973, Ronnie Tallon. Canyon-houses had been the subject of a travelling exhibition sponsored by the American company Bethlehem Steel in 1959 and here Tallon demonstrated that he could cantilever with the best of them.

Private House Rotterdam, The Netherlands, 1991, Mecanoo

contain storage cupboards and separate the bedrooms, bathroom and kitchen from the main living space. The latter rises to 4.5 metres (14.7 feet) while the service blocks are continuous with the enclosing walls. The only glazing is in four large square openings, placed at the intersection of the low walls and the main pavilion. They offer magical views through the walled spaces and generate what Baeza calls 'horizontal light', which by eliminating shadows has the effect of dematerializing rather than rendering form. In the Gaspar House, Baeza achieved an elemental simplicity and grandeur with modest means: it was built for a schoolteacher, and the accommodation occupies only 120 square metres (1291 square feet).

Architecture in the Minimalist vein was but one manifestation of the continuing interest in the high modern virtues of abstraction, transparency and spatial continuity. Miesian designs, indebted to the Farnsworth House and derivatives by Craig Ellwood in California, continued to be built into the 1980s. Some of the most elegant were the work of Ronnie Tallon in Ireland (a partner in Scott Tallon Walker): his own house, completed in 1970, was framed in white-painted steel and had an open living space with bedrooms at each end – just like a traditional old Irish house, he explained. Three years later, with the Goulding Studio, Tallon outdid the Americans at cantilevering a house off a steep, canyon-like hillside. At the same period, when Michael and Patty Hopkins built their house in Hampstead, London in 1977 they turned to the Eames House for inspiration.

While the Hopkins were happy to live with their young family in a fully glazed interior shielded and divided only by venetian blinds, other architects increasingly sought ways to retain the openness while adapting it to the needs of different sites and lifestyles. In 1991, in the Karlingse district of Rotterdam, Erik van Egeraat and Francine Houben (partners in Mecanoo before van Egeraat's departure), completed an urban house and studio for themselves which offered a lesson in combining privacy and openness. A two-storey living pavilion is placed above an enclosed garage and studio and kept as open as possible to enjoy views through to water on each side – service spaces are packed along the blank wall close to a neighbour to keep the volumes open. To the front, double-height glazing, set back behind shallow metal balconies, offers views north to a small lake, while to the rear an ad hoc arrangement of glazed and solid panels responds to the spaces within. The side elevation is closed at ground level by a plane of concrete, and above it a fully glazed wall is protected by bamboo canes which can be moved back and forth hydraulically in an aluminium frame: an inventive reinterpretation of the *shoji* screens seen on a recent trip to Japan. Although the architects denied any conscious attempt to link to Dutch traditions, the intricately layered and gridded composition also inevitably brings to mind Rietveld's Schroeder House.

The development of secondary, non-structural layers became a favourite device for controlling both solar penetration and transparency. In the Kern House (1997) in Lochau Austria, Baumschlager and Eberle wrapped a glass box completely with wooden louvres. Near the ground the louvres lie flat against the house and as they rise they gradually angle back, opening views out but still providing protection from prying eyes – and simultaneously recalling traditional log-built houses. The Rosebery House (1994–7) in Queensland, Australia by Brit

Above Private House, Rotterdam, The Netherlands, 1991, Mecanoo. Openness and transparency are adapted to an exposed urban site, with the glazed end wall screened by retractable bamboo canes inspired by Japanese shoji screens.
Right Kern House, Lochau, Austria, 1997, Baumschlager and Eberle. A glass house lurks behind the continuous screen of louvres, which angle back to open up views of the landscape from the first floor.

Top right Hopkins House, London, England, 1976, Michael Hopkins. The house was planned as a continuous gridded space, to be sub-divided as the needs of a growing family required, and built, like the Eames House, using standard steel components.

Andresen and Peter O'Gorman is similarly almost completely engulfed in vertical battens of Australian eucalyptus wood. Here the 'landscape screen', as the architects called it, mediates between the scale of the house and the landscape, filtering the passage of light in and views out and enabling the fully glazed pavilions to feel both open and protected.

On a densely wooded, lakeside site outside São Paolo in Brazil, Andrade Morettin achieved a similarly modified transparency using cellular polycarbonate panels. The D'Alessandro House, built for two young photographers in 1998, is a reworking of the Miesian glass box and consists of a transparent 'light box' and a 'thick wall' containing the bathroom and kitchen; at night, a retractable curtain defines a private cube for sleeping, and in one corner glass replaces polycarbonate to allow unmediated views of the lake. The main pavilion of the architect Barton Myers' own house, completed the same year in Toro Canyon, Montecito, California, builds on the tradition of seamless integration between interior and landscape established by Koenig's Case Study Houses. But here the delicate glass box has become an imposing, steel-framed loft space of distinctly industrial provenance, complete with large up-and-over glass doors and galvanized external roller-shutters to defend the interior against bush fires.

Spatially, none of the houses we have considered in this chapter moved beyond possibilities established half a century earlier, and even the most innovative designs of the last two decades are inventive developments and transformations of Modernist themes rather than radically new propositions. Two much admired houses in Belgium completed in the early 1990s, for example, reinterpreted classic Miesian and Corbusian types. The first, Villa Maesen by Stéphane Beel, built in 1992 in Zedelgem, is sited in the kitchen garden of a castle and approached along a beech-lined drive. In deference to this imposing context Beel stretched the classic flat-roofed pavilion, represented by the Farnsworth House, into a 7-metre- (23-foot-) wide wall of accommodation which he placed 7 metres (23 feet) from the rear wall of the garden, recreating the volume of the house as a void. A continuous suite of open plan spaces and private terraces – outdoor rooms reminiscent of Ando's walled courtyards – overlooks the garden, and the house is long enough to break through an old dividing wall, enabling occupants to walk between a formal garden and orchard.

The house in Brasschaat near Antwerp, completed in 1993 by Xaveer de Geyter, project architect for Rem Koolhaas's Villa dall'Ava, inverts the classic Corbusian villa. It is entered by vehicle at roof level, up a short ramp complete with official-looking entry barrier. On the roof sits the square steel-and-glass pavilion of the double garage, oddly angled like a Greek temple on its acropolis. Such angled alignments were the subject of a celebrated reverie in Le Corbusier's *Vers une Architecture* and here the element which the vulgar, *arriviste* houses of the wealthy neighbourhood seek to suppress is celebrated – and floodlit at night lest anyone miss the point. To enter the house you descend via a ramp into a plan which is more Koolhaasian than Corbusian, zoned in parallel bands divided by bookshelves and cupboards and articulated by varied materials – light blue-green tiles, wooden floors, profiled aluminium cladding.

Corbusian precedents are equally apparent in the Double House (1997) in

Opposite top Rosebery House, Queensland, Australia, 1994–7, Brit Andresen and Peter O'Gorman. The glazed elevations are screened by slats of local eucalyptus wood.
Opposite centre Villa Maesen, Zedelgem, Belgium, 1992, Stéphane Beel. The classic Modernist flat-roofed pavilion floating in the landscape is here stretched into a long, transparent 'wall' of accommodation.
Below and opposite bottom House in Brasschaat, near Antwerp, Belgium, 1993, Xaveer de Geyter. An upside-down version of the Corbusian villa, entered from a roof-top garage reached via a short ramp.
Overleaf Myers House, Montecito, California, USA, 1998, Barton Myers. The steel and glass Case Study House is transformed into a robust glass shed, industrial in feel and complete with boldly expressed metal shutters to protect the interior in case of brush fire.

Villa Maesen Zedelgem, Belgium, 1992, Stéphane Beel

Left Morrison House, London, England, 1992, Graham Morrison (Allies and Morrison). The brick walls, slate roof and rendered porch of the surrounding Victorian villas are transformed into a modern composition of volumes and planes.

Top Reid House, Johns Island, South Carolina, USA, 1987, Clark and Menefee. The elements are familiar from the region – from boarding to shed-roofed porch – but the proportions and refined detailing are unmistakably contemporary.

Above Private House, Bad Tölz, Germany, 1996, Fink and Jocher. The shallow-pitch roof, timber boarding and louvres echo the traditional log-built houses, and sliding shutters enable the house to turn into an almost solid wooden box, like an agricultural store.

Above Concord House, Concord, Massachusetts, USA, 1994, Machado and Silvetti. The New England vernacular is given a twist by boldly coloured trapezoidal volumes projecting from the façade.

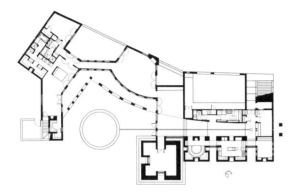

Above Fuller House, near Phoenix, Arizona, USA, 1984–6, Antoine Predock. The complex, processional sequence of volumes unfolds between sunrise- and sunset-viewing platforms.
Overleaf Zuber House, near Phoenix, Arizona, USA, 1989, Antoine Predock. The 'runway to anywhere', lit from below at night through cracks in the paving, projects out from one of two square towers which punctuate the bar of a T-shaped plan.

Menefee explain their Reid House, built on Johns Island, South Carolina in 1987, by reference to the shed-roofed porches, butane tanks and other accretions found on local rural buildings, but the house could never be mistaken for a traditional structure. The areas of glazing are too large, the detailing too delicate, and touches like the abstract acroteria too artful – but for all these refinements it still succeeds in feeling very much of its place. As, too, does Machado and Silvetti's Concord House of 1994 in Concord, Massachusetts, where the garden front juxtaposes the ubiquitous material of New England buildings – white-painted clapboarding – with two singular, trapezoidal volumes which grow unexpectedly from the main volume.

Faced with tough local planning requirements in Blackheath, London, Graham Morrison of Allies and Morrison had no option but to use traditional brickwork and a pitched roof for his own house, completed in 1992. In a further gesture to the context he included a white-rendered cubic version of the porches found on the surrounding Victorian villas, but by treating the walls and wafer-thin roof as planes he managed to achieve a convincingly modern expression. In a house completed in 1996 on the edge of an old village in Upper Bavaria, near the German Alps, Fink and Jocher responded to constructional forms evolved in response to the severe weather. But in place of horizontal logs or boarding they used narrow vertical strips; the roof is shallow pitched but with deeper than normal overhangs, painted white underneath to reflect light into the interior; and the glazed openings are far larger than in older houses, but can be protected by sliding timber shutters to restore the sense of solidity.

In America, the majority of the most innovative houses continued to be built as responses to rural rather than urban sites. Those of Antoine Predock, for example, seem inseparable from the deserts of New Mexico and Arizona. Like Wright before him, Predock is fascinated by the native adobe architecture, whose walls, he says, 'act as a bridge between earth and sky'. Given generous budgets and open, previously unsettled sites, many of Predock's houses are more like small settlements rather than individual buildings. The Treaster Gray Residence, completed in Tesuque in 1985, resembles a New Mexican village climbing the flank of a ridge, while the Fuller House of 1984–6, in the Sonoran desert north of Phoenix, Arizona is organized as a processional sequence of spaces in response to the passage of the sun. Between sunrise- and sunset-viewing platforms the house unfolds as an abstraction of the landscape, replete with an interior 'canyon' in which lie a channel of flowing water, a kitchen and dining 'boulder', and the miniature mountain of the pyramidal den – a rather inflated gesture for such a small room.

In the Zuber House, completed three years later on another desert site outside Phoenix, Predock abandoned adobe construction and references to pueblo architecture. The T-shaped plan is divided into a leg, deeply recessed into the mountain and constructed of rough concrete blocks whose aggregate echoes the mountain's colour, and a bar-shaped 'panoramic house' finished with grey-green stucco resembling the desert floor. The junction between the plan elements is marked by two square towers, rotated through 45 degrees. From one springs a metal bridge which ends poised high above the desert. It is aligned to local aircraft flight patterns and at night the open joints of the limestone paving are lit

from below, transforming the bridge that leads nowhere into an imaginary runway to anywhere.

Stanley Saitowitz's Halfway House in the Transvaal, which we considered in Chapter 4, is an outstanding example of site-specific design and in 1992, some years after moving to California, he completed the McDonald House, a vacation home in Stinson Beach a few miles north of San Francisco's Golden Gate Bridge. Before visiting the site he had visions of pounding surf and acres of open sand, but what he found was a placid lagoon – so he set about making the house a metaphor for the absent sea. The parallelogram-shaped plan, a Saitowitz trademark, harbours a full width deck and anchors the house to the water's edge. Inland, it has one rounded corner, like a sea cave scoured by water, while the flank walls run out to present raking, prow-like forms to the lagoon and protect the deck from wind. The redwood-sheathed walls will weather to what the architect calls 'a driftwood crust' and protect, shell-like, an iridescent white interior. Above, the roof ebbs and flows gently across, barely touching the walls and rising, like the crest of a gentle wave, to reveal a shallow triangle of light, echoed in triangular cut-outs in the walls which further dissolve the sense of enclosure. Detailed with refreshing simplicity, and animated by odd slices of sun and the play of light reflected from the water onto the ceiling, the interior perfectly captures the spirit of relaxation by the sea.

McDonald House Stinson Beach, California, USA, 1992, Stanley Saitowitz

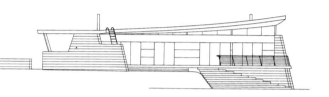

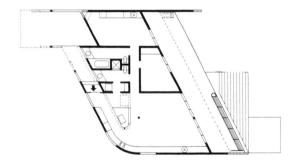

Above and opposite McDonald House, Stinson Beach, California, USA, 1992, Stanley Saitowitz.
Below Casa Garau-Agusti, Barcelona, Spain, 1988-93, Enric Miralles.

A glance at the plans of the Casa Garau-Agusti (1988–93) by Enric Miralles might suggest that they were inspired by the spirit of fragmentation discussed earlier, but in fact the complex geometry developed in response to the site. Situated on a plot in suburban Barcelona with mundane houses to either side and a view across a shallow valley to a picturesque church, the walls and windows twist and angle in search of views, to settle into the topography and to avoid visual contact with the neighbours. The approach has its roots in the work of Miralles's distinguished predecessor in Barcelona, Antonio Coderch, whose site-responsive Casa Ugalde we encountered in Chapter 4 (p. 100), and is echoed in the work of John and Patricia Patkau, for whom every project begins with a search for what they call its 'found potential'. Rejecting the universal models of Classicism and Modernism, they seek to ground their designs in the particularities of place, programme and materials, and to make them part of a continuum with the natural world.

The Patkaus' first decade of practice culminated with the completion of the Barnes House in 1992. Sited on the edge of an open, rocky outcrop in five acres of forested land, it enjoys outstanding views of the Strait of Georgia and mainland British Columbia to the north and the rocky shoreline of Vancouver Island to the north-west. The irregular, compacted form is itself boulder-like and emerges from a plan developed by wedging the spaces into the tapering ravine. Or so it appears: in fact, while following the nature of the site closely, the plans and sections also artfully juxtapose two geometries, two kinds of space: orthogonal and non-orthogonal, figurative and abstract, strong and weak. The ultimate roots lie in Aalto and the approach serves to heighten both the experience of the landscape and the feeling of interiority. The orthogonal spaces, their walls thickened by built-in cabinets, are cave-like retreats, while the weaker, non-orthogonal zones direct the eye to the spectacular views and defer to the

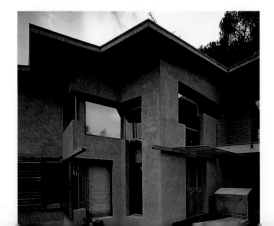

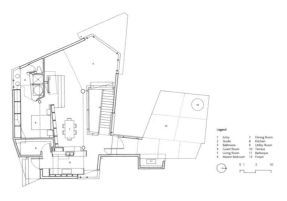

Busk House Bamble, Norway, 1987–90, Sverre Fehn

Above Busk House, Bamble, Norway, 1987–90, Sverre Fehn. The house seems to grow out of the rocky ridge, its solidity emphasized by the tree-like angled struts of the overhanging roofs and canopies.
Opposite Barnes House, British Columbia, Canada, 1992, Patkau Architects. Below the boldly structured folded plane of the roof, orthogonal cave-like rooms retreat from freely planned spaces which open to the landscape.
Below Brick House, Baerum, Norway, 1987, Sverre Fehn. The projecting, nose-like chimney marks one end of a central axis along which are ranged the elements of earth (walled garden), air (white-tiled court), fire and water (bath).

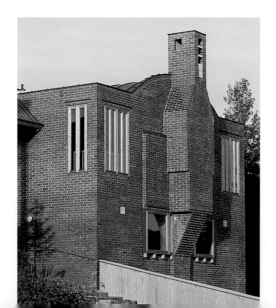

landscape which forms the visual boundary of these weakly defined spaces. Similar contrasts are cultivated in the construction. Delicately detailed steel railings and connections are set against the heavy, monolithic surfaces of the concrete floors, stucco-clad, timber-framed walls and substantial roof timbers, while a one-centimetre-thick (0.4 inch) steel-plate canopy projects dramatically beyond the large opening to the north-west, a thin, perfectly horizontal surface in sharp contrast to the thick, folded planes of the roof.

The Busk House, completed in 1990 by the Norwegian architect Sverre Fehn, expresses a similar concern to lock the design into the land. The site is a large area of rocky, tree- and scrub-covered terrain in the Oslo fjord and the width of the main body of the house was determined by a massive boulder that closes one end of the chosen location. The house's alignment follows the rocky terrain to the south-west, a sheer concrete wall rising directly from the granite and folding round at each end of the house to contain the fire at one end and a plunge pool off the master bedroom at the other. In a showhouse for the brick industry completed in Baerum in 1987 Fehn made an even more elemental celebration central to the design, organizing the rooms around an axis along which earth (garden), air (white-tiled atrium), fire (hearth) and water (the bath) were aligned.

The perceived solidity of the concrete wall of the Busk House is enhanced by the layered timbers and angled struts of the overhanging roof canopies and, on the opposite elevation, by a long, glazed colonnade. The line of columns springs from an existing tree on the site and takes the occupants metaphorically out into nature to move between rooms – and literally so at each end, where it is unglazed. To contrast with the linear main block, Fehn designed the children's bedrooms as a freestanding timber tower – 'a little fortress for the daughters' as he put it – linked by a glazed bridge and connected vertically by a spiral stair housed in a wooden cylinder, which rises into a fully glazed study. 'In Norway,' Fehn says, 'you are still aware that you have to destroy nature in order to build.' His work is both an attempt to minimize the inevitable damage and to celebrate nature by deriving the architecture metaphorically from her: in the Busk House, the terrain-hugging main block, colonnade and timber roofs read clearly as abstractions of rocks, tree trunks and branches.

Through his work and teaching as professor of architecture in Oslo Fehn has exerted a strong influence over a gifted new generation of young Norwegian architects, including Carl-Viggo Hølmebakk whose summerhouse in Risor was completed in 1997. The client loved the many pine trees so the site was surveyed with a computerized level to provide exceptionally detailed plans of both trees and topography. The plan locks itself around several pines, which are captured in courtyards or rise through decks, and a special foundation system was adopted using concrete stub columns whose position could be adjusted as necessary to miss tree roots. The heights of the rooms also varied, to slip under branches, and the openings were carefully attuned to the views, final decisions often being taken on site. In the same year, Lacaton and Vassal were faced with a similar brief – to place a house on a beautiful, pine-covered site overlooking the Bassin d'Arcachon in Bordeaux without destroying any trees. They opted for a lightweight aluminium box, elevated on columns and built around six trees. The

Above Doctor's House, Paderborn, Germany, 1998, Thomas Herzog. An accomplished modernist composition which is also designed to maximize the use of passive energy and renewable resources.
Opposite, top and bottom Private house, Cap-Ferrat, France, 1997, Lacaton and Vassal. The machine in the garden – a lightweight aluminium box skewered by mature trees.
Opposite, middle Summer house, Risør, Noway, 1997, Carl-Viggo Hølmebakk. Here the rooms and decks flow with calculated precision around and under the tree trunks and branches.
Below House in Regensburg, Germany, 1979, Thomas Herzog. An early example of passive solar design, demonstrative in its maximal exposure of sloping, south-facing glazing.

openings for the tree trunks were fitted with transparent plastic sheets and flexible rubber gaskets around the trunks enable the house to be sealed and the trees to move and grow. Below, the reflective surface of the corrugated aluminium cladding makes for a magical undercroft.

These two pine-respecting houses say much about the differences between the Nordic and French attitudes to nature – in which Romantic fusion and Classical counterpoint are still very much to the fore – and even more about the shift in values that had been apparent since the 1960s. As the environmental consequences of economies and value-systems predicated on unlimited growth became increasingly apparent the concern with 'green' issues gathered force. Initially, little of architectural consequence was produced. Houses were earth-sheltered, or buried, had 'passive' and 'active' solar collectors – such as conservatories and heat-absorbing solar panels – or were built with unusual materials like the straw-block house erected by Klas Anhelm at the Ararat Exhibition in Stockholm in 1976. These houses frequently showed little concern for the visual consequences of their green philosophy. Indeed they were sometimes designed to offend conventional sensibilities by rejecting the aesthetic norms that were considered as bankrupt as the ecologically destructive societies that produced them. This radical spirit lived on in an ecological community built in Torup in Denmark as late as 1991, based on that icon of alternative culture, the geodesic dome. But by then green issues had firmly entered the mainstream and during the final decade of the century competitions for model energy-efficient homes proliferated worldwide.

Among the first architects to produce a sustained and architecturally convincing body of work addressing environmental issues was Thomas Herzog, a professor of design at Munich Technical University. His house in Regensburg was completed in 1979 and used one of the classic strategies of passive solar design – a linear plan with a south-facing, fully glazed buffer zone. Running across the main, inner house this was designed to capture solar energy by absorbing it in the heavy stone floor. In the Regensburg project the glazing ran down to the ground as part of a triangular wedge, and the whole house was raised slightly off the site to protect tree roots and escape the high water table. In a house in Waldmohr completed five years later Herzog opted for a compact 'thermal onion' plan, placing the rooms requiring the most heat – such as bathrooms – at the centre of a square-within-a-diamond scheme. A two-storey conservatory fills the south-facing elevation, and the east and west sides are protected by trellises covered by deciduous climbing plants whose leaves drop in winter to allow useful solar gain.

Herzog's later house for a doctor near Paderborn in Germany, completed in 1998, does not appear overtly 'environmental', but on analysis proves to be as rigorously thought through as his more programmatic earlier projects. Two double-height pavilions are linked to each other and to an earlier surgery by an intermediate, single-storey space that is glazed to the south-east and runs along a heavily insulated wall providing protection from the road. The pavilions are fully glazed to the south and protected from solar gain by the projecting roof and climbing plants; service spaces such as the bathrooms and sauna are housed in small concrete boxes in the connecting space, which also acts as a gallery for the doctor's modern art collection. In winter it becomes like an orangery, with only background heating from an underfloor system.

In total contrast to Herzog's quiet, modestly scaled proposals is the Sun Valley House, completed in Idaho in 1986 by Arne Bystrom. A bold gesture addressing a vast landscape, it combines a heavy, bracketed timber roof – a familiar symbol of shelter from the Far East to northern Europe – with a Wright-inspired base variously cut into and projecting from the earth. Beneath the roof the plan is cranked 45 degrees to face due south; the mono-pitch roof slope exactly matches the low December sun to maximize solar gain, and it projects far enough to exclude the high summer sun from the interior. Heat gathered passively in the 'solar gallery' is stored in rock bins, and water circulates through an array of active metal-and-glass solar collectors which hang somewhat incongruously beneath the heavy timbers.

Sun Valley House Sun Valley, Idaho, USA, 1986, Arne Bystrom

While conspicuously living up to its name, the Sun Valley House also embodies a problem evident in much 'green' design, torn between our urge to go back to nature and to the earth, and our desire to sustain an acceptable standard of living using sophisticated high-tech devices. No such equivocation is apparent in the solar house at Breisach-am-Rhein, completed in 1996 by Thomas Spiegelhalter. This extraordinary deconstructivist collage, bristling with solar collectors and photovoltaic panels and writhing restlessly in response to aspect and prospect, inevitably raises other questions: it might harness energy efficiently, but its overall use of resources would hardly stand up to an environmental audit.

Demonstration eco-houses are particularly susceptible to the proliferation of environmental gizmos, often resulting, as James Wines recently observed, in 'too little home and too much technology'. The Australian 'House of the Future' (or Monier House), built in 1992 in Swan Valley to competition-winning designs by Kimberly Ackert and Robert Dawson-Browne, was an exception. It integrated a range of active and passive solar collectors without overwhelming the spaces, and insulated the cool, south-facing elevation with a rammed-earth wall composed of an iron-rich soil mixed with 4 percent cement – a modification of a traditional way of building that is gradually coming back into use in diverse climates.

Frustrated by the house-building industry's continuing reluctance to embrace technology wholeheartedly, the Austrian architects Driendl and Steixner built Standard Solar House in Langenschönbichl in 1992. To admit more light and simplify construction, it uses all-glass walls with full-height, solid, opening panels for ventilation on all but the heavily insulated north elevation. On the southern, living side familiar passive solar strategies are employed, with external aluminium blinds to exclude excess sun. Along the north side, sunlight enters through a high, south-facing clerestory to be absorbed by the thick stone cladding of the insulated concrete wall; the stone then gives up its heat to water circulating in pipes in the wall, which take it away to a ground storage tank. The architects claim the house undercut standard building costs by 20 percent and, occupied by a family of five, is costing 40 percent less than normal to heat.

In a private house in Lyon-St Just, Jourda and Perraudin took a different tack. Accepting at face value the tendency of passive-solar designs to turn into

Above House of the Future, Swan Valley, Australia, 1992, Ackert and Dawson-Browne. Unlike many exhibition designs bristling with environmental technology, this house manages to integrate active and passive devices successfully into a visually calm form.

Right Solar House, Breisach-am-Rhein, Germany, 1996, Thomas Spiegelhalter. Deconstructivist collage meets solar energy.

Opposite Sun Valley House, Idaho, USA, 1986, Arne Bystrom. The all-sheltering roof and pervasive forty-five degree geometry struggle to hold together an array of solar collectors and sun-spaces.

Above Private house, Lyon-St Just, France, Jourda and Perraudin. A standard greenhouse construction system is used to make an eco-friendly house with the addition of canvas, insulation and planting.
Right Architects' Own House, Lyons, France, Jourda and Perraudin. This cheap steel-framed box has a dramatic fabric structure to keep most of the rain off the roof membrane, and plywood barrel-vaults to expand the living space.

Above, below and overleaf

Crescent House, Wiltshire, England, 1999, Ken Shuttleworth. By the end of the century, efficient passive solar design could be effortlessly combined with Modernist abstraction in sophisticated designs such as this.

Crescent House Wiltshire, England, 1999, Ken Shuttleworth

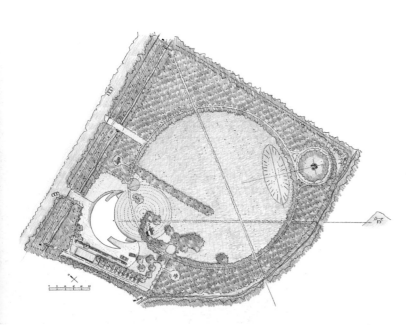

greenhouses, they built a simple, 21-metre- (69-foot-) long glass shed using a commercially produced system, and then modified it using a combination of fixed insulation panels, layers of canvas, and internal and external planting. In their own house in Lyons they opted for a simple steel frame and the cheapest of flat roofs, and then unfurled a dramatic fabric structure over the whole structure. Supported on a forest of light steel struts, the canopy provided protection from weather during construction, keeps most of the rain off the flat roof and offers solar shading. Plywood barrel vaults give added dignity and volume to the living/dining area, whereas in contrast the bedrooms are reduced to tiny pods. Jourda and Perraudin believe in providing only what is essential, and in minimizing a structure's impact on the earth: like Glenn Murcutt's elegant pavilions, whose work also demonstrates a serious concern with the use of resources, their house seems determined to 'touch this earth lightly'.

By the mid 1990s sophisticated software packages to predict the environmental performance of buildings were widely available and the basic principles of passive design were becoming a natural part of many architects' design processes, not the province of experts or the ideologically committed. At first sight Ken Shuttleworth's Crescent House (1999), with its artful crescent-moon plan, crisp white surfaces, unbroken glazed wall, open, light-filled interior and elegant formal landscape, might appear to be a sophisticated essay in late-Modern design rather than a serious attempt to address environmental issues: in fact it is both. To begin with, over a thousand deciduous trees were planted on the five-acre site, which lies in an area of outstanding natural beauty on the edge of the Marlborough Downs in Wiltshire in south-west England. The trees near the house reduce the chilling effect of the wind and provide welcome shade in summer, while allowing valuable sunshine through in winter.

Shuttleworth, a director of Foster and Partners, subjected the design to typically thorough technical studies which suggested that a south/south-east orientation was optimal for the large glazed wall, making the most of early morning gains but avoiding overheating in summer. The interior is generously day-lit and naturally cross ventilated, and even the chimney plays its part, acting as a ventilation stack in hot weather. Concrete was chosen as the main structural material because it was available from a plant across the road from the site, and secondhand timber from the run-down house which formerly occupied the land was used extensively in making the form-work. The heavy concrete walls, which store heat and even out thermal changes in the interior, are wrapped externally in 10 centimetres (4 inches) of CFC-free insulation; on the roof, the thickness of insulation is doubled. The building systems are designed to make use of photovoltaic panels, recycled rainwater and a nearby well when they become economically viable.

Crescent House, like the other houses we have considered in this final chapter, belongs to an evolving and increasingly mature, diverse and responsive tradition of modern architecture. Aesthetically, its roots lie in the abstraction explored in the 1920s, and to the majority of people such a thoroughgoing expression of modernity at the domestic scale remains alien, not least because it simply refuses to look like a 'proper house'. Herzog and de Meuron's Rudin House, built in 1993

Rudin House Leymen, France, ,1993, Herzog and de Meuron

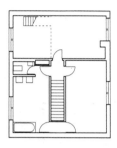

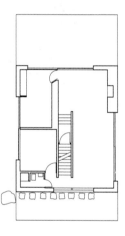

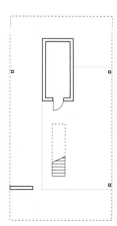

at Leymen in France, is in part a commentary on this dilemma. Seen across the fields it appears quintessentially house-like: symmetrical, gabled, rooted in the ground, and with holes for windows and doors, just like a child's drawing. Move closer, however, and it becomes utterly strange. It appears to be made of only one material, concrete (although in fact there is a membrane on the roof), and as a result looks unfinished; the openings are larger than normal and not neatly symmetrical; far from being rooted securely in the ground, it is raised precariously on a platform, like an architectural model on a cardboard base; and where, you suddenly wonder, is the front door?

The missing door turns out to be under the house, approached up a staircase which might be retractable but, like everything else, is made of concrete. Once inside you discover that the plan is ordinary, the section and finishes less so. The tall, narrow stairwell around which the rooms are organized reaches high up to a skylight, yet the daylight is mixed with the different colour spectrum emanating from a long horizontal strip of fluorescent tubes. The walls are lined with adobe, made with straw and loam from the surrounding land; on the lower floor, close to the fields, the finish is a natural sand colour, while the stairwell and upper floor are painted white. Despite your first impressions, there is little reassuringly conventional about the Rudin House, which has more to do with recent fine art practices than traditional house building. The mixture of natural and artificial light emulates the explorations of 'Light and Space' artists like Dan Flavin, while the adobe revetment of the ground floor echoes the emphasis on materiality in the work of American Minimalists such as Donald Judd, who built an adobe wall in the courtyard of the house he designed for himself in Marfa, Texas.

The Rudin House operates by different rules to the total works of art with which we began this exploration of the twentieth-century house, but it is still conceived as a work of art, a commentary on 'houseness' and also a house itself. As commonly understood, however, houses and works of art are very different creatures. A house should be accommodating and open to interpretation, allowing different occupants to change its decoration and adapt its rooms to their taste and requirements, not totally controlled from plan to teaspoon, or exquisitely tuned like a gallery installation. Culturally, it must be widely accessible, not the expression of abstruse ideas, and it should grow old with grace, not appear hopelessly outmoded by the next twist of fashion in a changing world. A work of art, on the other hand, can — and most contemporary artists and critics would doubtless say, should — be challenging and unconventional, and may legitimately make demands on its audience by way of attention and prior knowledge.

All architecture, to a greater or lesser extent, seeks to subject life to a system of spatial and aesthetic order, and the tension between the house as a work of art and a setting for everyday life runs acutely through the twentieth century. Even the supposedly liberating free plan could produce its own kind of tyranny: it is no coincidence that a disproportionate number of the houses we have explored are second homes, to be enjoyed in the more relaxed atmosphere of weekends or vacations, or are manifestos built by architects for their own occupation. The most eminently liveable of the great twentieth-century dwellings — one thinks of the Schröder and Sarabhai houses, many of Wright's, from Fallingwater to the

Opposite and below Rudin House, Leymen, France, 1993, Herzog and de Meuron. At first sight as house-like as any child's (or Post-Modernist's) dream, on closer inspection this all-concrete structure turns out to be a knowing exercise in late-modern design.

Usonians, the Villa Mairea, Niemeyer and Barragán houses, Utzon's Can Lis – succeed in reconciling these often conflicting poles, but the gulf between the ideals they represent and the general culture of housing hardly needs stating. The story of the twentieth-century house is an exhilarating journey through architectural ideas of great originality, and in the West, in the wealthiest society in history, the house's future as a vehicle for architectural expression and experimentation seems assured. Indeed, in an increasingly bureaucratized world it may prove to be the one building type over which the architect retains something close to traditional control.

further reading, index, credits, and acknowledgments

The literature on modern architecture is vast and a comprehensive bibliography of the houses discussed in this book could occupy many pages. These suggestions for further reading have been chosen for their accessibility and availability, to enable readers to broaden and deepen their interest in the work and ideas discussed in this book.

On modern architecture generally:
William Curtis: *Modern Architecture Since 1900* (London: Phaidon Press, 3rd edn, 1996)
Kenneth Frampton: *Modern Architecture: A critical history* (London: Thames and Hudson, 3rd edn, 1992)

On specific periods/styles:
Peter Davey: *Arts and Crafts Architecture* (London: Phaidon Press, 1995)
Lesley Jackson: *'Contemporary'* (London: Phaidon Press, 1994)
Richard Weston: *Modernism* (London: Phaidon Press, 1996)

Houses:
Esther McCoy: *Blueprints for Living: History and Legacy of the Case Study Houses* (Cambridge, MA: MIT Press, 1989)
John Welsh: *Modern House* (London: Phaidon Press, 1995)
Neil Jackson: *The Modern Steel House* (London: Spon, 1996)
Olivier Boissière: *Twentieth-Century Houses, Europe* (Paris: Terrail, 1998)
Anatxu Zabalbeascoa: *Houses of the Century* (Corte Madera: Gingko Press, 1998)
Clare Melhuish: *Modern House II* (London: Phaidon Press, 1999)
Susan Doubilet and Daralice Boles: *European House Now* (London: Thames and Hudson, 1999)
Robert McCarter, Richard Weston, James Steele: *Twentieth Century Houses* (London: Phaidon Press, 1999; Fallingwater, Villa Mairea, and the Eames House)
Nicolas Pople: *Experimental Houses* (London: Laurence King, 2000)

Theoretical/topical:
Christian Norberg-Schulz: *The Concept of Dwelling* (New York: Rizzoli, 1985)
Charles Moore, Donlyn Lyndon, Gerald Allen: *The Place of Houses* (New York: Henry Holt, 1979)
James Wines: *Green Architecture* (Cologne: Taschen, 2000)

Individual architects:
Richard Weston: *Alvar Aalto* (London: Phaidon Press, 1995)
Yukio Futagawa, ed.: *Tadao Ando, 1972–1987* (Tokyo: A.D.A. Edita, 1987)
Antonio Riggen Martínez: *Luis Barragán* (New York: Monacelli Press, 1996)
Pat Kirkham: *Charles and Ray Eames* (Cambridge, MA: MIT Press, 1995)
Eduard F. Sekler: *Josef Hoffmann* (Princeton: Princeton University Press, 1985)
William Curtis: *Le Corbusier: Forms and Ideas* (London: Phaidon Press, 199?)
Tim Benton: *The Villas of Le Corbusier, 1920–1930* (New Haven and London: Yale University Press, 1987)
Roberto Schezen: *Adolf Loos: Architecture 1903–1932* (New York: Monacelli Press, 1996)